THE BARD OF SAVAGERY

Thorstein Veblen and Modern Social Theory

John P. Diggins

THE BARD OF SAVAGERY

Thorstein Veblen and Modern Social Theory

A Continuum Book
THE SEABURY PRESS • NEW YORK

To my mother
and the memory
of my father

1978
The Seabury Press
815 Second Avenue
New York, New York 10017

Printed in the United States of America

Library of Congress Cataloging in Publication Data
Diggins, John P
The bard of savagery.
(A Continuum book)
Includes index.
1. Veblen, Thorstein, 1857–1929. 2. Social reformers—United States—Biography. 3. Economics—United States—History.
4. Social history. I. Title.
HB119.V4D46 330'.092'4 [B] 77-13319 ISBN 0-8164-9323-5

Contents

Preface: Social Theory and the Anthropological Imperative

The rich are different from you and me.
F. SCOTT FITZGERALD

Yes, they have more money.
ERNEST HEMINGWAY

In that short exchange, which is reported to have taken place between two of America's greatest modern novelists, we have a key to the entire social theory of Thorstein Veblen. Fitzgerald was fascinated by the rich and by the sociology of wealth. Hemingway could dismiss the charm of money only because he worshipped something even more romantic and more related to Fitzgerald's imagination than he was aware—the world of will, strength, and conquest. Driven by a compulsion to succeed, both writers were haunted by the shadow of failure. Perhaps only Veblen, both a genius and a failure, could see the connection between Fitzgerald's fantasy and Hemingway's masculinity, between the possession of wealth and the enjoyment of status, between money and power, love and glory.

Thorstein Veblen was an intellectual of many roles: ponderous critic of orthodox economic theory, witty castigator of class distinctions, champion of feminism against the "barbarian status of women," *enfant terrible* of the "higher learning," theoretician of industrialization and national power, exponent of scientific philosophy and economic anthropology, sociologist of status and anatomist of affluence, literary artist of irony and satire and stylist of playful solemnity. Previous scholarship on Veblen has generally focused on a single aspect of his thought to the neglect of other dimensions. In American intellectual history, for example, Veblen has often been dealt with as one of the chief social critics of the progressive era, a writer whose thoughts are best appreciated in the context of other reform movements such as liberalism and socialism. Although useful, such an interpretation slights Veblen's aloofness from reform movements, his critique of the theoretical foundations of socialism, and his real doubts about the powerful pragmatic creed that constituted the philosophical core of modern American liberalism.

The very name "Veblen" evokes various images. Among general readers it recalls the eccentric professor and caustic satirist of status climbing and "conspicuous consumption." Among the more informed the name conjures up the theoretician who saw in the ascendancy of the technical and scientific professions a radical hope for social transformation. But these impressions, which derive respectively from *The Theory of the Leisure Class* and *The Engineers and the Price System*, have the effect of obscuring rather than illuminating the depth and diversity of Veblen's unique analysis of modern industrial society. On the one hand Veblen emerges as but the mentor of Vance Packard; on the other as merely the precursor of James Burnham or the spiritual ancestor of John Kenneth Galbraith. So regarded, Veblen can easily be relegated to the footnotes of American intellectual history, an author whose works are frequently quoted and seldom read.

Part of the confusion about Veblen's reputation stems from the ambiguous nature of his own ideological legacy. On the left Marxists admire his critique of capitalism but are piqued by his rejection of Hegel and dialectical materialism; liberals value his attack on big business but are disturbed by his skepticism about historical progress; conservatives rejoice in his exposure of the foibles of mass society but are shocked by his disrespect for the rich and the powerful; and feminists esteem his understanding of the archaic basis of masculine domination but are puzzled by his own relationships with women. Veblen seems to delight everyone and satisfy no one.

I believe that the best way to transcend these ambiguities and to achieve a clearer sense of Veblen's achievements is to examine his thought in relation primarily to the theories of the two sovereign social thinkers of the age—Karl Marx and Max Weber. It should thus be stressed at the outset that this book has to do with social theory in general, with Veblen serving as the central focus, and Marx, Weber, Tocqueville, Durkheim, Simmel, Sombart, Mead, and others providing occasional comparative perspectives. I believe that this is how Veblen would have liked to be reconsidered, not merely as a tehnocratic reformer but as a wide-ranging scholar grappling with the same great issues of apprehending social reality that preoccupied other social theorists of the nineteenth and early twentieth centuries.

Viewed from this perspective, Veblen was almost alone in refusing to grant capitalism its historical legitimacy. He denied that it represented a "progressive" force that, whatever its negative features, had to be judged both productive and rational. He insisted, rather, that a large part of capitalist behavior is irrational and essentially hedonistic, an almost atavistic phenomenon reflecting not so much the cool prudence of bourgeois man as the residual habits of primitive societies.

Neither Marx nor Weber fully explored the possibility that modern capitalism could be interpreted as an anthropological problem, could be seen, that is, less as a unique historical "stage" or "spirit" than as a timeless mentality with roots not only in ancient, preliterate communities but also in the "barbaric" depths of contemporary man. As a result, both Marx and Weber underestimated the staying power of capitalism and fell short of perceiving the total reality of bourgeois culture. Marx concentrated on the economic forces of production to the exclusion of the sociological pressures of consumption, while Weber stressed the ascetic, as opposed to the acquisitive, nature of early capitalism, seeing the emergence of a new "ethic" rather than the reemergence of an archaic trait. It was precisely this determination to explain the "higher" by the "lower" that made Veblen the bane of capitalism and, as Perry Miller so aptly described him, "the bard of savagery."[1]

Any thorough evaluation of Veblen's achievements as a social theorist must begin with the recognition that he was the pioneer of the field of economic anthropology.[2] His criticisms of traditional economic philosophy mainly derived from his conviction that economic theory by itself failed to explain adequately everyday economic behavior. Hence orthodox economic theory had to give way to a more comprehensive theory of social phenomena, a theory grounded in the data of ethnology and anthropology. Consider, for example, the function of money. In its classical definition money fulfills three roles: it is a medium of exchange, a standard of value, and a store of wealth. Veblen found this definition too rational, based on the psychology of self-interest and economic calculation that characterized the prevailing orthodox assumptions about human behavior. For Veblen the important thing about money is the context in which it circulates, a social-cultural dimension which, once grasped, enables us to see money not primarily as a means of exchange but as an expression of power by means of its display-value. What is ultimately desired, under the name of profit or riches, is essentially power over men and women by those who possess the symbols of wealth. One of Veblen's many achievements was his demystification of the authority of wealth by exposing the psychological structure of an economic system that runs on non-economic motives. Even though he failed, perhaps not surprisingly, to drive home this message in an American culture obsessively devoted to the rule of commodities, the magnitude of his accomplishment is suggested by the fact that he was formally writing about economics, actually delving into anthropology, and ultimately making a major contribution to the sociology of human power relations.

To treat Veblen as a social theorist requires an expanded definition of the term "theory." Veblen himself never bothered to explain what he meant by the term, even when he used it in the title of his most famous book. I use it to refer not to a rigorous methodology, a simple point of view, a program of human liberation, or a theoretical "system" consisting of logically interrelated propositions subject to empirical refutation or confirmation. I use the term in a way that is bound up with the problem of consciousness. By the turn of the century, a period in which post-Marxist scholars like Weber, Durkheim, and Veblen were formulating their theories, society and consciousness of society had become problematic. It was increasingly felt that society should be explained, not by the notions of those who participate in it, but by the more profound causes which are unperceived by its members. Veblen, like Durkheim and other contemporary sociologists, perceived society as an independent power set over and apart from the individual, a power which endows the mind with concepts that subtly impose their hold as it molds the individual by means of the "forms" that arise from its inexorable socializing processes. To know society by means of theory was presumably to escape this epistemological circularity in which both the knowing subject and the object of knowledge have been ensnared. Theory, thought Veblen, would enable one to penetrate the underlying processes of society which are hidden from the more ordinary forms of consciousness.

Theory for Veblen, however, meant neither social involvement nor political activism but detachment, self-reflection, and an ironic perspective that seemed to negate everything and affirm nothing. Where Marxists believed that one knows the world by acting upon it and transforming it *(praxis)*, and where liberal pragmatists believed that social truth derived from social experimentation, Veblen held that "idle curiosity" offered the best hope of overcoming a condition of mind so alienating it is incapable of experiencing its own alienation. Marxists and capitalists alike were committed to changing the world. Veblen remained convinced that what could not be accurately interpreted could not be fundamentally changed. Before we can even begin to talk of overcoming *(Aufhebung)* alienation and exploitation we need to discover where such phenomena came from in early archaic society. It was this task that constituted the anthropological imperative of social theory.

To appreciate fully Veblen's contribution to modern consciousness one must engage in comparative social theory. There are hazards in this genre, not the least of which is the dubious promise of ultimate truth. "Comparison," wrote George Santayana, "is the expedient of those who cannot reach the heart of the things compared; and no philosophy is more external and egotistical than that which places the essence of a thing in its relation to something else."[3] Santayana's injunction may humble the philosopher; the social theorist and intellectual historian, concerned not with fixed "essences" or absolute truth but with the dynamic nature of social phenomena, recognize that we can understand social life only as a whole and that each part can be understood only by its relationships. What applies to reality applies to theory. To get at some approximate truth about social phenomena we must engage in comparative analysis. No social theory can be studied in isolation from its competitors, for it is only when theories are allowed to confront one another that we become fully aware of their limitations. This book is essentially an exercise in theoretical confrontations, an approach which is, by the way, entirely compatible with Veblen's own modes of analysis. More than any other contemporary American thinker, Veblen was a comparative scholar par excellence. His theory involved the determination of certain cultural traits in modern industrial society and the comparison of contemporary social relations with the behavior of archaic men and women in primitive societies. Probing the new data of ethnology and anthropology, Veblen offered fresh perspectives on social reality which merit but have not received systematic examination. I believe that Veblen achieved new and important insights into the nature of society, and the originality of his vision can only be made evident with the accumulation of different perspectives on it. When properly comprehended, Veblen's insights may, in the end, bring about a reorientation of modern social theory. Like the novelist of manners, he illuminated the deeper meaning of social behavior with imperishable perceptions. With the literary artist he recognized that truth may be approximated by means of satirical technique, by exposing cant and debunking the reigning misconceptions of "false consciousness." As a satirist as well as a social theorist, he remains a critical mind upon whose gaze nothing was lost.

A word about the book's organization. Part One, "The Milieu and the Man," seeks to introduce Veblen to the general reader through an elementary discussion of his writings, career, and the general historical context in which he moved. Part Two, "Theory and History," plunges into the deeper currents of modern social philosophy: theories of value, alienation, reification, mediation, hegemony, and history, and especially the sociological dynamics of capitalism in the course of American history. Part Three, "Inside the Whale," discusses Veblen's engagement with such contemporary social issues as higher education, the women question, and war and peace. The final chapter, "Disciples and Dissenters," deals with Veblen's legacy in American thought and social action, and the Conclusion, "Whither Capitalism?" offers a final estimate of the central question Veblen raised: How is unearned wealth and wasteful consumption legitimated in a culture supposedly devoted to the ethic of work and the value of efficiency?

Some of this material has appeared previously in the following journals: *Chronicle of Higher Education, History and Theory, The New Republic* and *Social Research*.

Several scholars were kind enough to read portions of the first draft of the manuscript. For their criticisms and suggestions I wish to thank Lewis Coser, Carl Degler, Anthony Giddens, Robert Heilbroner, Robert Huberty, Christine Hyerman, and Alan Lawson. Again I am indebted to my friend Gerald Meaker, who took time out from his own scholarship to give the manuscript a rigorous reading. The editorial suggestions of George Lawler are much appreciated, and so too the biographical information provided by Joseph Dorfman and the recollections of Veblen offered by Lewis Mumford. I am grateful to the John Simon Guggenheim Memorial Foundation for making possible my residence at Cambridge University where, as a Fellow at Churchill College, I worked on the book and benefitted from my conversations with Maurice Dobb, Moses Finley, Doug Gale, Tony Giddens, Jack Goody, Jack Pole, and Joan Robinson. A special note of thanks is due to David Reisman, who encouraged me to go beyond his own psychoanalytic interpretation of Veblen, doubtless realizing, as we all must, that even the revisers will be revised, not excluding, of course, this one.

Laguna Beach, 1977

List of Abbreviations

AO	*Absentee Ownership and Business Enterprise in Recent Times* (New York, 1923; Boston: Beacon edn., 1967).
BE	*The Theory of Business Enterprise* (New York, 1904; Augustus Kelley edn., 1965).
ECO	*Essays in Our Changing Order* (New York, 1934; Augustus Kelley edn., 1964).
EPS	*The Engineers and the Price System* (New York, 1921; Harcourt edn., 1963).
HL	*The Higher Learning in America: A Memorandum on the Conduct of Universities by Business Men* (New York, 1918; Hill & Wang edn., 1957).
IG	*Imperial Germany and the Industrial Revolution* (New York, 1915; Ann Arbor paperback edn., 1966).
IOW	*The Instinct of Workmanship and the State of the Industrial Arts* (New York, 1914; Norton edn., 1964).
LC	*The Theory of the Leisure Class: An Economic Study of Institutions* (New York, 1899; Mentor edn., 1953).
NP	*The Nature of Peace and the Terms of Its Perpetuation* (New York, 1917).
POS	*The Place of Science in Modern Civilization and Other Essays* (New York, 1918; Capricorn edn., 1969). Note: The Capricorn edition, used here, bears the revised title *Veblen on Marx, Race, Science and Economics*.
VI	*The Vested Interests and the Common Man* (New York, 1919; Capricorn edn., 1969).
Dorfman, I	Joseph Dorfman, *Thorstein Veblen and His America* (New York, 1934).
Dorfman, II	Joseph Dorfman, *Thorstein Veblen: Essays, Reviews and Reports: Previously Uncollected Writings* (Clifton, N.J., 1973).

THE BARD OF SAVAGERY

Thorstein Veblen and Modern Social Theory

Part One . . .

THE MILIEU AND THE MAN

1 . . Veblen's America

THE CRISIS OF THE REPUBLIC

Veblen's *Theory of the Leisure Class* was published in 1899, the eve of America's auspicious entrance into the twentieth century. Although many writers hailed the transition of centuries as a marvelous chronicle of progress, the various recent protest movements—free silver, the single tax, populism, socialism, and progressivism—strongly suggest that the majority of citizens felt themselves the victims of new, menacing economic forces they could neither comprehend nor control. While it is always difficult to explain precisely how "problems" enter first into social theory and then permeate the broader domain of public consciousness, if we scan the literature of the late nineteenth and early twentieth centuries we can discern the countercurrents of discontent under the surface of doctrine. Let us trace some of the revelations disclosed in the writings that appeared a dozen or so years before and after the publication of Veblen's great classic.

We first learn the lessons of power: that liberty has succumbed to the rule of plutocracy (James Bryce, *The American Commonwealth*, 1889), that the moguls of Wall Street produce nothing and control everything (William "Coin" Harvey, *Money, Trusts, and Imperialism*, 1900), that corruption is rampant in the highest levels of public office (David Graham Phillips, *The Treason of the Senate*, 1906), and that "nature is rich, but everywhere man, the heir of nature, is poor" (Henry Demarest Lloyd, *Wealth Against Commonwealth*, 1894). We next learn the lessons of history: that the democratic values that had sprung from the plenitude of land and space would decline with the closing of western territory to further settlement (Frederick Jackson Turner, "The Significance of the American Frontier," 1893), that ethnic minorities clustered in city ghettos had been denied access to the opportunities which made democratic values real and viable (Jacob Riis, *How The Other Half Lives*, 1890), that America's political values actually conceal the seamy side of American history (Charles Beard, *An Economic Interpretation of the Constitution*, 1913), and that traditional American values can mean nothing until the woman is liberated from the drudgery of domesticity (Charlotte Perkins Gilman, *Women and Economics*, 1898). Yet, turning to philosophers and social theorists, we realize that the raising of consciousness cannot be entertained until the mind attains a self-critical understanding of its own nature (William James, "Does Consciousness Exist?" 1904), that individual meaning and value may be impossible to establish since all knowledge depends upon customs that are relative, neither good nor bad but merely culturally pertinent to time and place (William Graham Sumner, *Folkways*, 1906), and that the individual has been absorbed into political society and can no longer be regarded as a discrete unit of investigation (Arthur Bentley, *The Process of Government*, 1908). Finally, reaching for religious help, we learn that man has succumbed completely to the temptations of the flesh (Max Nordau, *Degeneration*, 1895), that sin and suffering are real and can only be comprehended through faith in God (Josiah Royce, *Studies of Good and Evil*, 1898), that a revival of religious fervor and social duty offers the last chance for America to redeem herself (Walter Rauschenbusch, *Christianity and the Social Crisis*, 1907), but that human nature is incorrigibly venal (Mark Twain, "The Man That Corrupted Hadleyburg," 1899), and that Christianity is senile and God is dead (H. L. Mencken, *The Philosophy of Nietszche*, 1908).

Amidst this babel of wisdom from the intelligentsia, the American people remained as disturbed as they were delighted when they gazed forward into the new century. Three problems especially troubled them. One was the loss of individual freedom, the erosion of self-autonomy by the hierarchical structures of power that had arisen from the processes of modernization. As the country passed from an agrarian to an industrial economy, and as citizens migrated from the farms to the cities, more and more workers became dependent for their livelihood upon those who owned the sources of materials and the machinery of production. In turn ownership of these crucial means of economic life gravitated to a previously unknown entity which became, after 1880, the major locus of economic power—the corporation. Serving at first as an efficient instrument for channeling entrepreneurial activity, the corporate form of business came to be regarded by the popular mind as little more than a Leviathan of greed and corruption, the railroad conspirators well known to the readers of Frank Norris' *The Octopus* (1901), and the stock manipulators familiar to the readers of Theodore Dreiser's *The Titan* (1914). America had been predominantly a nation of farmers and small-town merchants devoted to a life of economic opportunity and competitive individualism. Americans came to take it for granted that property would be broadly distributed and political and economic power widely dispersed. The reaction against the sudden appearance, in the late nineteenth century, of the giant corporation reflected the widespread reaction against centralized economic power and revealed the strength of traditional American values. It was precisely Veblen's task to show that old ideals had to be overcome before new institutions could be effectively challenged.

→ Lynds

Workers and consumers were not the only ones threatened by the corporation. Advanced capitalism also rendered the independent businessman a casuality of progress. The disappearance of the self-employed artisan and storekeeper went on apace as corporate capitalism evolved ever more elaborate organizational techniques. This process culminated in the trust, a form of combination in which affiliated companies handed over their stocks and their power to a central board of trustees. John D. Rockefeller's Standard Oil trust, organized in 1889, was the first and most successful venture in large-scale credit control. Rockefeller and his defenders maintained that the competitive victories that produced his enormous wealth and power were due to his innovative marketing methods and entrepreneurial genius. It is significant that those who saw corporate power as a threat to individual freedom had no technical rebuttal to the capitalist's defense of business consolidation based upon efficiency and productivity. Indeed, it was typical of America that the only legislative response to corporate power was to restore the principle of competition by legal statute—a policy perhaps unique among the western nations. Yet the Sherman Anti-Trust Act (1890), designed to break up corporations into smaller units, was merely an attempt to remedy by more individualism the problems that resulted precisely from unfettered individualism. Veblen, on the other hand, formulated a unique refutation of the corporate ideology of concentration, one that argued the case against capitalism in terms of its own claims of efficiency and productivity.

If politically the American people sensed their loss of power under corporate capitalism, psychologically they became increasingly conscious of the affront of wealth and status. Gustavus Myers's three-volume work *A History of Great American Fortunes,* published in 1909 and 1910, served as a factual confirmation of popular outrage over the maldistribution of income. Myers may have not been entirely correct in assuming that the concentration of wealth resulted from the industrial growth of the post-Civil War period. Even during the Jacksonian era of the "common man," to go back no farther, the moneyed classes had comprised a social elite. What was new in the late nineteenth century was the growing depth of the abyss between the rich and poor and the manner in which wealth could be so blatantly flaunted. Mark Twain labeled these years the "Gilded Age" seeking to connote an era of lusty extravagance. "Society" became synonymous with newly risen pseudo-gothic mansions wherein gas lights flickered lasciviously over presumably endless revelries amid settings of crystal and silver, oak and mahogany, velvet and marble. New York, Chicago, and San Francisco—all great cities—had their "parlor houses," an euphemism for magnificent bordellos with hand-carved oak doors, walls paneled with satin-wood and lined with beveled mirrors, and, of course, polished mahogany bars at which "gentlemen" might savor imported champagne and oysters while boasting of commercial coups and erotic conquests. In an era of flamboyant sensibility it was natural that Jim Fisk, the talented *roué* who milked the Erie Railroad dry, should build the Grand Opera House in New York City as a splendiferous monument housing both the Erie head office and numbers of glamorous women who dressed in tights.

But Fisk and his cohorts Daniel Drew and Jay Gould, the miscreant millionaires of the "gold conspiracy" of 1869, found themselves frowned upon by the Rockefellers, the Vanderbilts, and other members of the upper stratum of the "old" *nouveaux riches* who believed their wealth reflected their accomplishments and character. These would-be pillars of society commonly announced their "arrival" by staging fancy-dress balls of considerable ostentation. Mrs. W. K. Vanderbilt hosted a housewarming in her Fifth Avenue mansion. It seemed that the Medicis had come to Manhattan. The halls and drawing rooms were lined with rose blossoms and the upstairs gymnasium was turned into a massive dining room set incongruously in the tropics. Mr. Vanderbilt dressed as Louis XIV and his wife as a Venetian princess. Such extravagance could be justified by conservative economists and custodians of culture. Luxurious expenditure, after all, served to circulate money; the construction of a 40-bedroom house involved the employment of labor, and exquisite decoration provided patronage for the arts and crafts.[1] But on rare occasions the public saw things differently. During the panic of 1897, the Bradley Martins decided to give a ball in order to help alleviate national unemployment. The lavish affair, held in the Waldorf Astoria, had an estimated cost of three hundred and sixty-nine thousand dollars. So great was the outcry in the press against such wasteful opulence that the Martins fled to Europe in disgrace.

The radical left exulted over this debacle, seeing in it the rumblings of class consciousness. Artist William Balfour was inspired to draw his famous picture of a dining room full of tycoons and matrons, resplendent in diamond-studded cuff-links and emerald-studded evening gowns, recoiling in well-bred horror from the powerful fist of a laboring man shown smashing up through the planks of the restaurant floor. The drawing, which showed the floor supported on the bowed heads and shoulders of the proletariat below, doubtless satisfied the aesthetics of class conflict. But it must be asked whether lower-class Americans actually desired to bring down the higher classes or merely to climb up into them? Were workers who constantly had to be reminded that the rich were unhappy and decadent psychologically capable of challenging the hegemony of capitalism? Did the labor movement in fact pose a real threat to the authority of wealth in America?

A third problem confronting the new American industrial society was the evident inadequacy of moral principles in the struggle against the power of big business. Contemporary ethical philosophy represented a curious amalgam derived from the utilitarian materialism of Franklin and the Founding Fathers, the spiritual idealism of Emerson and the Transcendentalists, and the amoral and competitive individualism of William Graham Sumner and the Social Darwinists. These doctrinal strands, offering the antithetical options of a materialization of mind, a mystical intuition of "spirit," or a commercial cult of action,[2] had nothing in common with one another except the most precious idea of all—the principle of self-reliance. But the attempt to apply this individualistic moral code, born of a swiftly passing agrarian society, to the realities of a highly industrialized and increasingly integrated social order had, in fact, proved futile. For while the traditional notion of morality rested heavily on personal responsibility, the anonymity of corporate organization served to obscure individual obligation and indeed to depersonalize the entire sphere of human relations. By the same token, the older idea of religious morality had implied that good and evil were easily recognizable; yet as the sociologist E. A. Ross noted in *Sin and Society* (1907), it was the essence of modern business life that it opened the gates wide to greed, liberated society from traditional restraints, and thereby freed behavior from the ancient burden of guilt. Moreover, although the older ethical codes of Jefferson and Franklin had presupposed an innate "moral sense," modern science and evolutionary thought denied the reality of man's spiritual conscience. In the universe of moral silence revealed by naturalistic thought, ethics seemed to follow the logic of power, not the power of logic or the promptings of compassion.

There was, no doubt, much more to late nineteenth and early twentieth-century America than rampant material greed, industrial conflict, ethical paralysis, municipal corruption, and unwashed immigrants. But this was the vision of American life that rose from the pages of Lincoln Steffens, Homer Lea, Ignatius Donnelly, Mary Lease, Brooks and Henry Adams, and, not least, Jack London. And it was this version which fueled the apocalyptic premonitions of representatives of the older Anglo-American order that was increasingly challenged by what seemed to be an unholy alliance of besotted Irish laborers and greedy Jewish bankers. Even the more benign and patrician utopians like Edward Bellamy and William Dean Howells felt the hot breath of impending social upheaval, and it was, indeed, this fear of catastrophe that underlay their obsession with harmony. Some progressives also felt a deep sense of fatalism before the sway of corporate power. Even the robust Theodore Roosevelt confessed his initial helplessness in his *Autobiography:* "A riot of individualistic materialism, under which complete freedom for the individual . . . turned out in practice to mean perfect freedom for the strong to wrong the weak. The power of the mighty industrial overlords . . . had increased with giant strides, while the methods of controlling them . . . through the government, remained archaic and therefore practically impotent."[3]

Roosevelt and many of the era's reformers were less interested in analyzing the deeper causes of capitalist power than in correcting its pernicious consequences. This approach put the solution before the problem. If the power of government could, perhaps, be wielded to curb the economic power of big business, what political means could be used to check the cultural authority of wealth? If indeed the "mighty industrial overlords" were so manifestly wicked and selfish, how did they come to gain such great influence and prestige that even Roosevelt, the President of the United States, could often feel dwarfed by their presence? It was above all this question that Veblen would seek to answer.

The Reform Persuasion

The republic's effort to save itself from the power of the moneyed classes and to restore the potency of the moral conscience gave rise in Veblen's era to two political movements, progressivism and socialism. Flowing through both of these movements were three intellectual currents that provided the impetus for reform and the inspiration for social change: liberal idealism, Christian humanitarianism, and science and social engineering.

The first of these currents surfaced politically during the progressive movement, finding a national platform in the administrations of Roosevelt and Woodrow Wilson. Both presidents desired to renew the moral fibre of the nation; neither proposed a basic restructuring of the economic order or a thoroughgoing analysis of its ideological foundations. Roosevelt was willing to use the power of the federal government to give a "square deal" to the laborer, the farmer, and the small businessman who was being eliminated by big business. Wilson wanted to use the state not to discipline business but to revive pristine American virtues. Roosevelt's sense of struggle and conflict and his condemnation of the "malefactors of wealth" resembled in some respects Veblen's Darwinian understanding of the power that the strong command over the weak. Wilson, on the other hand, believed that abusive power could be liquidated by restoring, through government regulatory agencies if necessary, competitive opportunities to business. Where Roosevelt felt that power could at best be curbed, Wilson remained convinced that it could be cleansed through a reinvigoration of the old values of individualism, initiative, and enterprise. "A people shall be saved," Wilson declared, "by the waters welling up from its own sweet, perennial springs. Not from above; not by patronage of its aristocrats. Everything that blooms in beauty in the air of heaven draws its fairness, its vigor, from its roots. . . . Up from the soil, up from the silent bosoms of the earth, rise the currents of life and energy. Up from the common soil, up from the quiet heart of the people, rise joyously today streams of hope and determination bound to renew the face of the earth in glory."[4]

The liberal tradition represented one source of reform, the religious heritage another. Radical Protestant idealism, with its moral indignation and evangelical promise of a better world, influenced both progressivism and Christian socialism. One of the most widely read books of the era was Edward Bellamy's *Looking Backward* (1888), a parable of spiritual communalism which called for, in the tradition of great revivals, "a melting and flowing forth of men's hearts toward one another." The Boston minister W. D. P. Bliss organized the journal *American Fabian* as a fusion of Bellamyite idealism and Christian socialism, and the Reverend George D. Herron, one of the leading figures of the American Socialist Party, identified Christianity and Marxism as equal evangels of the religion of humanity. The social gospel movement also brought its missionary zeal to bear upon public life, sending its disciples into the slums to study the labor question, boss politics, and absentee ownership. At the theoretical level, these ideas and activities culminated in Walter Rauschenbusch's *Christianity and the Social Crisis* (1907), a religious treatise that indicted capitalism for corrupting the spirit of men by encouraging such anti-Christian principles as aggression, covetousness, and pride.

Thorstein Veblen responded to the vast literature of moral reform with ennui and skepticism. From his perspective, both liberal progressivism and Christian socialism seemed like a futile attempt to march forward to yesterday, to revive as solutions the very notions that were part of the problem. Bourgeois individualism could hardly arrest the concentration of wealth and power, which resulted in large part from the technical imperatives of corporate organization. Nor could Protestantism restore the work ethic in a society in which leisure was increasingly becoming, if not a noble calling, an enviable life-style.

It was in the third ingredient of reform thought—science and social engineering—that Veblen found greatest hope for the future of industrial civilization. The prestige of science at the turn of the century was partly due to the great feats of engineering and medicine, whose achievements were regularly celebrated at world fairs and exhibitions. Accomplishments in these areas could not help but enhance the belief that the genius of scientific method could be used to illuminate the nature and workings of society as well. Ironically, this great dream of the eighteenth-century Enlightenment supported the position of several conservative social theorists, who assumed that an empirical study of "nature's" economic laws would justify laissez-faire doctrines and lead to a more rational and productive life for all. But the empirical method of analysis also inspired many radical critics who regarded socialism as the "science of society." At the turn of the century the intellectual left was fond of quoting Marx to the effect that scientists should "put their knowledge to the service of mankind." Veblen joined in espousing this synthesis of empirical knowledge and social progress. Despite his theoretical differences with the Marxists, he eagerly translated for American readers Ferdinand Lasalle's moving address, "Die Wissenschaft und die Arbeiter" ("Science and the Workingman").

Lester Ward, the father of American sociology, also looked to science as the foundation of modern society and the focus of modern social analysis. Ward was the liberal's answer to conservative Social Darwinism. His *Dynamic Sociology* (1883) urged Darwinists like Herbert Spencer and William Graham Sumner to appreciate the creative role of the mind and not to dismiss man as a passive creature in the evolutionary process. Laissez-faire economics led to chaos and strife, whereas genuine progress resulted only from man's calculated interference with nature. Thus the best agents of social progress were those who understood how man can control the forces of nature by deliberate artifice. "Before progressive legislation can become a success," Ward advised, "every legislature must become, as it were, a polytechnic school, a laboratory of philosophical research, into the laws of society and of human nature. No legislator is qualified to vote on or propose measures designed to affect the destinies of millions of social units until he masters all that is known of the science of society. Every true legislator must be a sociologist."[5]

What were these "laws of society and of human nature"? Ward believed that one could discover them through empirical research and theoretical analysis, and in so doing the sociologist could demonstrate man's cooperative and sociable nature and thereby lay the basis for the coming of the good society. Veblen was less certain that the "men of good hope" (Daniel Aaron's apt description) would win out over the forces of corporate power. Not only did such an optimistic view slight the burden of man's archaic heritage, it failed to consider how deeply assimilated was the ideology of capitalism in American thought and culture. No one was more aware of the preeminence of capitalist values than Veblen himself.

The Preeminence of Capitalist Ideology

In many respects Veblen was to nineteenth-century capitalism what Voltaire was to eighteenth-century Catholicism: the scourge, satirist, and *grand démolisseur* of dogmatic belief. Both the French philosopher and the American social theorist embraced modernity with some ambivalence, and both turned their sardonic wit on the fictions that sustained sacred institutions and on the inexhaustible foibles of the human race. But while Voltaire's ideas ultimately triumphed and found expression in the Enlightenment, those of Veblen proved, in the end, unable to survive the shifting interests and perceptions of several generations of American intellectuals. Whether the "grand man" Veblen was "buried by orthodoxy," as the British economist Joan Robison has lamented (in a conversation with this writer), or whether his ideas succumbed to inherent fallacies is a matter we shall take up later. The immediate aim of these early chapters is to explain Veblen's role in the liberation of American social thought in the first two decades of the twentieth century. To do this it is necessary first to understand the assumptions that underlay the hegemony of capitalist ideas and values. Those assumptions of late nineteenth-century American conservative ideology contained three dominant ingredients: the Protestant ethic, Social Darwinism, and political economy.

Although the Protestant ethic emerged in America in the sermons of the seventeenth-century Puritans, it would be erroneous—or at least a grave over-simplification—to view Calvinist theology as the midwife of capitalist ideology, as later scholars have been wont to imagine. For Calvinism scarcely instilled the bold confidence and unrestrained rationality that became characteristic of the bourgeois entrepreneur; nor were the American Puritans devoted to a life of economic individualism, competitive enterprise, and boundless materialism. On the contrary, their greatest dream lay in community, their greatest fear in discord. Nevertheless, although Puritanism and capitalism were historically distinct ideologies, they shared at least one common premise (which Veblen challenged in its later capitalist formulation): the "gospel" of work and wealth. Two centuries before Andrew Carnegie enunciated it we can find in the writings of Cotton Mather and other Puritan divines the doctrine of the two callings, the idea that a Christian can serve God while pursuing his own occupation. In this worldly formulation economic success could be regarded as a "sign" of salvation even though the claim of sanctification through work violated the doctrine of grace and carried with it the sin of pride. Puritanism was incompatible with capitalism in many respects, but in so far as it held out hope of salvation through practical Christian endeavor it encouraged an activist morality in which man eventually would, as the Puritans feared, be "swallowed up" by material desires and "drown'd in the Encumbrances of his Occupation."[6]

Ben Franklin was not the perfect American embodiment of the Protestant ethic. He was too much the hedonist, the public servant, and the curious scientist to "drown" himself in the single pursuit of capitalist acquisition. But Franklin's belief in character cultivation through hard work clearly had roots in Protestantism, and his "Way To Wealth" maxims set the tone for the "try, try again" injunctions of the McGuffey Reader, the "rags-to-riches" parables of Horatio Alger, and the self-help philosophy of Carnegie. The idea of individual success, the triumph of will over circumstances, soon permeated American thought and culture, high as well as low, as Veblen well knew. By the late nineteenth century the traditional Protestant ethic became almost synonymous with the lessons of Carnegie's famous "Gospel of Wealth": prosperity is evidence of character and virtue, poverty of laziness and vice.

The doctrine of Social Darwinism reinforced the Protestant ethic by translating a presumed spiritual truth into a presumed natural fact. The catchwords that derived from the theory of evolution—"struggle for existence," "natural selection," and "survival of the fittest"—gave scientific validation to the capitalist philosophy of life. For the central premise of both capitalism and Darwinism—a premise which Veblen challenged—held that life was a grim, competitive struggle over the limited resources provided by nature, a struggle in which nature, rather than God, would reward the strong, able, and industrious, while penalizing the weak, lazy, and careless. The great exponent of Social Darwinism in America was William Graham Sumner, a Yale scholar who had been brought up on the Protestant ideal that one serves God by being frugal and productive. Later, as a graduate student, Sumner abandoned Christianity for the teachings of the influential English philosopher Herbert Spencer. Spencer maintained that no one should attempt to interfere with the inexorable processes of nature, which, left to evolve according to their own "laws," would bring man closer to perfection. Spencer opposed government regulation of the economy, state-supported schools, aid to the poor, and even public-health laws, believing that nature was doing humanity a favor by "singling out the low spirited, the intemperate, and the debilitated as the victims of an epidemic."[7]

As Spencer's American disciple, Sumner attacked the reformers and socialists of the left, the "ignorant men of impossible dreams" who would try to defy nature by making the world over. To Sumner society could best be understood as an analogy to biology. The Darwinian principles of struggle persist and the cruelties of nature are necessarily reflected in society. The human animal is driven to compete only by the "iron spur" of scarcity; too many people and not enough land force men to struggle with one another over the means of subsistance. In this endless combat no one owes anything to anyone. The lone individual must practice the two great virtues of hard work and self-denial, human virtues which contribute to the economic resources of labor and capital. The "hero of civilization is the bank-depositer," Sumner declared, the man who, by his capacity for deferred gratification, saves and invests wisely, creates capital, and thereby forges economic growth. These moral lessons were the scientific truths that the left ignored. Motivated by the false doctrine of equality, the radical wanted to eliminate competition and to take from the productive and give to the unproductive. In destroying the sources of capital, the left would destroy the basis of civilization.[8]

Reinforcing the Protestant ethic and Social Darwinism was the third ingredient of American conservative thought, political economy.

Nineteenth-century American economic theory derived to a large extent from Adam Smith's *Wealth of Nations* and the eighteenth-century concept of natural law. As a discipline economics was deductive, based on the assumption of a natural order of things working through immutable laws that encompassed a universe of almost perfect regularity. From this assumption economists like John Bates Clark, the target of Veblen's attacks, could draw several corollaries. First, conservative economists believed that competition was the law of life, and they tended to see more order and harmony in this principle than did the Social Darwinists. "Rightly viewed," wrote the distinguished economist Francis A. Walker, "perfect competition would seem to be the order of the economic universe, as truly as gravity is the order of the physical universe, and to be no less harmonious and beneficent in operation."[9] Second, the "free market" was the institutionalized reflection of man's natural tendency toward self-assertion, and hence it could no more be eliminated than could the law of gravity. Third, free enterprise assures that the economy will function according to the laws of supply and demand, a self-regulating mechanism that governs price and wage levels to the benefit of the buyer as well as the seller. Fourth, since prices and wages follow a "natural course," the principle of laissez faire must be followed by a government whose only function is national security and protection of property. And fifth, since self-interest is and will always be the mainspring of human action, the behavior of "economic man" is rational and thus capable of empirical analysis and perhaps eventually of scientific predictability.

The tenets of the Protestant ethic, Social Darwinism, and political economy were shared not only by conservative economists but by such titans of capitalism as John D. Rockefeller, James J. Hill, Commodore Vanderbilt, and J. P. Morgan. Although the well-read Carnegie knew his Spencer, it is highly doubtful that other business giants were steeped in the literature of political economy or Social Darwinism.[10] Nor did the captains of industry seriously try to reconcile the ingredients of conservative thought. Hence Rockefeller could draw upon Social Darwinism to explain why the classical principle of competition was not fit for survival in the modern era of business consolidation.

> The growth of a large business is merely a survival of the fittest. . . . The American beauty rose can be produced in the splendor and fragrance which bring cheer to its beholder only by sacrificing the early buds which grow up around it. This is not an evil tendency in business. It is merely the working-out of a law of nature and a law of God.[11]

Without once calling business an "evil tendency," Veblen was able to contradict flatly almost every premise and assumption upon which the ideology of capitalism rested.

2 . . . Enter Veblen: "Disturber of the Intellectual Peace"

THE STATUS OF LEISURE AND THE STIGMA OF LABOR

Veblen's better-known works—*The Theory of the Leisure Class, The Theory of Business Enterprise, The Engineers and the Price System,* and *Absentee Ownership*—were attempts to expose the value system of modern industrial America as described above, while his theoretical essays and his most ambitious philosophical treatise, *The Instinct of Workmanship,* may be read as attempts at developing an alternative explanation to the three reigning social theories of his era: the neoclassical school of economics, the Marxist philosophy of history, and the Weberian interpretation of capitalism and the Protestant ethic. We shall deal first with Veblen the demolisher, and we begin at the beginning, with the origins of property. To deconstruct the ideology of capitalism Veblen posed a simple question: How was property originally acquired?

According to orthodox theory, possession of goods was somehow related to the moral worth of the possessor, the assumption being that capitalist man had created wealth by virtue of his labor and superior intelligence and character. This notion, prevalent in the nineteenth-century, had its rationale in the philosophy of Locke and the classical thought of the eighteenth century. But Veblen felt no need to return to classical thought in order to question the legitimacy of property as a reward for labor. Drawing instead from contemporary anthropology, he pointed out that property was frequently seized, appropriated either by stealth or brute force. Rather than being an honorable feat of production, private wealth often originated in an act of aggression.

To support this impious thesis Veblen discussed two types of contrasting communities which anthropologists had only begun to study in depth. He discovered, in feudal Japan, in the Polynesian islands, and among the Icelandic tribes, the existence of a "leisure class," that is, war lords and tribal chieftains who lived off the labor of their own people. More provocatively, Veblen claimed to find among some little-studied peoples just being researched by anthropologists—such as the Pueblos, various other North American Indians, the Andamans, the Todas, the Ainu of Asia and Africa, and "some Bushman and Eskimo groups"—communities which seemed to lack an exploiting class altogether, communities which were invariably small, sedentary, and collectivist. The distinguishing characteristics of these latter communities were their marginal subsistence economies, their peaceful character, and the absence of all formal claims to private property. In the leisure-class societies, however, property was a central feature, and indeed one of the earliest expressions of ownership was the possession of women by the stronger men of the village. The seizure of females in tribal clashes marked the lower stages of "barbarian culture," an act possibly related to the origins of slavery. Veblen speculated that women were most likely captured because of their "usefulness as trophies," and this appropriation of humans was eventually extended to other "useful things" in archaic economies that were advancing beyond the edge of bare survival. Thus even in its most primitive form the struggle for wealth was not, as some classical theorists had assumed, merely a struggle for subsistence. Nor could the economic history of man be read, as it had been by Veblen's popular contemporary Simon Patten, as the story of the triumph of a "pleasure" or surplus economy over a "pain" or deprivation economy. On the contrary, in societies where bare survival had given way to a measure of abundance, struggle continued to express itself in a desire for power and prestige, and the possessions of the ruling members derived not from labor but from "force and fraud." The leisure class was not idle; it busily accumulated servants, slaves, women, ornaments, garments, and other artifacts of status; but its activities had little to do with the actual creation of wealth through productive labor. In a word, the leisure class was predatory.

That property is theft was hardly a revelation in radical social thought, nor did the idea seriously touch the theoretical justification of ownership as a reward for work and savings, at least in empirical economics wherein the motives of individuals were irrelevant. But neoclassical economists and defenders of modern business enterprise assumed that capitalists enjoyed deference because the public recognized their contribution to the general welfare. Veblen's anthropological explorations led to a strikingly different conclusion. Although tribal chieftains did little to enhance the public good, they could seize goods and flaunt their expropriated wealth with the smiling approval of the whole community. Why? The deferential status of the leisure class, Veblen pointed out, resulted from changes in economic conditions. The shift from a sedentary agricultural existence to one of pursuit of large animals and the conduct of tribal invasions and conquest meant that the skills of the hunter and warrior would now be prized in the eyes of the community. In this shift away from "peaceful savagery" lay not only the origin of the leisure class but the distinction between male and female occupations. The position of the woman laborer, who had at one time tilled the soil and nurtured the harvest on an equal basis with males, now declined as her work came to be seen as dull and routine compared to the adventurous exploits of the powerful male. "The warrior and hunter alike reap where they have not strewn. Their aggressive assertion of force and sagacity differs obviously from the women's assiduous and uneventful shaping of materials; it is not to be accounted productive labor, but rather an acquisition of substance by seizure."[1]

The prestige of the warrior and hunter was further enhanced by the rise of the tendency toward "emulation." With the passing of the peaceful economy of the savage state and the coming of the predatory stage of existence, the emergence of objects of desire and envy first took root as a social phenomenon. Booty, trophies, and other paraphernalia came to be prized as evidence of the "pre-eminent force" of the possessor. Far back in the history of archaic cultures Veblen discovered in the psychology of emulation a key to the riddle that troubled Marx—the "fetishism of commodities."

The emergence of the possessor to a position of power and eminence brings us to one of Veblen's greatest insights, the cultural revolution in man's attitude toward work that accompanied the advance of modern economic society. With the growing esteem of predatory wealth came a growing disdain for productive labor. Obtaining goods by methods other than seizure came to be regarded as unheroic and mundane, while the acquisition of wealth by force was increasingly regarded as honorable and dignified. Eventually all productive work, even employment in personal service, suffered the same odium for the same reason. As abundance increased labor was no longer honored by the community; it became an occupation fit only for men and women of lower station. And the pleasures of productive work were lost sight of as the community came to look upon it as sterile drudgery. Yet the activity of labor—and this was the crux of the matter—is not dull and grinding because of its inherent nature but rather because society had deemed it as such. "Labor," Veblen noted in challenging the orthodox assumption that man had no innate love for work, "acquires a character of irksomeness by virtue of the indignity imputed to it."[2]

Although seemingly remote from contemporary economics, Veblen's anthropological observations aimed to show that the predatory traits of primitive man were continued in the pecuniary habits of modern "civilized" man. These archaic traits manifested themselves in several ways. For one thing, leisure as an expression of social superiority and labor as a form of debasement remained characteristic of modern industrial life. Every evidence of abstention from productive work "is beautiful and ennobling in all civilized men's eyes." The contemporary man of wealth, no less than his tribal forebear, makes every effort to demonstrate he is not engaged in constructive employment. This behavior can be seen in the genteel manners that distinguish the leisure class. Refined tastes and sensibilities are evidence of good breeding, the cultivation of which can only be achieved by those who are free from the more practical demands of life. The hiring of servants is also evidence of the social status of the master of the house, and the wealthier the master, the more idle the servants. The housewife, too, becomes the lady of leisure whose frivolous activities serve the ceremonial function of dramatizing the husband's reputable standing. Even more obvious is the dress style of the leisure class. Elegant clothes serve the purpose not only of advertising extravagant expenditure but of demonstrating that the wearer is exempt from personal contact with productive labor. The "charm" of the spotless shirt, the neatly pressed suit, the uncomfortable starched collar, the shining patent leather shoes, and the "lustrous cylindrical hat" suggests that the gentleman so attired cannot stoop to useful employment.

While the leisure class manifests its privileged position by refraining from all socially useful activities, it magnifies its pecuniary power by consuming what others have produced. To Veblen the phenomenon of "conspicuous consumption" was symptomatic of the superfluous life-style of the rich. Wearing diamond-studded jewelry, overindulging in luxurious foods and alcohol, and maintaining a livery of racing horses were the perquisites of men of gentle breeding whose lavish parties and well-publicized feasts redounded to their glory. Veblen conceded that certain art objects possessed by the rich contained intrinsic aesthetic value, but their artistic worth could not explain their inordinate commercial price. Even great works of art do not become great until they are discovered, until the "canon of expensiveness" makes them "beautiful." Above all, objects of conspicuous consumption must be without function and serviceability; since their social value lies in their having no practical use whatsoever, only those who can squander wealth can afford them. "In order to be reputable it must be wasteful." To embellish this dictum Veblen subjected the economic mores of upper Victorian society to a wicked and hyperbolic utilitarian criterion. The spacious, manicured lawns that surround the palatial mansions of Newport and Hyde Park, for example, were not kept up by the grazing of cattle, for that would suggest thrift and utility, inexpensive therefore indecorous. Similarly with animals. No reputable household would dare contain such useful creatures as sheep, goats, hogs, draught horses, and barnyard fowls, but instead would adorn its premises with fancy-bred pets. And the rich, Veblen wryly noted perhaps more with amusement than accuracy, are temperamentally ill-suited to the cat, who (except for the Angora) is too independent and self-sufficient; they prefer the dog, either the pedigree who symbolizes the owner's wealth and breeding or the trained hound who symbolizes the master's pastime as a huntsman, the leisure activity of the predator. The dog, Veblen chided, is said to be "man's best friend," which can only mean that the "filthiest" and "nastiest" of domestic animals has "the gift of unquestioning subservience and a slave's quickness in guessing his master's mood."[3]

In view of the enormous profits accruing to today's pet food industry, market analysts might well read Veblen's account of household animals as conspicuous consumers. But in Veblen's time economists had their eyes fixed on charts and statistics while he studied primitive behavior in order better to understand the motives behind modern behavior. To most nineteenth-century thinkers the development of modern society had been regarded as further evidence of historical progress, an assumption shared alike by capitalists and Marxists. Veblen was almost alone in seeing continuity and persistence where others saw change and progress. The leisure class, for example, not only continued to follow its ancient predatory instincts, it was still esteemed by the community because of the mindless admiration of personal strength that is the residue of barbarism in contemporary life. The "modern survival of prowess" could be seen in the leisure class's traditional preference for fighting and dueling, its martial spirit, and its aggressive patriotism. Veblen acknowledged that the high-bred gentleman and the rowdy both have a bellicose temperament; but fighting for the "lower-class delinquent" may be a brief reversion brought on either by momentary irritation, alcoholic exaltation, or by the instinct of self-preservation; for the leisure class fighting is a natural way of life, an honorable occupation which for centuries had been the only profession worthy of a gentleman. The clearest artifact of this behavior is the walking stick, which serves not only as a symbol of peripatetic leisure but as an actual weapon of self-defense.

Nowhere is the barbarian prowess of the leisure class better illustrated than in the field of sports. The zeal of athletic games is further evidence of the survival of the combative instinct. Boxing and bullfighting of course are only of vicarious significance to the rich, and indeed to all who call themselves civilized. For these spectacles enable modern man to experience the triumph of strength and the infliction of pain without admitting these desires within himself. Other activities, like hunting, shooting, and angling, are reputable both because they represent the continuation of the older useful pursuits through which primitive man won status and because they have come through the ages to be identified with the life of the landed gentry. These activities meet the two requirements of "proximate purposefulness and ulterior wastefulness." If fox hunting is economically useless but socially honorable, it also suggests that the play of man has an amazing survival value because the instinct of *homo ludens* originally served the biological purpose of supplying food. But other sports are reputable because they dramatize man's combat with fellow man, an engagement in "emulative ferocity" that requires such skills as cunning and pugnacity. Of all the predatory sports football seemed to Veblen the clearest example of a return to *ferae natura*. To the argu-

w. contrast James

ment that collegiate football builds character, Veblen replied: "It has been said, not inaptly, that the relation of football to physical culture is much the same as that of the bull-fight to agriculture."[4]

An integral aspect of sport is chance, which may signify the element of personal danger, as in football or big-game hunting, or simply the element of gambling. But whether the thrill of adventure or the psychology of betting is involved, the belief in luck represents for Veblen another continuation of barbarian habits. The gambler, seeking to overcome the "prosy mediocrity" of modern industrial life, finds alleviation from mechanistic routine by believing that the unpredictable and the unknown can be ascertained by means of wearing charms, having faith in mascots, or devising a "system" to outguess the roulette table. The gambling proclivity in sport suggests its relationship to the capitalist ethos of success through risk taking and speculation; it also suggests its relationship to boyhood fantasies. A youthful addiction to athletics as well as to betting is a form of adolescence that "marks an arrested development of the man's moral nature." It is characteristic of those prone to adventure, histrionics, and make-believe, as well as to clannishness, swagger, and toughness. Indeed it is the hero worship of the strong that the leisure class and the working class have in common, and what is mutually admired are the archaic traits of childish aggressiveness and competitiveness that are destructive of mature social life. Veblen's observations are too telling to paraphrase:

> As it finds expression in the life of the barbarian, prowess manifests itself in two main directions—force and fraud. In varying degrees these two forms of expression are similarly present in modern warfare, in the pecuniary occupations, and in sports and games. Both lines of aptitudes are cultivated and strengthened by the life of sport as well as by the more serious forms of emulative life. Strategy or cunning is an element invariably present in games, as also in warlike pursuits and in the chase. In all of these employments strategy tends to develop into finesse and chicanery. Chicanery, falsehood, browbeating, hold a well-secured place in the method of procedure of any athletic contest and in games generally. The habitual employment of an umpire, and the minute technical regulations governing the limits and details of permissible fraud and strategic advantage, sufficiently attest the fact that fraudulent practices and attempts to overreach one's opponents are not adventitious features of the game. In the nature of the case habituation to sports should conduce to a fuller development of the aptitude for fraud; and the prevalence in the community of that predatory temperament which inclines men to sports connotes a prevalence of sharp practice and callous disregard of the interests of others, individually and collectively. Resort to fraud, in any guise and under any legitimation of law or custom, is an expression of a narrowly self-regarding habit of mind. It is needless to dwell at any length on the economic value of this feature of the sporting character.
>
> In this connection it is to be noted that the most obvious characteristic of the physiognomy affected by athletic and other sporting men is that of an

extreme astuteness. The gifts and exploits of Ulysses are scarcely second to those of Achilles, either in their substantial furtherance of the game or in the éclat which they give the astute sporting man among his associates. The pantomime of astuteness is commonly the first step in that assimilation to the professional sporting man which a youth undergoes after matriculation in any reputable school, of the secondary or the higher education, as the case may be. And the physiognomy of astuteness, as a decorative feature, never ceases to receive the thoughtful attention of men whose serious interest lies in athletic games, races, or other contests of a similar emulative nature. As a further indication of their spiritual kinship, it may be pointed out that the members of the lower delinquent class usually show this physiognomy of astuteness in a marked degree, and that they very commonly show the same histrionic exaggeration of it that is often seen in the young candidate for athletic honors. This, by the way, is the most legible mark of what is vulgarly called "toughness" in youthful aspirants for a bad name.

The astute man, it may be remarked, is of no economic value to the community—unless it be for the purpose of sharp practice in dealings with other communities. His functioning is not a furtherance of the generic life process. At its best, in its direct economic bearing, it is a conversion of the economic substance of the collectivity to a growth alien to the collective life process—very much after the analogy of what in medicine would be called a benign tumor, with some tendency to transgress the uncertain line that divides the benign from the malign growths.[5]

In *The Theory of the Leisure Class* Veblen cited sport, war, government, and religion as the chief occupations of those who do not contribute to an increase of wealth by productive effort. In order to establish a continuity with the barbarian past it was necessary for him to discuss those activities that most reveal the traits of predatory man: political deceit and manipulation, military and athletic exploit and domination, and extravagant religious ornamentation and superstition on the part of the "priestly class." But the real villain in Veblen's theory of history is the modern businessman, the captain of industry who stalks the pages of his subsequent books like a threatening specter. If *The Theory of the Leisure Class* could be read as a harmless satire, *The Theory of Business Enterprise* was deadly serious, and *The Engineers and the Price System* and *Absentee Ownership* gravely portentous.

The Engineers and the Price System

The Theory of Business Enterprise was published in 1904, five years after *Leisure Class* deflated the pretensions of the rich and powerful. Veblen's second book lacked the playful irony and mordant humor of the first, but its implications for the theory of capitalism were even more devastating. In *Business Enterprise* Veblen turned from the *haute culture* of capitalism to the decisive economic role played by the heroes of that culture. The context is crucial, for Veblen's second book was written against a dense background of tendentious economic theory that placed the businessman at the forefront of historical progress. Every major economist from the time of Adam Smith had regarded the capitalist as the driving force in the process of industrialization; even Marx hailed the capitalist as the demiurge of history. The businessman was the prime mover, the entrepreneurial genius who sensed the right opportunities, applied his organizational talents, drew upon his imagination and vision, and thereby initiated the various processes of modernization that created the "wealth of nations." Veblen turned this entire picture upside down, making an old hero into a new villain.

It was not businessmen, Veblen argued, but men of industry—inventors, engineers, technical experts—who did the intellectual work, devised the blueprints, developed the techniques, and even provided the expectations for economic gain that made the modern industrial system possible. The scientist and technician must first create the mechanical possibility of new and more efficient methods of producing before the businessman's eyes are opened to new investment opportunities. But is the businessman at all interested in productivity? Not always. Veblen drew a sharp distinction between the engineer and the capitalist, between what he called the "industrial and pecuniary employments," between those who make goods and those who make money. Arrayed against the engineer and his concern for productivity, serviceability, and efficiency, stands the businessman and his concern for optimum prices and maximum profits. Occasionally the two interests coincide, particularly in the early stages of industrialization; but more often they come into conflict, at which point the interests of capital take precedence over the interests of science. Whenever there is a cleavage the businessman may curtail supply in order to maintain high prices, transfer funds from productive operations to speculative investment, deliberately mismanage the company's affairs so as to create "a convincing appearance of decline or disaster" in order to deceive competitors, and in general engage in a number of unconscionable activities which Veblen described, with characteristic irony, as a "conscientious withdrawal of efficiency." Accordingly, the profit system had little or nothing to do with achieving and sustaining maximum industrial productivity in the interests of getting the largest amount of goods to the greatest number of people at the lowest possible price.

The technician is the pioneer who paves the way toward industrial progress, just as the ancient grower was the innovator who experimented with soil and seed and the craftsman of the handicraft era was the artisan who provided new production methods. But the communal interests of the producer are frustrated by the predator who arrives upon the scene to conspire against maximum output and to seize profits for himself. Thus technology does not determine capital; on the contrary, industry is carried out for the sake of business. At every turn the "pecuniary expert" who has come to dominate economic life functions to disturb, upset, or block the industrial process at some point of production. The logic of money triumphs over the logic of machinery.

Is capitalism itself logical? Veblen was fond of using the terms "capitalist," "entrepreneur," and "undertaker" interchangeably, for no doubt he saw the capitalist system, though not its culture, as engaged in a slow dance of death. He might have said of the capitalist what Jefferson said of the *homo sapiens:* he is the only member of the species who preys upon and levies war against his own kind. It is not only that technological efficiency results in greater consolidation of business units and thus the eclipse of the free market. The irony is that businessmen themselves, in so far as they see the profitability of standardizing their operations, want to do away with as many business transactions as possible. The purpose of management is to coordinate, not to oppose, and thus competitive capitalism has as its logical outcome the elimination of competition, the ruination of the presumed lifeblood of capitalism itself (at least for the Social Darwinist if not the industrialist). Businessmen as a class want to see less of their kind, and they cheerily preside over their own demise. As the system of private enterprise is said to be advancing, opportunity for private enterprise is actually disappearing. "The heroic role of the captain of industry," mocked Veblen, "is that of a deliverer from an excess of business management. It is a casting out of businessmen by the chief of businessmen."[6]

If competition is the guillotine of capitalism, the credit system is its modern gas chamber. In classical economic theory it was assumed that the use of loan credit facilitates investment, extends the time element before profits must be made, enhances the earning potential of private enterprise, and thereby contributes to the health of industrial society. Veblen was not so sure that this was the case. In the first place, credit is necessary only to modern business transactions and control, not to modern industry; it may serve the volume of business as long as prices rise, according to Veblen, but it does not necessarily add to the aggregate industrial equipment or to the degree of efficiency with which industry is managed. Moreover, to the extent that business enterprises come to depend upon credit, their competitive bidding raises interest rates, and in response companies overcapitalize their stock, whose money value is based on nothing more than their ability to obtain further credit. Eventually the entire operations of companies are placed on a credit basis that has nothing to do with their actual earning capacities. When this discrepancy arises, a period of liquidation begins, and as creditors call in loans there takes place a transfer of ownership to large financial corporations. Furthermore, expansion of the credit system brings about, in Veblen's scenario, a separation of management from the ownership of property. The managers of money enjoy enormous discretionary power, so that the material processes of industry are now actually run by those who control its immaterial assets (common stock, securities, good will). Finally, the entire process of credit expansion culminates in what might be called Veblen's theory of business crisis. Credit is extended in prosperous times, but its limited supply forces interest rates up, leading overcapitalized companies to raise prices, which in turn lessens demand for goods and hence lowers the volume of sales. As profits decline loans become tighter, and the businessman panics when he sees the structure of prosperity toppled by a discredited credit system.

Pessimistic about the future of business capitalism, Veblen could be optimistic about the future of industrial society. In 1904, when *The Theory of Business Enterprise* appeared, the United States was in the midst of what appeared to be a sweeping protest against the power of big business. President Theodore Roosevelt, stirred both by the public's outrage and by his own aristocratic disdain for the business class, denounced the "malefactors of wealth" to the cheers of progressives. The interests of corporate capitalism did not, of course, really suffer under the administrations of Roosevelt or his successors Taft and Wilson. But its image as a benevolent and enlightened institution was subject to exposure and ridicule by muckraking journalists and liberal reformers. At the same time capitalism was being challenged by a socialist movement that was experiencing its "golden age" in the first decade of the twentieth century, with its national leader Eugene Debs drawing almost one million votes in the elections of 1900 and 1912. If any age in modern American history seemed to offer hope for radical social change and reform it was the progressive era. Yet Veblen placed little faith in liberal reform and still less in Marxist socialism. He looked instead to a new functional element in modern society that capitalism itself had produced: the engineer.

In *Business Enterprise* Veblen devoted two chapters to explaining the impact of "the machine process" on modern industrial society. The machine emerges as the historical agency of redemption, fulfilling much the same role as Marx's proletariat. The machine is the antithesis of business enterprise. Not only does technology strive for efficiency and productivity while capitalism aims simply at profits, but two different mental attitudes separate the world of science from the world of business. The capitalist ethos depends upon the psychology of status and personal prestige and the economics of leisure and wasteful consumption, all of which are easily exploited by advertising and salesmanship. Science, on the other hand, issues in a "matter-of-fact" mentality, a mode of intelligence that enables man to be critical and analytical, concerned primarily with accuracy, precision, and objectivity. The "discipline of the machine" induces the mind to think in terms of "opaque, impersonal cause and effect, to the neglect of those norms of validity that rest on usage and on the conventional standards handed down by usage."[7] So endowed, those who come in contact with the machine will eventually be liberated from all that is false and superstitious, particularly from ideas like natural law that serve as the theoretical rationale for capitalism, and from social customs like leisure and consumption, the class distinctions of manners and taste that gave capitalism its cultural legitimacy. Only scientific knowledge can penetrate the origins and nature of the social compulsions of behavior and thereby lay bare the irrationality of an economic system driven by non-economic motives. Thus Veblen looked forward to the emergence of a society characterized not so much by class conflict as functional division: the scientist against the salesman, the technician against the priest, the general, and the politician, the engineer against the financier.

Veblen could entertain such a vision of social reality for the first two decades of the century. His sense of the functional contradictions of capitalism became more pronounced after the outbreak of World War I and more optimistic with the Bolshevik Revolution. During the years 1917–1920, Veblen found encouragement in the upheavals spreading through eastern Europe. Bolshevism seemed to him a challenge to the vested interests, a genuine revolutionary movement led by a dissident intelligentsia which desired to democratize the industrial system. But Veblen remained skeptical that engineers elsewhere in the world would succeed in seizing political power even though they held the real power of technical expertise in their own hands. In 1921, when *The Engineers and the Price System* appeared, Veblen admitted that the establishment need not fear the revolution and he could only advise the left not to hope for it in the near future.

Meanwhile Veblen's attack on business enterprise remained as hostile as ever. The *sangfroid* response of capitalists to the suffering of displaced Europeans and unemployed Americans aroused further his ire during the period of postwar depression. The cupidity of a business system that would go to any extreme to maintain prices was matched only by its desperate chaos. Thus Veblen opened the book with a chapter on "Sabotage," a term that had been popularly associated with the incendiary *élan* of the radical left, particularly the syndicalist-inspired Wobblies. Veblen admitted that the strike constituted an act of sabotage, but insisted that there were other forms of sabotage that were sanctioned by law and by public conscience: the industrial lockout and layoff, and the financier's tactic of restricting and delaying production. Again Veblen returned to the credit system as the source of the problem, but he now included the role of the investment banker, the chief figure, in his postwar analysis, of the syndication and pooling of corporate finance through the recently established Federal Reserve System.

In 1922 Veblen published his last book, *Absentee Ownership and Business Enterprise in Recent Times*. It was his most somber work, his final indictment against a business civilization about to receive its coronation under the Calvin Coolidge administration. Here Veblen first expressed explicitly what had been at the back of his mind for two decades, namely that the engineering class was too integrated into the business system to constitute a negation of it, and that the underlying populations would continue to put up with the "imbecilic institutions" of capitalism because they had absorbed its cultural ethic of individualism and materialism. In chapter after chapter Veblen unfolds a grim story of the expansion and control of the "money power," of the conspiracies of trade and the imposition of advertising costs upon the consumer, of the plight of the independent farmer too self-reliant to organize against organized capital, of the centralization of corporate power, and of the wasteful exploitation and growing exhaustion of America's natural resources by absentee owners. What infuriated Veblen most was the disparity between what he regarded as the businessman's actual saboteur role and his image as an astute entrepreneur who had rejected the reckless ventures of buccaneer capitalism and "settled down to the wisdom of 'Watchful Waiting.'" The new businessman may appear a beaver of industry; in reality he functions as nothing more than a lazy reptile with a territorial claim to the public domain:

> Doubtless this form of words, "watchful waiting," will have been employed in the first instance to describe the frame of mind of a toad who has reached years of discretion and has found his appointed place along some frequented run where many flies and spiders pass and repass on their way to complete that destiny to which it has pleased an all-seeing and merciful Providence to call them; but by an easy turn of speech it has also been found suitable to describe the safe and sane strategy of that mature order of captains of industry who are governed by sound business principles. There is a certain bland sufficiency spread across the face of such a toad so circumstanced, while his comely personal bulk gives assurance of a pyramidal stability of principles.[8]

In the 1890s Veblen had hoped that his exposure of the leisure class and capitalism would stir some response at least among the scientists and the intellectual community. A quarter-century later he described an America mesmerized by the wonders of business enterprise, captivated by the parasites who enjoyed the image of feudal princes. In Veblen's tired mind an America that could applaud Coolidge's declaration that "the business of America is business" could only deserve what it got: all power to the predators. Veblen's analysis of why the capitalist classes could establish their hegemony will be explored in a subsequent chapter. It is only necessary here to mention that Veblen saw the masses as eager participants in their own servitude. There is some need or instinct within human nature, Veblen suggests, which causes men to admire strength and success and thereby attribute the highest of motives to the most powerful of rulers. Thus the captains of industry have attained both the economic power with which they can exploit and drain the public's interests and the social status with which they can appear to be acting in the interests of the common good. Veblen found ample precedent for this phenomenon in previous eras of history: the war lords of the barbarian raids, the barons of the Middle Ages, the prince of the epoch of state making, the priesthood of early and late Christendom, and the Mikado in the times of the Shogunate. In modern times the capitalist has inherited the role of the benevolent protector and provider, and by no means are his real exploits threatened by the rise of mass democracy. Indeed, democracy is the medium in which deference flourishes, and absentee ownership, not production and workmanship, is the most honored of all the occupations. Observing this development in corporate society in the twenties, Veblen's witty irony could no longer conceal his despair:

> So the captain of industry came into the place of first consequence and took up the responsibilities of exemplar, philosopher and friend at large to civilised mankind; and no man shall say that he has not done as well as might be expected. Neither has he fallen short in respect of a becoming gravity through it all. The larger the proportion of the community's wealth and income which he has taken over, the larger the deference and imputation of merit imputed to him, and the larger and graver that affable condescension and stately benevolence that habitually adorn the character of the large captains of solvency. There is no branch or department of the humanities in which the substantial absentee owner is not competent to act as guide, philosopher and friend, whether in his own conceit or in the estimation of his underlying population,—in art and literature, in church and state, in science and education, in law and morals,—and the underlying population is well content. And nowhere does the pecuniary personage stand higher or more secure as the standard container of the civic virtues than in democratic America; as should be the case, of course, since America is the most democratic of them all. And nowhere else does the captain of big business rule the affairs of the nation, civil and political, and control the conditions of life so unreservedly as in democratic America; as should also be the case, inasmuch as the acquisition of absentee ownership is, after all, in the popular apprehension, the most meritorious and the most necessary work to be done in this country.[9]

One must ask, in view of Veblen's somber reflections on the triumph of capitalist ideology, whence sprang his vision of hope? What sustained his faith, however guarded, that capitalism as a theory could not withstand the test of facts? Against the hegemony of capitalist culture, how could reality be apprehended? For Veblen there remained only one answer: science. Because Veblen's social analysis is bound up with his philosophical conception of science, we need to examine his view of the nature of scientific thought and its presumed liberating function in modern society.

Science and Liberation

Veblen was well prepared to argue the case for the philosophy of science. In the 1880s, as a graduate student at Johns Hopkins University, he took classes from Charles Sanders Peirce, the founder of American pragmatism, who, as epistemologist, logician, and semiologist, has come to be recognized as one of the most gifted philosophers in modern times. Veblen also wrote his dissertation on a philosophical subject, "Ethical Grounds of a Doctrine of Retribution." This work, completed at Yale in 1884, has been lost to posterity. But while working on his dissertation, and later as a post-doctoral student, Veblen had been immersed in the evolutionary ideas of Herbert Spencer and the epistemological ideas of Immanuel Kant. The British materialist appealed to him no less than the German idealist. For Veblen saw no conflict between science and philosophy, between empirical knowledge and theoretical understanding.

Veblen's first major essay, published in the *Journal of Speculative Philosophy* in 1884, was on "Kant's Critique of Judgment," the title of Kant's last book still untranslated. Veblen pointed out that Kant in his final work was attempting to mediate between the strict determinism of the *Critique of Pure Reason* and the imperative of moral freedom of the *Critique of Practical Reason*. Veblen recognized the problem of reconciling science and ethics, and he appreciated Kant's effort to rescue human freedom from natural causality. He also admired Kant's metaphysical humility before the intractable dualisms of philosophy, the fact that subject and object are divided, that man perceives the world with the help of a mental apparatus which imposes its own forms upon the raw data of life. This subjective aspect of Kantian philosophy would remain with Veblen, who would never forget how important are the mediating functions of human apprehension and how paramount is the mind's power of judgment. But whereas Kant had turned inward to develop objective principles of moral law, Veblen believed there was no escape into the interior of mind to avoid the flux of change and experience. It is true that the mind desires to bring order and systematic coherence into the knowledge it acquires. But the mind can only "reflect and reflect upon the materials given it"; it can never comprehend teleology, the purpose and the why of things. With Peirce Veblen maintained that knowledge of things arises out of a feeling of dissatisfaction with the incomplete perception of things, but this epistemological tension is all that experience can provide. The mind, stirred to inquiry by emotional needs, can never be gratified; it will always ask for more than knowledge can give.

If pure reason contributes nothing to the empirical act of knowing, as Kant insisted, and if the mind tends to make impossible demands upon experience, how can we know anything about the world? Veblen's answer was to follow Kant back to Locke and to the sense experience that supplies the origin and content of our knowledge of nature. Drawing upon the British empiricist tradition, Veblen substituted method for mind, inductive, tentative reasoning for deductive, absolute knowledge. Induction alone can "reduce things to systems and connexion," bring phenomena under "definite laws of interaction," and thereby enable us to begin the attempt at scientific explanation and prediction. The Baconian method of induction, of reasoning from particular facts to general principles, may not lead us to the ultimate truth of things; but it is the only mode of cognition of any immediate useful value, "the only knowledge which can serve as a guide in practical life, whether moral or otherwise."[10]

In 1908, speaking before the Kosmos Club at the University of California in Berkeley, Veblen spelled out in greater detail his philosophy of science and nature in an address entitled "The Evolution of the Scientific Point of View." Here Veblen seems to have been attempting to carry out Kant's effort at salvaging scientific knowledge from the philosophical skepticism of Hume. Although a great admirer of Hume—that "placid unbeliever" whose acid-like skepticism dissolved "everything that was well-received"[11]—Veblen denied Hume's argument that the concept of causation was essentially metaphysical or psychological, a matter of imputation rather than of observation. Modern science, Veblen maintained, took as a postulate the fact of "consecutive change," a nexus of sequences based upon the relation of cause and effect. Nature is a "process" that can be ultimately understood in terms of temporal cumulative and causal sequence, even thought inquiry begins with the itch of metaphysical curiosity. Darwinism offered proof of this revolution in epistemology. Pre-Darwinian science was content with taxonomy, the classification and definition of phenomena, and with "natural laws," principles as much causal as static that assume immutable relations in which things "naturally" stood one to another. Post-Darwinian science, on the other hand, shuns presupposed metaphysical structures and offers a theory of consecutive change, an evolving process that is self-continuing and self-propagating, with no final causes and no ultimate goals.

The liberating power of modern science lies in its demand for a genetic account of the phenomena it investigates. This empirical imperative differs from the primitive system of knowledge which is constructed on "animistic lines." *Animism,* a term central to Veblen which we shall explore more thoroughly in later chapters, is the tendency to attribute personal qualities to the impersonal data of nature. In Veblen's analysis animism is cited to illustrate how modern man, just as his primitive ancestors, contrives cosmological systems and theological doctrines, how he disassociates reality from fact and hence separates the scheme of life from the scheme of knowledge. Modern science, Veblen was convinced, emancipates historical man from superstition, myth, lore, magic, and all the animistic forces of authority and tradition. Science analyzes the hitherto sacred imponderables, applies the acid test of skepticism to all existing institutions, and destroys false ideas and values by explaining their natural origins.[12]

Veblen's philosophical dream was Henry Adams' metaphysical dread. Adams believed that modern thought had so assaulted authority that legitimacy had been reduced to nothing more than sheer power. Veblen embraced modernity to bring about precisely this effect. He was eager—perhaps too eager—to desanctify authority through scientific analysis and lay bare its brutish nature, to strip existing institutions of their ideological veils. Veblen's idea of "critical theory" contained the critical sting of skepticism. So corrosive was his empirical temperament that even the "authority" of Marxism could not survive his analysis. What then was Veblen's idea of authority? Did he desire to destroy existing institutions in order to bring about a new technological society governed by a managerial elite? It is necessary to raise this question here, and to return to it in later chapters, for this is the essential charge made against Veblen by some of his more severe critics, on the left as well as on the right.

Veblen was by no means unambiguous in his advocacy of the emerging rationalized society. He welcomed the advent of the "machine process" in modern life as an answer to cultural lag, but he was dubious about the engineers as an independent profession and had mixed feelings about technology as an autonomous force. We shall discuss these matters in detail as we explore his many books and essays. It is enough to suggest here, in our discussion of Veblen's epistemological stance, that he seemed to resist rationalization nearly as much as he advocated it, just as he was capable of embracing both progress and primitivism. It is perhaps for this reason that he attempted to turn utilitarianism on its head by claiming, against every canon of empiricism, that science progresses only to the extent that it serves no immediate useful purpose. In "The Place of Science in Modern Civilization," one of Veblen's most theoretically intriguing articles, the concept of "idle curiosity" was first introduced. Although never clearly defined, the concept was variously referred to as a "more or less irrelevant attention," a behavior closely related to the "aptitude of play" in man and in the lower animals, and an activity that "seems peculiarly lively in the young, whose aptitude for sustained pragmatism is at the same time relatively vague and unreliable." Veblen's attitude toward the philosophy of pragmatism has troubled scholars, particularly the disciples of John Dewey. On the one hand Veblen admitted that the pragmatic dictum that mind is functional and knowledge instrumental is, if not "the whole truth . . . at least goes nearer to the heart of the epistemological problem than any earlier formulation." On the other he seemed to chide pragmatic philosophers for misunderstanding the foundation of intelligence, which presumably lay not in problem-solving activity, but in pure wonder and innate curiosity.[13] Veblen's reservations about pragmatism may be interpreted as a critique of the potential appropriation of science for purposes of social control. For one aim of "idle curiosity" was to assert the playful, spontaneous nature of knowledge against the pretensions of exact science and objective consciousness. In this respect Veblen's protest against utilitarianism can also be extended forwarded and directed against the behavioralism that came into vogue in the 1920s and was, unfortunately, to be associated with his name. The mind can be controlled only if the social scientist is willing to extinguish the spark of human curiosity that has generated progress through the ages. If intellectual history teaches anything, Veblen argued, it is that science cannot be both an instrument of domination and an agency of enlightenment, for it advances in defiance of immediate political interests and answers to man's natural instinct of playful speculation.

Veblen, to be sure, revealed a somewhat cavalier unconcern about the technical and logical problems inherent in scientific method, and his conviction that change could be easily explained in causal terms seems naive. Any assessment of his early epistemological essays must take these deficiencies into account. But Perry Miller is close to the truth when he says that "The Place of Science in Modern Civilization" is a protest against "applied science" by the "bard of savagery," an attack on the over-systematization of empirical procedure by a "romantic" who wants to save the mind from enslavement to the "passionless matter-of-fact." Veblen's profound essay is, Miller observes, "a *cri de coeur* of humanity; it looks like an attack upon Pragmatism for not taking sufficient account of the ineradicable propensity of the human animal for self-delusion, and so, by providing facile formulas for the fixation of belief or the will to believe, aiding that mechanization of society against which the primordial instincts revolt."[14] "Idle curiosity" might be regarded as Veblen's version of the doubting and negating function of "critical theory." In so far as it can help check both the Deweyite determination to make all knowledge expedient and the Jamesian desire to allow man to believe in what he wills to believe, "idle curiosity" may serve to curb both instrumentalism and myth making and thereby secure some sphere where mechanization and scientific rationality cannot absorb the questioning mind.

It was, perhaps, the residue of Kantianism in Veblen that led him to see science as practically liberating only so long as the mind remained theoretically free from the demands of practicality. Science is a mode of cognition, not a means of economic exploitation or technological domination. Its potential for human emancipation lies in its ability to explain genetically the origins of ideas and institutions, and, by explaining them, demystifying them. Paradoxically, science, the latest and highest achievement of the modern mind, would enable contemporary man to begin the return home to his natural state of innocence and harmony, the healthy state of savage life.

Who was this "bard of savagery," this thoroughly modern thinker who combined positivist realism with primitivist dreams? No one knows for sure. If his writings are ambiguous, his character and life are a legend shrouded in myth and enigma.

3 . . . The Social Scientist as "Stranger"

The Man Nobody Knows

The scene is a New York City bookstore; the time is the immediate aftermath of the First World War; the speaker is Madge Jenison, the proprietress:

> A man used to appear every six or eight weeks quite regularly, an ascetic, mysterious person with keys to unlock things, I took him to be, and with a gentle air. He wore his hair long and looked Scandinavian. I do not know just why or when I made him a Swedenborgian minister. He always bought interesting things—Greek texts, the less read work of William Morris; and when we did not have what he wanted, he asked us to order it, and a long-legged rosy young girl with long straight braids came for it. His niece, I thought. I decided he lived with his sister—a spare woman with a cool bright face, serious not cold, and eyes like clear glass, very erect and with a small hat like a Zorn portrait of a lady I had once seen at a Swedish exhibition. I used to try to interest him in economics. The clergy should be informed on these things, I thought, and he was an especially remote clergyman. I plied him from time to time with important importations. I even once tried to get him to begin with *The Theory of the Leisure Class*. I explained to him what a brilliant port of entry it is to social consciousness. But it became clear that if he was ever to be interested in sociology and economics, he would not be interested in them by me. He listened attentively to all I said and melted like a snow drop through the door. One day he ordered a volume of Latin hymns.
>
> "I shall have to take your name because we will order this expressly for you," I told him. "We shall not have an audience for such a book as this again in a long time, I am afraid."
>
> "My name is Thorstein Veblen," he breathed rather than said.[1]

This recollection suggests Veblen's elusive character and temperament. Quiet, aloof, uninvolved, unfathomable, mischievous, often somber, occasionally whimsical, Veblen is surely one of the more baffling figures in American intellectual history. Even when he attained the status of an intellectual celebrity he always remained the mysterious stranger. Nearly everyone respected him but hardly anyone knew him. And this is how he wanted it. It is often said that writers seek immortality through their work; Veblen struggled to sustain personal obscurity even as he gained a scholarly reputation, and in the end the secrets of his life went to the grave with him, as he requested in his will:

> It is also my wish, in case of death, to be cremated, if it can conveniently be done, as expeditiously and inexpensively as may be, without ritual or ceremony of any kind; that my ashes be thrown loose into the sea, or into some sizable stream running into the sea; that no tombstone, slab, epitaph, effigy, tablet, inscription or monument of any kind or nature, be set up in my memory or name at any place or at any time; that no obituary, memorial, portrait, or biography of me, nor any letters written to or by me be printed or published, or in any way reproduced, copied, or circulated.[2]

Veblen had the manner and physiognomy of a Norwegian peasant. A rare photograph shows him stolid and quizzical. His shrewd eyes peer out from a lean, rough face. His hair is slightly disheveled, his beard unkempt, and his moustache full and defiantly bristling. Students remember his slow, lethargic movements, which made him seem half asleep, and his rumpled clothes, which looked as though they had been slept in. His collars were usually several sizes too large, his trousers baggy, and his thick woolen stockings invariably supported by pins clipped to his pant legs. Scornful of ostentation—this does not surprise us—he wore no rings or jewelry of any kind, carrying his watch on a length of black ribbon which he hooked to the front of his vest by a large safety pin.

Veblen was surely one of the strangest creatures ever to walk in the groves of academe. He led a bizarre life that scandalized the academic world of his time. When teaching at a midwestern university, he lived in the basement of a friend's house, entering his domicile by crawling through a window. Years later, retired in California, he lived in a shack surrounded by a jungle of shrubs and weeds. "The house," recalled a friend, "was bare and barnlike, inside and out; dusty, and so devoid of ordinary comfort that one felt as if someone from a very alien culture were camping in it—someone to whom our chairs and beds and tables are but useless curiosities."[3] Although an ardent advocate of technology and mass production, Veblen chose to make his own furniture out of dry-good boxes and burlap sacks, and even proposed making clothes out of paper. He refused to have a telephone, kept his books stacked against a wall in unpacked cartons, and amused himself by taking apart clocks to see how they worked. Uneasy with any form of domesticity, he set an example for the liberation of women by practicing the gospel of efficiency. Regarding the daily making of beds as a wasteful ritual, Veblen simply threw the blankets down over the foot in the morning and drew them up again at night. Dishes were a tedious nuisance; he allowed them to stack up alarmingly in the tub and, when he was finally out of cups and saucers, washed the whole greasy pile by turning the garden hose on it.

Veblen was eccentric and unpredictable. He could take warmly to children and delight in the playfulness of animals. But his own sense of fun verged on the sadistic. Once he borrowed a sack from a nearby farmer and returned it with a hornets' nest inside, saying, "Thank you." He spent most of his life railing against "absentee ownership," but his own property was another matter. When he returned to the small cabin he owned in the West after 20 years and mistakenly believed that someone else had appropriated the land, he "took a hatchet and methodically broke the windows," according to his biographer Joseph Dorfman, "going at the matter with a dull intensity that was like madness, the intensity of a physically lazy person roused into sudden activity by anger."[4] He was severely critical of contemporary economists for discoursing in a manner that claimed objectivity while concealing value judgment; he himself claimed nothing but concealed everything. "Do you take anything seriously?" a student once asked Veblen. "Yes," he whispered furtively, "but don't tell anyone." He was eager to penetrate the social world with his writings, but kept his own thoughts on any given subject virtually impenetrable. On one occasion a friend picked up a copy of Dmitri Merezhkovsky's *Birth of the Gods* and read Veblen the preface, which ends with the declaration that "the living world is the abstract space in which the body of Christ is being formed." He then asked Veblen, as a scholar, what the preface was about. Veblen answered: "It is about four pages and a half."[5]

The Satire of His Presence

Thorstein Veblen was born on a frontier farm in Wisconsin in 1857. He came from the same Middle Border that produced such eminent contemporaries as Charles Beard, Vernon L. Parrington, Simon Patten, Frederick Jackson Turner, and Lester Ward—historians and sociologists who would mount a far-reaching assault on the economic and cultural values of the East. Veblen, however, was a stranger not merely to the eastern establishment but to the country as a whole, and this more profound alienation was mirrored in his unprecedentedly harsh and thoroughgoing critique of American society.

Veblen was the fourth son and sixth child of an immigrant Norwegian family. His parents, Thomas Anderson Veblen and Kari Bunde Veblen, had arrived in America ten years before his birth, bringing with them harsh memories of the old country. Veblen's grandfather had been tricked out of his inheritance of the family land and suffered a painful decline in status when he was forced to become a humble tenant farmer. His mother's father had also lost his land to lawyers and, depressed by this setback, died a young man, leaving Veblen's mother an orphan at the age of five. In Minnesota the Veblens encountered similar troubles with land speculators and money lenders. Yet these experiences did not infect the young Veblen with the genteel anti-Semitism that cast its shadow over the minds of contemporaries such as Henry Adams and Frederick Jackson Turner. The roots of greed and speculation lay neither in the Jew nor in capitalism. It went deeper than race and extended far beyond the bounds of economic institutions.

Veblen's father was an aloof man with a slow but keen mind. His mother was energetic, tender, and passionate. Pioneer austerity shaped the character of the household: clothes were handmade, coffee and sugar were luxuries. To his frugal and hard-working family Thorstein seemed an odd youth, lazy, impish, irreverent. He preferred reading in the attic to daily chores, fought with boys, teased girls, and pestered elders. Above all, he was precocious. "From my earliest recollection," a young brother recalls, "I thought he knew everything. I could ask him any question and he would tell me all about it in detail. I have found out since that a good deal he told me was made of the whole cloth, but even his lies were good."[6]

In 1874, Veblen's father, now relatively well off, decided that his sons should attend college and escape the limited opportunities of farm life. One day Thorstein was simply called from the field to find that his belongings were packed and waiting in the family buggy. He never knew his destination until he arrived at Carleton College, a Congregational outpost of New England culture on the Minnesota prairies. Thorstein was being sent there in the hope that he would enter the Lutheran ministry. But, not surprisingly, the budding iconoclast found the pious atmosphere stultifying. The curriculum revolved around moral philosophy, particularly the common-sense doctrines that Thomas Reid and William Hamilton had developed to counter the skepticism of Hume. Natural science was all but neglected. Yet Veblen managed through voracious independent reading to acquire his own education, and he was impressed with his teacher John Bates Clark (later a distinguished economist and an object of Veblen's theoretical critiques), who liked the "misfit" youth with "a mind clothed in sardonic humor." Veblen caused an uproar among the missionary-oriented faculty with his addresses on a "Plea for Cannibalism" and an "Apology for a Toper," which justified the eating of human flesh and the drinking of spirits. Carleton officials were not a little relieved when the young eccentric graduated in 1880.

Veblen left Carleton looking forward to an academic career. Now began his long, wretched apprenticeship in what might be termed the survival of the unfittest. His first post, at Monona Academy in Wisconsin, came to an end within a year when the school closed. Veblen decided to follow his brother Andrew (father of the mathematician and Princeton colleague of Einstein, Oswald Veblen) to Johns Hopkins to study philosophy. He took courses from the Hegelian philosopher George Sylvester Morris and from the liberal political economist

Richard T. Ely, neither of whom had any significant impact on his thinking. The only man who made an impression was a temporary lecturer in logic, Charles Sanders Peirce. Veblen tried for a scholarship at the recently opened Johns Hopkins University, but despite glowing recommendations from his teachers he was turned down (as was John Dewey in the same year). Veblen then decided to transfer to Yale to study philosophy under its president, the Reverend Noah Porter. Here he found himself drawn to the Olympian figure of William Graham Sumner, the conservative Social Darwinist who was fighting to radicalize the religion-centered curriculum by introducing more courses in modern science. Veblen also steeped himself in Kant, gained recognition for his philosophical acumen despite his habitual irreverence, graduated in 1884 with a Ph.D. but without any prospects of academic employment.

He returned home to Minnesota jaded, bitter, and less inclined to hard labor than ever. He insisted that he was not well and needed to be cared for; his family suspected laziness. "He read and loafed," wrote a brother, "and then the next day he loafed and read." In between walks in the woods and tinkering with inventions, Veblen read anything and everything: political tracts, botanical studies, treatises on anthropology, economics, and sociology, even Lutheran hymnbooks. In the meantime he married Ellen Rolfe, the niece of the president of Carleton College and the daughter of one of the leading families in the Middle West. Her father, a grain-elevator and railroad magnate, was angered that his daughter had married an unemployed academic and atheist. But he accepted the *mésalliance*, which is what it indeed turned out to be, and allowed the young couple to settle on one of his Iowa farms. But despite his Ph.D., his wife's connections, and his letters of recommendation, Veblen continued to have bad luck in obtaining an academic position or even landing employment as a railroad bookkeeper. Meanwhile he and his wife read about the populist movement that was sweeping through the Middle West and poured over Bellamy's *Looking Backward*, "the turning point of our lives," Ellen later wrote. Excited by the wave of the agrarian unrest, Veblen began a serious study of economics and considered resuming his formal education. Finally, after seven years of premature retirement, he was encouraged by his family to return to graduate study, at the age of 34, and to make one more attempt to break into the academic world.

In 1891, a lean, pale man attired in coonskin cap and corduroy trousers walked into the office of Cornell professor J. Laurence Laughlin and announced, "I am Thorstein Veblen." Although a pillar of conservative economics, Laughlin was strangely impressed by Veblen and almost immediately secured him a fellowship. Finding encouragement at last, Veblen began to reflect upon his vast reading and to write some theoretical and technical articles for *The Quarterly Journal of Economics*. When the University of Chicago opened the following year and hired Laughlin to head the economics department, he invited Veblen to come with him. Thus in his 35th year Veblen finally acquired his first job, at a salary of $520 a year.

Veblen stayed at the University of Chicago for 14 years, a difficult period for both the school and the scholar. His unorthodox manners and ideas, his uninspired teaching and inspired love life led to frequent clashes with university officials. Veblen would later write a scathing book describing the "higher learning" as a form of cultural barbarism. But notwithstanding his bouts with bureaucrats and administrative entrepreneurs, Veblen was fortunate in having a stimulating intellectual environment peopled by such distinguished scholars as John Dewey in philosophy, William I. Thomas and George Herbert Mead in sociology, Jacques Loeb in psychology, and Franz Boas in anthropology. When *The Theory of the Leisure Class* appeared in 1899, Veblen himself suddenly became famous. The book, which Lewis Mumford would later liken to a stick of dynamite wrapped in candy paper, became overnight the sensation of the intelligentsia, being warmly praised by William Dean Howells and Lester Frank Ward alike. "Veblenism" came to connote wickedly satirical and pungent observations on all that had been sacred and secure. Veblen's second book, *The Theory of Business Enterprise* (1904), failed to win the enthusiastic acclaim that had greeted his first work. His opaque, convoluted style, marked by polysyllabic neologisms and esoteric terminology, pleased neither radicals expecting a recipe for revolution nor conservatives hoping for a refutation of socialism. Above all, there were few general readers who could decipher the author's intent. The book contained a savage indictment of the "pecuniary motive," yet one reader wrote Veblen asking his advice on how to make money.

Officials at the University of Chicago took pride in Veblen's scholarly fame, but the publicity created by his unconcealed womanizing could not, in the end, be tolerated. When pressure was exerted on him to conform to the canons of academic propriety, Veblen defied his superiors and chose to look for another position. In 1906 he went to Stanford, but his libertinism there fully confirmed the notorious reputation he had brought with him, and within three years he was asked to resign. Veblen now applied for posts at a number of schools, only to receive vague, bureaucratic rejections. Finally, a former student and enduring friend and admirer, H. J. Davenport, helped him obtain a position at the University of Missouri in 1911.

That same year his wife divorced him.* Free of marriage, Veblen

* On Veblen's domestic life and relations with women, see below pp. 253–256; for further information on his academic career, see pp. 265–290. It should be stressed that no attempt is being made to write a biography of Veblen, a task performed in exhaustive detail in Joseph Dorfman's *Thorstein Veblen And His America* (1934); nor am I attempting a psychological explanation of this eccentric personality, the aim of David Riesman's provocative *Thorstein Veblen: A Critical Interpretation* (1953). My purpose in sketching his life and character is to provide a portrait of this strange man before undertaking a deeper exploration of his equally intriguing ideas and theories.

suffered a severe isolation in Columbia, living as a recluse among the Rotarians and Philistines. Residing in Davenport's cellar, lonely, embittered, and seemingly defeated, Veblen in fact experienced a remarkably productive period at the University of Missouri. He finished two of his most important works, *The Instinct of Workmanship* (1914) and *Imperial Germany and the Industrial Revolution* (1915). Few readers bothered with the former book, an unfortunate slight of his most searching attempt to explore in anthropological terms the origins of alienation; but *Imperial Germany,* with its implications for the great war in Europe, was widely read and regarded by some reviewers as a work of genius. In 1918, he published two more books, *An Inquiry Into The Nature Of Peace* and *The Higher Learning in America,* the latter having been conceived and partially written during his Chicago days. His subsequent books were either collections of previous essays, like *The Vested Interests and the Common Man* (1919) and *The Place of Science in Modern Civilization* (1919), restatements of previous theses, like *The Engineers and the Price System* (1921) and *Absentee Ownership* (1923), or posthumous publications like *Essays In Our Changing Order* (1934). He wrote, in all, 11 books and more than 150 articles and reviews.

When America entered the war in 1917, Veblen decided to move to Washington and offer his services to the American cause. He wrote several reports on the manpower shortage for the Food Administration, and was generally shifted about by government bureaucrats who paid little attention to his papers. He also prepared several memoranda for Colonel House's "Inquiry," a study group of intellectuals that the President had asked to explore the terms of a possible peace settlement. Several of these documents, which will be discussed in a future chapter, were also ignored.

The following year Veblen came to New York to write for *Dial,* the literary organ of the liberal intelligentsia. Veblen's articles, which called for the liquidation of the business system as an essential prerequisite to a permanent peace, were, for a time, widely discussed; and the journal, which also featured articles by Dewey, Mumford, and Randolph Bourne, was soon being referred to as "the Veblenian *Dial*." In the aftermath of the war Veblen's cynical writings found sympathy among the liberal intellectuals disillusioned with Wilsonianism, while his positive response to the Bolshevik Revolution pleased the Marxist left. But interest in Veblen declined as the *Dial,* with the war over, concerned itself more with literary matters and less with political causes and economic issues. The recently established New School for Social Research came to Veblen's support with the offer of a position that had been partly funded by a former student and admirer. The New School had on its faculty such personages as Charles Beard, Harold Laski, Wesley Mitchell, and Horace Kallen. Veblen was now a star among stars. But he was also a tired man, and his lectures, at first packed with curious students, turned out to be boring ordeals. As at Chicago, Stanford, and Missouri, Veblen continued to mumble while his enrollments steadily dwindled.

By the mid-1920s Veblen was nearly 70, and the years had begun to take their toll. He felt increasingly lonely in New York. Earlier his second wife, whom he married in 1914, suffered a mental breakdown and had to be committed; his first wife, Ellen, died in 1926. Veblen still had many admirers and disciples, and a number of academic economists joined together to sign a petition recommending his name as president of the American Economic Association. Veblen declined, commenting, "They didn't offer it to me when I needed it." Severing his last ties with the academic world, he returned to Palo Alto and settled in his small cabin on the outskirts of town, living in total isolation yet hungering for companionship and conversation. He lived on—this prophet of technological utopia—amid his rude furnishings, wearing rough clothes purchased through a Sears, Roebuck catalogue, increasingly lost in thought, oblivious to the occasional wood rat exploring his cabin or to the skunk that brushed against his leg as he sat in reverie in his handmade chair. Shortly before his death, on August 3, 1929, a neighbor visited him. Veblen told her that "he heard members of his family, long since dead, speak to him in Norwegian, as exactly and clearly as I was speaking to him then."[7]

The Intellectual Wanderer

Who was this man? To ask the question is to admit that Veblen continues to elude us, and this is as true of his mind as his personality. If his character could be the subject of psychohistory—an enterprise handicapped by the loss of his private papers—his ambiguous thoughts and writings remain a challenge to the student of intellectual history. One former pupil has described well what might be called "the Veblen problem":

> Veblen's explanations were seldom simple. His major thesis often seemed to be a result of long reflection. His supporting data frequently offered a remarkable evidence of wide erudition. But his argument was not straightforward proof. He devised twists and turns in the discussion, which threw the unwary off their stride, and brought up the rash doctrinaire with a surprising jolt. If a type of thinking can be symbolized by another form of activity, Veblen's course might be compared with the running of a fox—swift get-away, clever doubling, use of heavy cover, sharp holding-in.[8]

The student's perplexity was shared by several of Veblen's admirers (one of whom referred to him as "the man from Mars"). The British sociologist Graham Wallas once pleaded for someone to write "a 'Secret of Veblen,' summoning up (with an index!)" his mischievous books. Actually Veblen himself provided the best clue to his character in a curiously revealing essay written in 1918, "The Intellectual Pre-eminence of Jews in Modern Europe." Here we have the closest thing to a self-portrait that Veblen ever committed to print.

In common with such Jewish savants as Marx, Freud, and Einstein (the latter was one of Veblen's great admirers), Veblen hailed science as the benign destroyer of pernicious illusions and thus the indispensible harbinger of modern consciousness. Like the Jews, with whom he obviously identified, Veblen saw himself as a marginal man, the eternal outsider with no enduring ties to the prevailing culture and dominant institutions of his time. He saw as well the unmistakable advantages of his own and the Jews' lonely and rootless existence. For estrangement fostered a questioning frame of mind, which explained why the Jew was in "the vanguard of modern inquiry." The lonely intellectual, exempt from widely shared preconceptions, filled with "skeptical animus, *Unbefangenheit* [and] released from the dead hand of conventional finality," was the creator of new knowledge and fruitful insights. Disinherited, the wandering Jew remained the enemy of all inherited habits and thoughts and hence the friend of unmediated facts. Culturally uprooted, the Jew may never again be wholly assimilated. "One who goes away from home will come to see many unfamiliar things, and to take note of them; but it does not follow that he will swear by all the strange gods whom he meets along the road."

Veblen's analysis of the deracinated Jew bears remarkable likeness to Georg Simmel's essay on "The Stranger." In Simmel's treatment the "stranger" is not merely a wanderer "who comes today and goes tomorrow"; rather he is a "person who comes today and stays tomorrow," a person who is "an element of" society but not fully part of it. Other contemporary sociologists like Karl Mannheim and Max Weber also described the peculiar status of the "free-floating" intelligentsia and the *Benufsmensch* (man of vocation). Simmel believed, as did Mannheim, that the outsider enjoyed a privileged "objectivity" because he is not "bound by commitments which could prejudice his perception, understanding, and evaluation of the given."[9] Veblen could agree that certain intellectual benefits derived from social alienation. "The intellectually gifted Jew," he wrote,

> is in a peculiarly fortunate position in respect of this requisite immunity from the inhibitions of intellectual quietism. But he can come in for such immunity only at the cost of losing his secure place in the scheme of conventions into which he has been born, and at the cost, also, of finding no similarly secure place in that scheme of gentile conventions into which he is thrown. For him as for other men in the like case, the skepticism that goes to make him an effectual factor in the increase and diffusion of knowledge among men involves a loss of that peace of mind that is the birthright of the safe and sane pietist. He becomes a disturber of the intellectual peace, but only at the cost of becoming an intellectual wayfaring man, a wanderer in the intellectual no-man's land, seeking another place to rest, farther along

> the road, somewhere over the horizon. They are neither a complaisant nor a contented lot, these aliens of uneasy feet.[10]

The pain of Veblen's own alienation made him acutely aware that objectivity could not be won without paying a terrible price in ostracism and disquietude. As a free mind in a structured society, he was, like the Jew, "a sceptic by force of circumstances over which he has no control." Lonely, curious, detached, he was "in" the world but not "of" it. He did not choose the modern world of industrial capitalism; it chose him, and in it he remained the cerebral immigrant whose escape lay in serious inquiry, the obligation of the intellectual, and mordant humor, the refuge of the non-conformist.

Part Two . . .

THEORY AND HISTORY

4 . . . Economics and the Dilemma of Value Theory

BENTHAM OR HEGEL? VEBLEN'S CRITIQUE OF MARX'S ECONOMIC THEORIES

A good example of Veblen's own "skeptical animus" may be seen in his approach to the economic theories of his age. Indeed Veblen was perhaps the only American social scientist of the nineteenth century who was intellectually prepared to challenge the economic theories of Karl Marx on their own terms. Like Marx, Veblen came to economics by way of philosophy, a discipline that seeks to expand the horizons of knowledge while at the same time asserting the limits of what can be known. Both men used their training in logic and epistemology to question the reigning ideas of their day, and both set out to refute orthodox economic theory. But a half-century separated the young Marx (1818–1883) from the young Veblen (1857–1929). Thus when Marx studied the ideas and theoretical assumptions of capitalism, his economic analysis took its point of departure from the modern natural rights tradition of the Enlightenment and the utilitarian thought of Adam Smith and David Ricardo. When Veblen studied economics toward the end of the nineteenth century, the discipline was in a state of ferment and confusion. A chief source of controversy was the theory of labor value expounded by Marx himself.

Value, the constituent of anything that renders it desirable and useful, does not merely happen; according to Marx, it is created by the processes of human labor. The idea of locating value in man's productive efforts was hardly original with Marx. In the seventeenth century John Locke defended private property on such grounds; and in the eighteenth century David Ricardo advanced the idea that "the value of a commodity" depended "on the relative quality of labor necessary to its production."[1] Marx embraced these ideas of value only to turn the proposition on its head. If the whole value of a product is determined by the labor that goes into making it, should not the full value be paid to the men who had produced the commodity? Capitalism cannot allow such remuneration, Marx insisted, for it lives and thrives on profits, the difference between wages and prices.

Marx was by no means so naive as to claim that the value of goods could be measured by the time it took to produce them, in which case a lazy worker could create more value than an efficient one. Instead he introduced the ingenious notion of "labor power," the number of hours required by a man to work to earn a wage that would enable him to subsist and procreate. Man can earn enough to keep alive by working a limited number of hours, let us say a half-day. But in capitalist society he lacks the right and the power to contract so short a shift. The difference between the amount of time he must work to support himself and the extra time the employer requires him to stay on the job is the measure of the worker's exploitation. Marx calls this difference "surplus value," for the value produced by a man working 12 hours far exceeds the value he produced in six hours, and yet only the capitalist can sell the full-labor time embodied in the goods that the worker himself has produced. Forced to work a longer time than their mere subsistence warrants, workers are cheated by a wage system that conceals the distinction between the value they created in the period of "socially necessary labor" and the value created during the period in excess of it, between paid and unpaid labor time, between the cost of wages and the price of commodities.

The Marxist theory of value appeared simplistic to the economists who were contemporaries of Veblen. Marx's insistence that labor constituted the sole source of value and that the workers' pay would always gravitate to the subsistence level was subjected to wide criticism. Such economists as Böhm-Bawerk, Stanley Jevons, Carl Menger, and Leon Walras shifted from the Richardian-Marxist focus on production to the actual operations of the market place. With this shift, variously referred to as the "Jevonian Revolution," the "Austrian School," or "marginal utility analysis,"[2] attention now concentrated on the attitude of individual consumers toward commodities that satisfied human desires. So reoriented, the discipline of economics could demonstrate that prices do not necessarily reflect the costs of production and that value functions as a response to demand. This shift toward a "subjective theory of value" played down the processes of production in favor of the pull of demand and the utility of consumption. Yet the more that contemporary economists speculated about the problem of value, the more its precise solution seemed to elude them. Air, for example, may have utility even though it lacks labor value because no effort has gone to produce it; on the other hand, a work of art may require years of labor but possess no value because there is no demand for it. What then remains of Marx's conviction that value derives from labor alone?

Marx's position was actually quite complex, indeed so ambiguous that academic economists and social theorists are still debating its proper interpretation.[3] Perhaps a better approach to the issue is to suggest that Marx was less concerned with the problem of how value is created than with the process by which it is lost. In Volume I of *Capital* he attempts to relate value to prices, but he does so not to establish a law of value but to find out how the "form" of *exchange value* operates when commodities are sold. He was convinced that a separate theory of value had to precede a theory of prices and that there exists a single quality, or "essence," which inheres in commodities and governs their exchange. The task of the economist is to penetrate to the internal connections behind the "necessary appearances" of exchange ratios governing commodities to discover why value congealed in labor becomes alienated and projected onto things, the objects of wealth which consumers demand. This phenomenon was subsumed under the well-known rubric of the "fetishism of commodities," a concept which by no means validates the labor theory of value but dramatically transfers the problem from the sphere of economics to that of "social relations." Marx, then, was not seeking to substitute a "law of value" for market prices according to the traditional principle of supply and demand; rather he set out to discover why classical theory failed to describe what it purported to explain, a search in which the truth would reveal itself through philosophical reflection as well as empirical investigation. It is significant that Veblen alone among contemporary economists fully understood Marx's heroic effort, an act of empathy that would make Veblen's own critique all the more discerning.

Veblen's two-part essay, "The Socialist Economics of Karl Marx and His Followers," is the most penetrating discussion of the subject ever to come from an American scholar. The paper, which appeared later in the *Quarterly Journal of Economics,* was first presented as an address at Harvard University in 1906, about the same time that Jack London spoke before the Intercollegiate Socialist Society on the glories of class warfare. No doubt Veblen's dry mumbling scarcely matched London's oratorical power, but what Veblen had to say still bears pondering.

Veblen deeply admired the "boldness of conception" and "great logical consistency" in Marx's writings. He therefore wanted first to defend Marx against his contemporary critics and then to show where the hidden flaw in Marxism actually lay. Marx's opponents erred in trying to examine his economic theories as a set of independent principles, and as a result these "hostile" scholars "commonly lost themselves in a tangled scrutiny of supposedly abstruse details." Properly conceived, Marxism is a synthetic construct, not an analytic mode of explanation. "Except as a whole and except in the light of its postulates and aims, the Marxian system is not only not tenable, but it is not even intelligible. A discussion of a given isolated feature of the system (such as the theory of value) from the point of view of classical economics (such as that offered by Böhm-Bawerk) is as futile as a discussion of solids in terms of two dimensions." Marx's critics had also identified his theories with those of Ricardo, but even though Marx himself acknowledged the identity, it was of "superficial coincidence." Marx's idea of labor is based on the intrinsic value of work, value that becomes the quantum of congealed labor in the commodity; whereas with Ricardo the main characteristic of labor is its "degree of irksomeness," a negative quality which suggests that labor does not possess the unique property of being able to produce more value than is required for subsistence. Thus the notion of surplus value cannot be derived from Ricardo's position. What can be derived is exchange value, a matter of distribution rather than production. The exchange ratio of goods is compatible with classical economics, where the market determines commodity value, but for Marx exchange value is merely the "phenomenal form" of real value. And this distinction between the differing loci of value is the source of confusion among those who equate Marx with Ricardo in order to bury them both:

> Marx's critics commonly identify the concept of "value" with that of "exchange value," and show that the theory of "value" does not square with the run of the facts of price under the existing system of distribution, piously hoping thereby to have refuted the Marxian doctrine; whereas, of course, they have for the most part not touched it. The misapprehension of the critics may be due to a (possibly intentional) oracular obscurity on the part of Marx. Whether by this fault or their own, their refutations have hitherto been quite inconclusive. Marx's severest strictures on the inequities of the capitalist system is that contained by implication in his development of the manner in which actual exchange value of goods systematically diverges from their real (labor-cost) value. Herein, indeed, lies not only the inherent inequity of the existing system, but also its fateful infirmity, according to Marx.[4]

Veblen could agree with Marx that capitalism is inherently unjust, but it did not follow that it was fated to self-destruction. That capitalism "ought" to collapse is no reason for believing that historically it will do so. Veblen could also accept Marx's "law of the concentration of capital," the tendency toward industrial monopoly and merger that was familiar to progressive critics in America. But the "law of capitalist accumulation" hardly seemed persuasive. According to Marx, competition forces the capitalist to install more and more labor-saving machinery to produce more goods at a lower cost and thereby sustain his profit margin. In making this transition to machinery, however, he actually undermines his own position, for he has substituted non-profitable means of production for exploitable ones, human workers. To Veblen, who waxed rhapsodic about the "machine process," it made no sense at all to claim that technology could not create value. Even more vulnerable was the "law of increasing misery," the progressive distress of the proletarian class *(Verelendungstheorie)*. Veblen did not argue, as did many revisionist Marxists and humanitarian reformers, that working class conditions were actually improving, a fact that had little bearing on the theoretical premises of Marx's philosophy of history. Instead he simply made two observations that revealed the tenuous reasoning behind Marx's theory of a swelling "industrial reserve army." First, the theory implies that the number of factory workers will increase despite the decline in their means of existence, an assumption about the redemptive claims of poverty that defies the Darwinian notion of survival. Second, the notion that the pauperization of the workers will lead to a revolutionary situation is based on the dubious Hegelian premise that historical movements reverse directions, that the very powerlessness of the worker will produce its opposite effect and bring forth the power of proletarian class consciousness. Such a situation would be possible if life imitated philosophy, but history generally defies dialectics. "Experience, the experience of history, teaches that abject misery carries with it deterioration and abject subjection. The theory of progressive distress fits convincingly into the scheme of the Hegelian three-phase dialectic. It stands for the antithesis that is to be merged in the ulterior synthesis; but it has no particular force on the ground of an argument from cause to effect."[5]

Although the triadic *schema* of the dialectic is not as central to Marx as Veblen maintained, the Hegelian philosophy surely is, and Veblen, along with Benedetto Croce in Italy, was among the first social theorists in the 1890s to see the illusions of a historical materialism deified by German idealism. Veblen remained convinced that the scientific revolution ushered in by the theory of biological evolution had completely naturalized modern thought and thus rendered obsolete the Hegelian-Marxist categories of understanding. Veblen and Marx subscribed to two contrasting philosophies of history, the Darwinian and the dialectical. But it was not only Veblen's empirical temperament that caused him to be skeptical of Marxism as a theoretical proposition. Such an empirical stance characterized the position of many "scientific" socialists around the turn of the century. Probing considerably farther than other contemporary critics, Veblen discerned two irreconcilable principles in Marx's economic theories that exposed the contradictory foundations of Marxist socialism itself.

The postulates and preconceptions of Marx, wrote Veblen, are drawn from "two distinct lines of antecedents—the Materialistic Hegelianism and the English system of Natural Rights." From the former he derived his theory of historical development as self-actualizing, a movement unfolding by "inner necessity." From the latter he arrived at his theory of value and his conviction that the worker is entitled to the whole product of his labor. The problem arises when Marx tries to synthesize these two contrary traditions in the doctrine of class struggle. For in the Hegelian scheme the "dialectic of movement of social progress . . . moves on the spiritual plane of human desire and passion, not on the (literally) material plane of mechanical and physiological stress, on which the developmental process of brute creation unfolds itself. It is sublimated materialism, sublimated by the dominating presence of the conscious human spirit." The class struggle, on the other hand, "proceeds on motives of interest, and a recognition of class interest can, of course, be achieved only by a reflection on the facts of the case." Indeed, the doctrine of class struggle is of "utilitarian origin and of English pedigree, and it belongs to Marx by virtue of his having borrowed its elements from the system of self-interest. It is in fact a piece of hedonism, and is related to Bentham rather than to Hegel. It proceeds on the grounds of the hedonistic calculus, which is equally foreign to the Hegelian notion of unfolding process and to the post-Darwinian notions of cumulative causation."[6]

The problem of history is the problem of consciousness. Class consciousness was the great ideal of Karl Marx. But can a notion rooted in Hegel's "pious fancy" of the human spirit realizing itself be reconciled with a movement grounded in the utilitarian egoism of working class demands? If class consciousness can never rise above class interests, if the ideal can never transcend the real, if Bentham can be absorbed in Hegel, how can the proletariate liberate all mankind in the revolutionary act of self-liberation?

The Metaphysics of Normality: Veblen's Critique of Classical Economics

Veblen brought to bear upon classical economics the same critical spirit he revealed in his analysis of Marxist economics. Much of this skeptical acumen flowed from his own personality, that of the village iconoclast who loved to turn all answers into questions. But, beyond that, Veblen's training in philosophy equipped him for any theoretical system he might encounter. He had studied under Peirce, and it may have been from that philosopher that he gained his critical attitude toward hedonism and the utilitarian idea of happiness. He was also an admirer of Hume, who made him even more aware of the importance of being "irreverently skeptical . . . to the need or the use of any formulation of knowledge that outruns the reach of . . . matter-of-fact, step-by-step argument from cause to effect."[7] And from Kant, the subject of his graduate work, Veblen learned that human understanding rests upon preconceived categories of thought and that the mind is active and not a passive receptor of sensations. Veblen appropriated these philosophical positions in his analysis of contemporary orthodox thought in "The Preconceptions of Economic Science," a series of three articles in the *Quarterly Journal of Economics* that elaborated the arguments presented in his better-known essay, "Why Is Economics Not An Evolutionary Science?"

Why not? Because the discipline has failed to stay abreast of the physical sciences in adopting an evolutionary methodology. Veblen did not accuse economists of ignoring factual data, nor were they negligent in formulating a body of theory to explain growth and development. The difference is that the modern scientist is "unwilling to depart from the test of causal relation or quantitative sequence," whereas the economist wants to "go back of the colorless sequence of phenomena and seek higher ground for their ultimate synthesis." The scientist keeps his eyes on the long-range development of natural phenomena, trying carefully to discern in its cumulative processes a theory of causal relation. The economist, on the other hand, stretches the limits of causal understanding and unconsciously looks beyond nature to discover the personal meaning of impersonal events. This penchant for ascribing moral significance to natural phenomena Veblen labelled "animistic." Just as primitive man attributes human values to trees and other material objects, so does the "modern" economist read into nature his own emotional needs for order and symmetry. Among the seventeenth-century Physiocrats this tendency expressed itself in the idea of an *ordre naturel* and a *loi naturelle*. Among nineteenth-century economists it still found expression in the assumptions of an "unseen hand" and in the supposedly controlling laws of "natural" wages and "normal" value.

Classical political economy is also scientifically pre-revolutionary because it rests upon what Veblen called a "taxonomic" habit of mind. Instead of treating economic phenomena as dynamic and interrelated in line with evolutionary conceptions, economists approach the content of their discipline as an exercise in static analysis, classification, and disembodied abstraction. This attitude in turn leads to the assumption that equilibrium will always reestablish itself in a "frictionless competitive system" (the phrase is John Bates Clark's), and that any aberration may be dismissed as merely a "disturbing cause" that only proves the system's capacity for self-correction. The notion of a "hypothetically perfect competitive system," Veblen observed in his trenchant essay on Clark, rests on a body of logically consistent propositions concerning the "normal relations of things"; it rests, that is, within the deductive, model-building mind of Clark himself. This point is important to note, for Veblen's critics, like the Parsonian student Arthur K. Davis, have maintained that "rigorous adherence to Veblen's methodology would result in no science at all" since science requires hypotheses, abstractions, and systems models.[8] It is not at all clear that Veblen is denying models as such; indeed his own anthropological speculations are as questionable as the "conjectural history" he accuses economists of practicing. But Veblen does want to show that when contemporary economists formulate an ideal situation—"if perfect competition prevailed," "if buyers and sellers were governed by one motive," etc.[9]—it is because that ideal represents what they think should exist.* He criticizes them for speaking as scientists while behaving as moralists. As for those economists who continually build models and invoke the "normal case" to better escape the abnormalities of everyday life, Veblen satirically responded by asking what in the world they could explain by fleeing from the world by means of a paradigm that not only fails to represent reality but is linguistically bankrupt:

> But what does all this signify? If we are getting restless under the taxonomy of a monocotylednous wage-system and cryptogamic theory of interest, with involute loculicidal, tomentous and monoloform variants, what is the cytoplasm, centrosome, or karyokinetic process to which we may turn, and in which we may find surcease from the metaphysics of normality and controlling principles.[10]

Classical political economy was not only abstract and escapist, it was narrow and cautious. The marginal utility school of thought, for example, held that each succeeding unit of capital and labor is less productive than the preceding one because of the limits of demand, and that consumer behavior is rational and can therefore be scientifically calculated in terms of the diminishing utility of goods consumed. Veblen agreed that consumption is the proper focus, but the marginalists shut off inquiry just where it should begin, in the culture and mores of a consuming society. Veblen wanted to see a "genetic account" of the origins and development of this phenomena rather than a taxonomic description of cost-price theory. He wanted to expand the scope of investigation to include the sociological implications of economic behavior. But contemporary economists like Clark were timid precisely where they should be bold, prosaic where they should be imaginative. They were still laboring under "a metaphysics of normality which asserts no extra-causal constraint over events, but contents itself with establishing correlations, equivalencies, homologies, and theories concerning the conditions of economic equilibrium." So blinded, the economist will see in the most unusual economic behavior the most uniform laws of nature, and every and any situation will be a mere reflection of his own preconceptions, his own inner need for the "metaphysical postulates of congruity." "A gang of Aleutian Islanders," scoffed Veblen, "slushing about in the wrack and surf with rakes and magical incantations for the capture of shellfish, are held, in

* "This Order of Nature, or realm of Natural Law, is not the actual run of material facts, but the facts so interpreted as to meet the needs of the taxonomist in point of taste, logical consistency, and sense of justice. The question of the truth and adequacy of the categories is a question as to the consensus of taste and predilections among the taxonomists; i.e., they are an expression of trained human nature touching the matter of what ought to be." Veblen, "Professor's Clark's Economics," *POS*, p. 191.

point of taxonomic reality, to be engaged in a feat of hedonistic equilibration in rent, wages, and interest."[11]

At the basis of the whole structure of classical political economy is its one-dimensional conception of human nature. This conception proved too profane even for one of the most irreverent scholars of the Victorian era:

> The hedonistic conception of man is that of a lightning calculator of pleasures and pains, who oscillates like a homogenous globule of desire and happiness under the impulse of stimuli that shift him about the area, but leave him intact. He has neither antecedent nor consequent. He is an isolated, definitive human datum, in stable equilibrium except for the buffets of the impinging forces that displace him in one direction or another. Self-imposed in an elemental space, he spins symmetrically about his own spiritual axis until the parallelogram of forces bears down upon him, whereupon he follows the line of the resultant. When the force of the impact is spent, he comes to rest, a self-contained globule of desire as before. Spiritually, the hedonistic man is not a prime mover. He is not the seat of the process of living, except in the sense that he is subject to a series of permutations enforced upon him by circumstances external and alien to him.[12]

Much of Veblen's description of political economy was pure caricature; it fails to do justice to the richness and complexity of nineteenth-century economic thought. But why did Veblen, who saw hedonism as an archaic trait, and who indeed subsumed it under his own analysis of consumption, find the hedonistic conception of modern "economic man" so repugnant? For one thing, such a conceptualization tended to reorient economics so that the discipline concerned itself almost solely with distribution, with matters of ownership, income, prices, and acquisition. Marginalists like Clark, for example, analyzed production in terms of value, when value is primarily a matter of distribution. Thus Clark and others confused the two spheres of activity with the "theorem of equivalence," the presumed equality established between productivity and remuneration, between the aggregate output of collective effort and the even distribution according to individual contribution. The theorem implies that the workers get as much as they produce and produce as much as they get and that consumers pay as much as the commodity is worth and give what they are willing to pay. To Veblen such a formulation not only compares incomparable activities, it ignores the absence of freedom among the members of economic society and the necessity of conforming to external pressures. The norm is competition, the reality may very well be coercion. "There can be no balance, and no commensurability, between the laborer's disutility (pain) in producing goods and the consumer's utility (pleasure) in consuming them, in as much as these two hedonistic phenomena lie each within the consciousness of a distinct person." Hence, "the wages of labor (i.e., the utility of the goods received by the laborer) is not equal to the disutility undergone by him, except in the sense that he is competitively willing to accept it; nor are these wages equal to the utility got by the consumer of goods, except in the sense that he is willing to pay them."[13]

To try to systematize desire and discomfort was to try to eliminate the human element from economics, to allow the model to absorb the man. This was Veblen's severest criticism. Classical political economy not only assumed an equitable balance between work and reward, it so hypostatized the "laws" of economic behavior that it could understand everything but man himself. Veblen noted that John Stuart Mill had challenged the utilitarian calculus by supplementing the quantitative hedonism of Bentham with qualitative distinctions between different kinds of pleasures that motivate conduct. Veblen also observed, perhaps drawing upon Kant, that the associational psychology buttressing hedonistic economics reduced mind to a passive component of matter. But the human mind was more than a conditioned entity responding to external stimuli. Even the making of associations suggests the activity of mind. "Similarity of impressions," wrote Veblen, "implies a comparison of impressions by the mind in which the association takes place, and thereby implies some degree of constructive work on the part of the perceiving subject." The mental organs of the body respond to the environment, but in a selective manner, indicating a purposeful, discretionary quality. For evidence of this observation Veblen cited Dewey's revision of the "reflex arc concept," noting that the causal sequence between impact and response is continuous while the mind deliberates before it acts. The mind, then, is less a useless epiphenomenon than a vital "tropismatic complex."[14]

Translated into economic theory, Veblen's discourses in modern psychology enabled him—or so he thought—to demolish the utilitarian concept of man. Underlying the assumption of hedonism is the notion that the love of pleasure and the fear of pain determine what man does. Veblen turned this proposition on its head. "Instead of pleasure ultimately determining what human conduct shall be, the tropismatic propensities that eventuate in conduct ultimately determine what shall be pleasurable." Veblen even denied that pleasure can be regarded as an end in itself, arguing that it was "the feeling concomitant of certain states or modes of activity," a kind of spin-off satisfaction. Veblen was far from clear on his own conception of human nature, as we shall see; but like Peirce he was convinced that man could not be motivated merely by something so crass as happiness, nor could he be regarded simply as an inert creature of comfort. By taking economists outside of their discipline, Veblen was attempting to demonstrate that modern psychology and anthropology had expelled hedonism as an explanation of human activity and had provided the contemporary economist with an entirely different conception of human nature. "According to this conception, it is characteristic of man to do something, not simply to suffer pleasures and pains through the impact of suitable forces. He is not simply a bundle of desires that are to be saturated by being placed in the path of the forces of the environment, but rather a coherent structure of propensities and habits which seek realisation and expression in unfolding activity."[15]

The last statement suggests that Veblen the staunch evolutionist is closer to Hegel than to Darwin: man is less the creature of the environment than the agent of self-realization. This is not the only time Veblen shifts philosophical ground to strengthen his economic attack, or, for that matter, anthropological ground to enhance his critique of modern culture. This problem will be observed again in subsequent chapters. Presently it is necessary to evaluate Veblen's arguments against classical political economy.

Value Theory and the Fetish of Productivity

From the perspective of intellectual history Veblen's critique of present contemporary theory almost reads like a parody of past ideology. Lumping the whole tradition of classical political economy under the rubric of "hedonism" may have served a useful polemical purpose, but it was hardly a fair or accurate characterization. It is doubtful that Malthus and Ricardo can be placed squarely in this scheme, which has all orthodox economists seeing progress and purpose ("teleology") arising out of the interplay of self-interests. It is even more doubtful that the economics of self-interests and the psychology of hedonism are one and the same. In his *Theory of Moral Sentiments* (1790), Adam Smith stated that "Nature" had endowed man with an "original desire" to "feel pleasure" in winning the favorable regard of others; he did not advise that this "very best passion of human nature" could be realized by competing with others and acting on motives of interests alone.[16] Whether the psychology of capitalism developed along this sociological dimension is another matter, one we shall explore in a later chapter. More immediately, when one compares Smith's *Moral Sentiments* to his *Wealth of Nations*, one must raise a telling question: Did classical economists really believe that economics itself should be allowed to determine behavior? Hardly. Almost all the British theorists (Smith, Locke, Hume, et al.) counted upon social authority to restrain individual activity and private judgment. Not only squalid profits but a socialized conscience would govern civil society. Indeed, the same Veblenian ideas of social esteem, emulation, and appropriation also comprised the social psychology of Locke's *Second Treatise*, Mandeville's *The Fable of the Bees*, John Adams' *Discourses on Davila*, and, of course, Ben Franklin's *Autobiography*. In his social psychology of envy and status Veblen is closer than he is aware to the hated classic tradition from which he tried to liberate economics.

Veblen's attempt to use John Dewey to refute Jeremy Bentham also contains some embarrassingly ironic implications. First is the matter of inconsistency. In one of his "Preconceptions" essays Veblen hails the "new psychology" for introducing "personality" into modern social science; two pages later in the same essay he hails "modern mechanical industry" for the "elimination of personality" in favor of a cause-effect "process" of thinking that is "non-teleological."[17] He liberates man from hedonism only to turn him over to mechanism; or, more precisely, he desires to see "economic man" free and self-activating while at the same time demanding that the economist adjust his thoughts to the deterministic principles of science. This ambivalence may be due to Veblen's attempt to assimilate Kant and Darwin. Whatever the source of the ambivalence, it points up again the tension in Veblen's thought between humanism and behaviorism, between his wish to see man autonomous and his wish to understand man in empirical terms. Far more serious, however, is Veblen's seeming unawareness of the ultimate implications of the psychology he wanted to bring to bear upon economics. The "new psychology," in so far as it introduced "personality" as a factor in economic behavior, undermined the very argument Veblen was trying to make. From John Dewey to Charles Cooley and George Herbert Mead, and, more recently, to David Riesman, we have a progression from the original psychological discovery of "personality" and the "self" to the social psychology of the "social self," the seeking of identity through the "generalized other," the interactive "looking-glass self," and ultimately the "other-directed personality." Thus while Veblen cited the "new psychology" to demonstrate to neo-classical economists that human conduct is not necessarily determined by what is pleasurable, the same economists could cite the same psychology to demonstrate what the older classical economists knew all along—that conduct is indeed determined by what is sociable. Economic man is dead, but sociological man lives, and interest behavior finds its "higher" expression in status behavior, in the social determinants of personality. The "invisible hand" of economics has been replaced by the mirrored reflections of society. Veblen could hardly resist this conclusion; he himself desired to bring to consciousness the social compulsions of economic behavior. Thus his use of psychology had the ironic effect of relegating the locus of value to precisely the place from which he had tried to liberate it—society.

Veblen's unconscious proximity to classical economics in the area of social psychology appears also to be the case in an important area of economics, value theory. Veblen wanted an economics of production rather than consumption, an empirical system that dealt with the real tangible process of output rather than a market exchange that involved the artificial whims of consumption and status. As a result he could not move into the twentieth century with the marginal theorists who stressed the subjective nature of value. Thus the logic of his position, if not his temperament, required that he turn economic analysis "back" to the eighteenth century where value was located solely in the objective factors of production, the rational variables which, it was held by Ricardo and others, determine the distribution and consumption of wealth. Yet Veblen was not interested, as were the classical economists, in the relation of land, labor, and capital to rent, wages, and profits. Indeed he was not even interested in establishing an approximate remunerative norm for labor. "The divergence between the usefulness of work and the wages paid for it," he wrote in a footnote in *Business Enterprise*, "seems wide enough to throw the whole question of equivalence out of theoretical consideration."[18] Indifferent to the necessity of a wage scale, Veblen could also innocently call for an end to the price system. All that remained in Veblen's technological utopia is production for the sake of production, a state of syndicalist bliss that has only been achieved in wartime (Veblen would appreciate the irony), when a nation's efforts are devoted to the output of a few vital materials. But no industrial society can endure for long without a rationale for allocation and distribution. As Daniel Bell has observed, "Any complex planning mechanism seeking to distribute resources efficiently (i.e., to assess relative costs) in the production of tens of thousands of *different* products can do so, as even the socialist economies have discovered, only through a price system."[19]

Other difficulties arise in Veblen's analysis of modern business behavior. Focusing solely on the tangible aspects of production, on workmen and their machinery, he neglected the non-engineering activities that also contribute to the output of goods, the managerial functions of finance, personnel, and administrative coordination. Moreover, while Veblen was sensitive to the pressures of status, he never acknowledged that the modern businessman may be driven by pride to achieve productive efficiency as well as profit. The principle of optimization by productive agents Veblen confined to the technicians; he never explained why businessmen would also not want to enhance their prestige by a display of workmanlike efficiency. Veblen remained convinced that leisure-class values had triumphed over the instinct of workmanship. Yet even in American culture Andrew Carnegie emerged as the model of entrepreneurial genius and rationality, not Jay Gould and Jim Fisk. Similarly, Veblen's entire analysis presumed the existence of monopoly, and while this presumption is understandable in the light of the great mergers taking place during his time, it led Veblen to pay too little attention to the positive role of the market, if not in price competition at least in quality of production. As Kenneth Arrow has noted, Veblen yearned for the early communal spirit of the "handicraft era," and thus failed to consider that the protected, fraternal enterprises characterized by the intimacy of personal relations between buyer and seller may shelter incompetence and shoddy quality.[20]

Today economic theorists like the Nobel-prize scholar Arrow still find considerable reward in reading Veblen's theory of business cycles. What they lament, and what they tend to criticize institutional economics in general for, is Veblen's indifference to price theory. It might be said in Veblen's behalf that in a paradise of economic abundance there would be no need for a price system or even a value theory. For without scarcity there is no struggle over priorities and hence no pressing need for valuation of the costs of production and utility of consumption. Contemporary socialists, for example, could cite Bellamy's parable of the water tank to make the point that plenitude would solve the problem of distribution (and in our time Michael Harrington has tried to make a similar argument against competition).[21] But Veblen, the castigator of wasteful affluence, could hardly look to the advent of abundance as an answer to the theoretical problems in economics. Thus he could neither go forward nor backward to find the basis for a value system. At first glance the logic of his dilemma seems to call for a retreat. Since he assumed the priority of labor to commodity, of human effort to ownership and expenditure, it would seem that his only recourse was to return to Marx and attempt to salvage the labor theory of value. This he refused to do. On the other hand, he would not even allow a modicum of legitimacy to the sphere of market values that classical and neo-classical economists had tried to systematize. Such efforts, he charged, are concerned only with the "reaction to pecuniary stimulus," not with the creation of value, the "valuer" himself. Classical political economy offers "a theory of valuation with the element of valuation left out—a theory of life stated in terms of the normal paraphernalia of life."[22] Veblen might have said, to borrow from Oscar Wilde's definition of a cynic, that economists who fix their eyes solely on the market can tell us the price of everything and the value of nothing. But no amount of satire or irony can hide the fact that Veblen himself had no answer to the problem of valuation.

When we descend from the heights of theory into the worldly operations of business we find much in Veblen's writings that is strikingly accurate. He could not give much credence to a competitive price system in an era when United States Steel and Standard Oil held vertical and horizontal control over almost all phases of production and distribution. A half-century after *Business Enterprise* was published the American public learned that prices were indeed being "administered" by conspiring firms, a condition that prevailed in the steel and auto industries for several years until the Kefauver Committee investigations of 1958. None of this would have surprised Veblen, nor would he have been amazed at the huge growth of corporate assets. For Veblen was one of the first economists to perceive the implications of the emerging concept of intangible property, the present value of expected future profitable transactions. Veblen regarded this "intangible" value as "pecuniary" since it represented not so much capital in the traditional sense of corporeal property but rather purely monetary estimates by businessmen of the strategic power of manipulation afforded by corporate securities, credit, monopolistic privileges, franchises, good will, advertising, public relations, and, to bring the list up to date, tax shelters, depletion allowances, government contracts, and the like. Those who live in and off the world of intangible wealth are speculators in securities, attorneys, real-estate agents, bankers, brokers, financiers—those concerned primarily with exchange and market value. Such business activities, Veblen insisted, are "lucrative without necessarily being serviceable to the community." Veblen spelled out his case in his articles on "Credit and Prices," "The Limits of Marginal Utility," and "On The Nature of Capital," brilliant essays which attempted to demonstrate that inflation can cause high prices without necessarily expanding industrial output, that credit extension can increase profit margins without bringing new products onto the market, that, in short, man can make money without making goods. Veblen's articles were influential,* and today even scholars critical of Veblen express admiration for his contributions to the study of the modern transition from corporeal to intangible property. "The efforts of conventional economists to derive monopolistic profits from 'entrepreneurian wages,' or watered stock from 'good will,' are exposed," wrote David Riesman, "in all their feebleness."[23]

Veblen's understanding of the coming nature of advanced industrial society is remarkable. His observations of two developments in the American economy reveal much prescience. One development is the separation of management from the ownership of the means of business enterprise and the coming domination of the economy by an oligopolistic nucleus of giant corporations, a development verified three decades later in A. A. Berle's and Gardiner Means' *The Modern Corporation and Private Property* (1932). Veblen's second observation relates to his theory of business crisis, an anticipation of the great depression which in some respects is remarkably similar to John Maynard Keynes' famous treatise, *General Theory of Employment, Interest and Money* (1936).[24]

Although the two personalities differed strikingly, both Keynes and Veblen could agree about the impermanent nature of prosperity and economic stability, the absence of effective demand to support overproduction, and the psychological consideration of profit expectations on the part of panic-struck businessmen. But while Veblen leaned toward a devil theory of depression with real villains, Keynes naturalized the whole phenomenon. In Veblen's analysis depression arises

* As John R. Commons noted, the Supreme Court arrived at some of Veblen's conclusions about intangible property when ruling that taxes could be levied against a corporation's expected earning capacity based upon its vast market value of stocks and bonds. See Commons, *Institutional Economics: Its Place in Political Economy* (Madison: University of Wisconsin Press, 1959), pp. 651–53.

from an inflated credit system in which corporations borrow on overvalued intangible assets, commit themselves to future high level earnings based on the assumption of continued rounds of prosperity, which, if temporarily realized, leads to even more capitalization, a situation that cannot be sustained because technological innovation lowers prices and corporations can only expand by competing with one another; hence, a general drop in profits and a continual decline in values until the entire system collapses, not in a massive upheaval as Marx envisioned, but in a dull thud. Keynes' analysis starts with the movement of income and investment and the relation of these factors to saving and spending, and then charts the contraction and expansion of the rate of the flow of money through the entire economy, from buyers to producers to earners. Where Veblen believed that business would conspire to restrict production, Keynes maintained that business first decides not to reinvest and expand output because the consumption of specific goods had reached its limit, either due to the saturation of the market or the fall in consumer purchasing power, or both. With Veblen, then, the cycle downward may be deliberate "sabotage"; with Keynes, it is simply natural stagnation. Similarly, where Keynes looked to government investment to take up where private enterprise left off, Veblen assumed that the most likely way out of a depression would lie in "some form of wasteful expenditure, as, e.g., a sustained war demand or the demand due to the increase of armaments, naval and military."[25] It is perhaps not surprising that Veblen would underestimate the role of government spending as a means of stimulating income flow and consumption in order to bring about an increase in employment and general business recovery. Yet a prosperity based on mass consumption and military production was not beyond Veblen's imagination, which could grasp the rationale for everything, even the "normality" of waste and war.

Marx would have happily called our contemporary federal programs of Keynesian economics a "contradiction," Veblen, more pessimistically, a "chronic derangement." For neither Marx nor Veblen believed that private property, competition, and the profit system had much to do with the real meaning and value of life, with man's potential for full human development. Where, then, can that meaning and value be found, and how was man's capacity for self-realization thwarted in the first place?

5 . . . Marx, Veblen, and the "Riddle" of Alienation

The necessity of a comparative approach to intellectual history is impressed upon the historian by one question: Why is man alienated? An examination of different perspectives may deepen our understanding of alienation as a historical phenomenon. This chapter attempts such a study by contrasting Marx's and Veblen's analysis of the origins of property and by examining the far-reaching sociological ramifications of that development. By no means do I mean to imply that Marx or Veblen had an answer to the very problems they had uncovered. My aim is more modest: to suggest that Veblen had a different, and perhaps keener, grasp of these problems because, among other things, he had access to anthropological data of the late nineteenth century unavailable to Marx.[1] Both Marx and Veblen came to the study of economics by way of early training in philosophy, but Veblen extended his analysis of economic behavior into the relatively new disciplines of anthropology, ethnology, psychology, and sociology. In exploring these developing fields, Veblen discovered new ways of looking at contemporary social relations by rediscovering the old ways people related to each other in early primitive communities. Marx called upon man to draw his "poetry" from the future; Veblen drew his insights from the past.

Alienation and the Origins of Property

Marx's description of the process by which man becomes alienated, and his dialectical explanation of that process, appears questionable when juxtaposed to a Veblenian approach to the causal sequence of historical phenomena. To Marx, alienation originates in the emergence of private property and the division of labor. Denied the fruits of his labor and the right to determine the mode of work, man becomes estranged from himself and from others. Under capitalism, observed Marx, workers experience work not as creation but as coercion; and forced labor dehumanizes personal relationships because the introduction of the "alien intermediary" of money assumes all value and hence devaluates man. But why does alienation occur at all? "What a contradiction it would be," confessed Marx in his 1844 notebooks, "if the more man subjugates nature through work . . . man should renounce his joy in the producing and the enjoyment of his product for love of these powers." In acquiring the power to conquer nature, how did man lose the power to master himself? "How, we ask now, does it happen that *man externalizes* his *labor,* alienates it. How is this alienation rooted in the nature of human development?" With the question dramatically posed, Marx continues, "Let us consider more clearly these relationships." At this point the manuscript breaks off—unfinished.[2]

The same difficulties remain when Marx turns from questions about human behavior to the behavior of history itself. Marx begins his exploration into the processes of history by focusing on that which supposedly governs all human relations, productivity. Both the production of the means to support life and the exchange of the things produced occupy Marx's attention as he studies what he regards as the four basic historical epochs: "the Asiatic, the ancient, the feudal, and the modern bourgeois modes of production."[3] The scheme is ingenious, but one wonders whether it is merely a description masquerading as an explanation. Consider, for example, the communal society that Marx believed characterized ancient Slavic villages and certain Asiatic communities (to which Engels added the Iroquois of North America). In this historical stage land is held and tilled in common and products are shared communally in a society in which hunting, fishing, and cattle raising are the chief occupations. Why does this system, which Engels would term "primitive communism," break down and give rise to new forms of production that are no longer collectively owned? Marx was "thin on pre-history," Eric Hobsbawn noted;[4] he wisely avoided the question, perhaps realizing that any answer would be nothing more than guesswork. But Engels took the basic Marxist presupposition that private property emerges when production surpasses subsistence and tried to apply it to early primitive society. "The advent of private property in herds of cattle and articles of luxury," he wrote in *The Origins of the Family,* "led to an exchange between individuals, to a transformation of products into commodities. Here is the root of the entire revolution that followed." We are indeed on the verge of discovering why a supposedly non-exploitative communal society could be transformed into its opposite. However, the more Engels searched for the origin of this phenomenon, the more it eluded him. "How and when the herds were transformed from the collective ownership of the tribe . . . to the proprietorship of the heads of the families is not known to us," concludes Engels, who rests his case with a remark which reveals the theoretical impasse in which he finds himself: "The herds drifted into the hands of private individuals."[5]

In many of his excursions into classical antiquity and pre-history,

Marx focused on land as the crucial factor in the evolution of private property. It was on privately owned plots that slaves produced the surplus above that required for their own subsistence. Land became identical with wealth and society became differentiated on the basis of property. But in his *Economic-Philosophical Manuscripts,* in contrast to his historical studies, Marx saw alienation as logically prior to land ownership. Here he suggests that instead of asking "What is the origin of private property?" we should ask, "How can we explain the alienation that broke out in the course of human development?" How, indeed?

It is no surprise that this question should pose less difficulty for the philosopher than for the historian. The former may reason his way out of the dilemma; the latter cannot, or should not, permit logic to substitute for evidence. Small wonder that many contemporary scholars, especially students of classical antiquity, have shied away from the search for the origins of things that occupied the speculations of late nineteenth-century anthropologists and historians. The contemporary philosopher, however, and especially the Marxist, rushes in where the historian fears to tread. Thus the relationship between man's alienation and the emergence of property and the division of labor is scarcely a problem, either theoretical or factual, to the Yugoslavian philosopher István Mészáros. That the means of man's dehumanization—the productive forces of history—would also serve as the means of man's rehumanization is an aspect of the human struggle for freedom that must be grasped as a "dialectical reciprocity," Mészáros advises.[6] Similarly, the American philosopher Bertell Ollman informs us that since Marx never offered any "details" on how the original transfer from common to private property occurred, we need not bother with the question, at least not in historical terms. Ollman's learned discussion of the issue, however, shows that he himself is aware of the awesome dilemma Marx has left to students of history: if private property and the division of labor are "identical expressions" (Marx's phrase), and if private property is the term Marx used to describe the objects produced by "alienated labor," it would seem to follow that we need to know which came first, whether private property makes man alienated or whether unalienated man makes private property and hence produces the condition of his own alienation. Marx addressed himself directly to this "riddle":

> Private property is thus the product, the result, the necessary consequence of alienated labor, of the external relation of the worker to nature and to himself. Private property thus results by analysis from the concept of alienated labor—i.e., of alienated man, of estranged labor, of estranged life, of estranged man. True, it is as a result of the movement of private property that we have obtained the concept of alienated labor (of alienated life) from political economy. But on analysis of this concept it becomes clear that

> though private property appears to be the source, the cause of alienated labor, it is really its consequence, just as the gods in the beginning are not the cause but the effect of man's intellectual confusion. Later this relationship becomes reciprocal.

Ollman, after quoting the above passage from the 1844 notebooks, argues persuasively that Marx was correct in asserting that alienation cannot be formulated in the familiar terms of causal understanding:

> This "reciprocal effect" between private property and alienated labor is given the distinction of being called the "secret" of private property, where Marx says, "on the one hand it is the product of alienated labor, and . . . secondly it is the means by which labor alienates itself, the realization of this alienation." The logical tie which Marx posits between the two makes it impossible for one to appear without the other, and makes any attempt to establish historical primacy a fruitless task.[7]

From the Marxist perspective, then, alienation is a process in which its activity and its consequence are one and the same, in which the traditional notion of cause and effect must be seen dialectically as two forces which are at the same time themselves and each other. The phenomenon of private property can be grasped from the same perspective. As Marx observed, it is connected with the disintegration of primitive society; it evolved "side by side" with the "communal and state property of antiquity" that culminated in Roman society; and it developed along with the social division of labor between town and country, the separation of industrial and commercial activities from those of agriculture.[8] Such events can be understood without determining the necessity of their origins; for the attempt to establish the "historical primacy" of these relationships is, the philosopher advises, "a fruitless task." Seen from this privileged epistemological position, private property appears, emerges, unfolds, grows, and develops, relating to everything in general and originating in nothing in particular. The "secret" of private property is illuminated philosophically, if only by ignoring it historically.

The Beginnings of Ownership: The Anthropological Dimension

Such a resolution of the "secret" of property and the "riddle" of alienation could hardly be entertained by Thorstein Veblen. A Darwinist rather than a dialectician, Veblen remained convinced that the scientific revolution ushered in by the theory of biological evolution had completely naturalized modern thought and all but rendered obsolete the Hegelian-Marxist categories of understanding. As we have seen, it was Marx's attempt to salvage a value theory from orthodox economics that Veblen found most troublesome. In attempting to transcend the ethic of capitalism, Marx may have only absorbed its ethos; for he extended the Ricardian analysis of the factors of production by formulating a theory of value in which labor, whether free or coerced, possesses the unique property of being able to produce more than is required for subsistence. In the *Grundrisse* as well as in *Capital* Marx insists that exploitation and alienation derive from property, which itself must be seen as an outcome of human effort, and he explains why all other factors which may contribute to the "human condition" must be excluded, even the factor of consumption:

> *We reduce this property to the relation to the conditions of production.* Why not to consumption, since the production of the individual is originally restricted to the reproduction of his own body through the appropriation of ready objects prepared by nature itself for consumption? Even where the only task is to *find* and to *discover*, this soon requires exertion, labour—as in hunting, fishing, herding—and production (i.e., development) of certain capacities on the part of the subject.[9]

Veblen rarely used the word "alienation," and when he did so it usually meant to him, as it did to other social philosophers of his era, a political disinheritance involving natural rights. But there can be no doubt that Veblen was deeply occupied with the same phenomenon that had obsessed the early Marx. In his lesser-known but perhaps greatest book, *The Instinct of Workmanship and the State of the Industrial Arts*, Veblen observes that the suppression of this instinct, even though it may have been a necessary outcome of cultural and technological growth as man left the stage of primitive communal life, represents man's loss of freedom over his means of freedom, and this "supersession" is "the most universal and most radical mutation which human culture had undergone in its advance from savagery to civilization."[10] In Veblen's analysis of the source of alienation the loss of "free workmanship" lies not so much in production as in consumption, in the possession of wealth rather than in its creation, in the way in which goods come to be, not made, but owned.

Where Marx and Engels believed that private property emerges from the division of labor and the product of surplus value, and where the classical economists maintained that property was founded on productive labor and social contract, Veblen perceived the beginnings of the institution in the act of conquest.[11] Veblen, however, was not wholly convinced that property could be explained simply by tracing it to the act of seizure without exploring the sociological implications of the act itself. It is significant that when he addressed himself to this problem he refrained from using the term property and titled his article "The Beginnings of Ownership," thereby taking the issue out of the Marxist and liberal perspectives and grounding it in new anthropological concepts. Veblen wanted to demonstrate, first of all, that in many archaic cultures the subjective apprehension of external objects was so strong that "the relation of any individual to his personal effects is conceived to be of a more intimate kind than that of ownership simply." The items that we see as lying objectively apart from man are seen in primitive society as extensions of human personality. In ancient tribal villages the "congeries of things," such as clothes, ornaments, and weapons, are not what modern economists would call commodities. To primitive man these articles "are conceived to be his in much the same sense as his hands and feet are his, or his pulse-beat, or his digestion, or the heat of his body, or the motions of his limbs or brain." So closely linked is the psychological relationship of person to thing that the idea of ownership can scarcely be said to exist. "Such meagre belongings of the primitive savage as would under the nomenclature of a later day be classed as personal property are not thought of by him as his property at all; they pertain organically to his person."[12]

How then did the idea of property arise? It could not have had its roots in the breakup of primitive communism. Seen from the eyes of primitive man, communal ownership is a contradiction in terms: the very idea of ownership implies an individual possessor. The sequence must be reversed; communalism is of "relative late growth," perhaps a conscious response to an earlier non-communal stage. Nor is ownership an "instinctive notion," an innate idea deeply implanted in man's nature. On the contrary, it is an acquired cultural trait that must be learned. Neither could the concept of property have resulted from the growing uncertain status of articles and things, for a given object may even change hands "without passing out of the quasi-personal fringe" of the original owner. Possession is not necessarily synonymous with property. Slaves, for example, have use of their master's tools and thus possess the means of production but in no way do they own or control them. Yet it is in the institution of slavery, and later of serfdom, that one sees a key connection: ownership begins where workmanship ends. But the connection is complex. "It will hold as a rough generalization," Veblen notes cautiously, "that ownership does not begin before the rise of a canon of exploit; but it is to be added that it also does not seem to begin with the first beginning of exploit as a manly occupation." The first ventures of exploit relate to hunting and growing, self-sustaining occupations the products of which are consumed collectively. Veblen cites two reasons why the practice of seizing, accumulating, and privately claiming such products could not have begun under the "peaceable communistic regime of primitive savagery." First, the dissension resulting from such acts would have been fatal to the tribe. Second, the "primitive fighting horde still needs to consume its scanty means of subsistence in common, in order to give the collective horde its full fighting efficiency. Otherwise it would succumb before any rival horde that had not yet given up collective consumption." Even though predatory activity increases as life passes from peaceful savagery to barbarian exploitation, individual possession does not result from plunder alone, for the goods that are seized, weapons and food, continue to be essential to the survival of the conquering group. Thus in order for the idea of ownership to have arisen, the development of economic life must have reached a level where goods are durable rather than perishable. Yet economic growth is only a necessary and not a sufficient cause; even with abundance the idea of property may remain stillborn. Property itself is not the cause of alienation, a phenomenon that must be grasped as something more than a series of predetermined economic developments.

We must understand property, Veblen seems to say, not in the way it is presented to experience, particularly the experience of nineteenth-century economic theorists. Rather we must grasp the way it was apprehended at its very inception. In Veblen's analysis the birth of private property must await a change of consciousness, and the reorientation of human apprehension occurs when the primitive horde seizes not goods but people, not the products of man but man himself. "Captives are items that do not fit into the communal scheme of consumption, and their appropriation by their individual captor works no manifest detriment to the group. At the same time these captives continue to be obviously distinct from their captor in point of individuality, and so are not readily brought in under the quasi-personal fringe. The captives taken under rude conditions are chiefly women."[13]

Why women? Curiously Veblen attributes no sexual motive to the capture of women. Instead he suggested that except where there is a slave class of men, women are more useful since their labor is worth more than their maintenance and less "formidable" since they bear no weapons. But the sociological import of the capture of females is more significant than the economical or sexual. Women serve the symbolic function of "trophies" that attest to the prowess of their capturer. "They are fit subjects for command and constraint; it ministers to both his honor and his vanity to domineer over them, and their utility in this respect is very great. But his domineering over them is evidence of his prowess, and it is incompatible with their utility as trophies that other men should take the liberties with his women which serve as evidence of the coercive relation of the captor." A captured woman is not to be shared as a captured good is consumed collectively in primitive society. She is the one subject which predatory man can claim by virtue of his demonstrated strength; and as this practice hardens into a custom, the "customary right of use and abuse over an object which is obviously not an organic part of his person constitutes the relation of ownership as," Veblen ironically adds, "naively apprehended."[14]

Ownership soon extends to claims upon the products of labor performed by the person owned, hence the birth of exploitation. At the root of such predatory behavior is not merely the pure impulse of economic profit but the deeper emotions of pride and "emulation." Women are first seized as prizes, human badges signifying that the owner, unlike "all the non-combatant or ignoble" members of the community, is too eminent and powerful to engage in productive labor. Whatever the relationship of slavery to property or capitalism, human captivity could scarcely have been possible without the contempt for manual labor, a contempt rooted, as we shall see, in the contamination of man's instincts for workmanship and parental benevolence. And the first sign of wealth was subjugated women, the only real "goods" which primitive man could possess. In this formulation of the problem of alienation Marx's sequence of historical phenomena is reversed: the lust for things, the "furies of interests," is the result of the seizure of persons, not the cause of it.

Veblen's interpretation of the origins of property and slavery, though possibly original in nineteenth-century economic and social theory, was not without antecedents. Plato's theory that the state originates through the subjugation of sedentary populations by nomads and hunters was later discovered by Hume, who criticized the classical, liberal version of the social contract on these grounds. Veblen had been influenced by Hume, and it is quite likely that the same skepticism shaped his attitudes toward liberal theories of property, attitudes readily reinforced by his Darwinian sense of struggle. Today, contemporary scholars of ancient history have noted the relationship between slavery and the demand of the ruling classes for servants who are desired less for economic than for social reasons. Enslavement of persons and their conversion to property was a frequent occurrence in classical Greece; and in Rome, where the material level of life was better, and the lavish expenditures and military conquests brighter, the proportion of slaves to free populations was also greater. "Casual enslavement of individual outsiders, especially of captive women, went as far back as our evidence goes," writes M. I. Finley, a leading authority on slavery in classical antiquity. Finley is understandably intrigued by the motives for enslavement, and, after cautioning that the Greeks themselves engaged in no systematic discussion of the institution, he observes: "Yet somehow one must grasp the psychology of Xenophon when he made the proposal in all seriousness that the Athenian State acquire enough publicly owned slaves to work in the mines so that 'every Athenian be maintained at public expense.' "[15] No doubt Veblen would grasp that "psychology" of conspicuous disassociation from all manual labor, an attitude that somehow, despite the high esteem in which work was held by the pre-Socratic and Hippocratic philosophers, gained social acceptance through the writings of Plato and Aristotle.[16]

Veblen's explanation of the beginnings of ownership, which locates the source of private property not in alienated labor but in the activities of nomads, hunters, and warriors, thus bears some resemblance to the subjugation theory of the state, a school of thought which spans the whole course of western intellectual history, from Plato and Aristotle to Nietzsche and Toynbee—a theory, one should add, that is unacceptable to Marxists.[17] Veblen's observations may have also been familiar to some nineteenth-century anthropologists, and they resemble some of the theories of the contemporary anthropologist Claude Lévi-Strauss, who likewise sees women as the first expression of property exchange by archaic man (a subject to which we shall return in another chapter); and those of the Spanish philosopher Ortegay Gasset, who is convinced that the state not only had its origins in sexual aggression—the thesis also of Freud's *Totem and Taboo*—but that the very meaning of wealth evolved from the authority of the conqueror.*

Aside from the difficulties of verifying historically such speculations, Veblen's thesis must be judged in light of its internal coherence. Veblen may have revised Marx by showing that the capture of men and women precedes the passion for the objects produced by the captured person, that domination and exploitation have little to do with the labor theory of value, that, in short, oppression antedates alienation. Yet Veblen himself faced the same predicament as Marx. Veblen too believed that primitive society was peaceful, communal, and productive. Hence the paradox. If "natural" man enjoys workmanship, why does he feel compelled to capture women as trophies and servants to demonstrate that he no longer stoops to productive labor? If property is founded upon conquest and seizure, must we conclude that man is aggressive and acquisitive?

HUMAN NATURE AND THE STATE OF NATURE: VEBLEN VERSUS HOBBES

Veblen tried to answer such questions in *The Instinct of Workmanship and the State of the Industrial Arts* (1914). The book opens with a description of man as "conditioned by the complement of instinctual proclivities and tropismatic attitudes." The human animal is at the mercy of his instincts, but fortunately those instincts are impersonal, benevolent, and teleological, "conscious" tendencies that contain the potential for contributing to the material welfare of the community. Earlier, in his essay on "Why Is Economics Not An Evolutionary Science?" Veblen had described man as "not simply a bundle of desires

* "For those who are interested in such questions I will add in brief terms an equation which suggests the same origin of the state among Germanic tribes. The props of the German State are the *Recken*, that is to say, the young stalwarts like Siegfried and in general the nobles of the epics. *Recke* is the same word as rich; his power is the *Reich*, and the realm reached by his power the *Reichland*. *Rike*, rich, we see, does not mean being possessed of property. The *Recke* was not 'rich' because he owned the means of production; on the contrary, he disposed of wealth because he was *rike:* valiant, warlike." Ortega y Gasset, *History as a System and Other Essays* (New York, 1962), p. 40.

that are to be saturated . . . but rather a coherent structure of propensities and habits which seek realization and expression in an unfolding activity." He was now obliged to explain how these propensities, bents, and instincts will aim man toward altruistic ends. The two major dispositions conducive to the common good are workmanship and the parental bent. The former instinct, like the latter, is part of man's native endowment, and it functions so that man sees himself as "a center of unfolding impulsive activity—'teleological' activity. He is an agent seeking in every act the accomplishment of some concrete, objective, impersonal end. By force of his being such an agent he is possessed of a taste for effective work, and a distaste for futile effort. He has a sense of the merit of serviceability or efficiency and of the demerit of futility, waste, or incapacity." The parental bent as an "instinctive disposition" implies more than a solicitude for the welfare of children, and it is not to be confused with "the quasi-tropismatic impulses to the procreation of off-spring." Rather the parental bent, especially as it flowered in archaic cultures, reaches out not only to the community but to future generations. It represents a "solicitude for the welfare of the race at large," and in so far as it guides man toward more efficient and productive activities in the interest of posterity, it reinforces the sense of workmanship. So closely connected are the two instincts that Veblen suggests that workmanship can be regarded as the means by which the ends of the parental bent are realized.[18]

Veblen's theory of instincts brings a wince to the face of many modern scholars. The terminological confusions of his hopelessly interchangeable phrases—"propensity," "bent," "drive," "habit," "proclivity," "sense," "tropismatic attitude," etc.—have led some sociologists to dismiss his work as unsophisticated.[19] But Veblen well knew that instinct theory was "a concept of too lax and shifty a definition to meet the demands of exact biological science,"[20] and he used the term with great caution and qualification in the book (later he told a friend that he meant "by instinct a direction—*anlage*.")[21] There are confusions about the purpose as well as the precision of Veblen's concepts. Talcott Parsons, for example, likens Veblen's instinct of workmanship to Max Weber's idea of "the calling."[22] The parallel is dubious. In Weber, work is an exercise in repressive moral duty; in Veblen, it is an expressive "unfolding activity," a totally secularized concept innocent of the psychological and spiritual anguish supposedly associated with the "Protestant ethic." We should also be wary of equating Veblen's idea of workmanship with Marx's idea of man's basic nature as that of a *homo faber*. Veblen compared the workmanship instinct to the capacity for "play" and "idle curiosity" (more on this later),* which

* Veblen stressed the creative and expressive character of work in order to refute the notion of the "irksomeness of labor" in the doctrine of classical political economy. Yet while Veblen was fond of equating work with the capacity for play and even idle

suggests that the formative element in culture lay not only in the biological necessity of production, as Marx would have it, but in various activities of symbolic expression as a means of human development—a point made by Veblen's greatest scholarly disciple, Lewis Mumford.[23]

Veblen's theory of instincts postulates an antagonism between natural man and the culture which he himself has erected. In reinforcing the instinct of workmanship, the parental bent "continually reasserts itself in its native and untaught character," struggling to break out of the confines of modern institutions and the cluster of sanctioned habits and thoughts. Yet only in the early neolithic time were men and women at one with their instinctual nature, with "those activities and mutual relations that would further the life of the group." Veblen believed that man is born with instincts that enables him to shape life to human ends. But there was some strange twist, an "ironic inversion" in man's native endowment, so that the congruity between man's original nature and primitive life eventually gives way to discord, and in the end institutions triumph over instincts, death over life. Perhaps it is more than coincidence that Veblen's *Instinct of Workmanship* appeared in 1914. In that fatal vear western civilization seemed to be in a state of Spenglerian doom. Veblen too was haunted by the long shadow of "barbarism," but instead of sensing an abrupt "decline" of the West he seemed to express a stoical melancholy reminiscent of Santayana meditating on human destiny:

> In the course of cultural growth most of those civilizations or peoples that have had a long history have from time to time been brought up against an imperative call to revise their scheme of institutions in the light of their native instincts, on pain of collapse or decay; and they have chosen variously, and for the most part blindly, to live or not to live, according as their instinctive bias has driven them. In the cases where it has happened that those instincts which make directly for the material welfare of the community, such as the parental bent and the sense of workmanship, have been present in such potent force, or where the institutional elements at variance with the continued life-interests of the community or the civilization in question have been in a sufficiently infirm state, there the bonds of custom, prescription, principles, precedent, have been broken—or loosened or shifted so as to let the current of life and cultural growth go on, with or without substantial retardation. But history records more frequent and more spectacular instances of the triumph of imbecile institutions over life and culture than of peoples who have by force of instinctive insight saved themselves alive out of a desperately precarious institutional situation, such, for instance, as now faces the people of Christendom.[24]

---

curiosity, he never waxed exuberant about work as pure pleasure, and in several instances he described as one characteristic of the instinct of workmanship "the proclivity for taking pains." (Veblen, *IOW*, p. 33.)

Veblen's dichotomy between man's instinctual nature and the institutionalized creature that man has become resembles Freud's conflict between the id and the super-ego, between the self and the outer world. But for Freud the problem lies in man, who is divided against himself in the very structure of his psyche; for Veblen, it lies in the "imbecile institutions" which represent the alienation of reason from its human origins. Whereas Freud saw culture arising to repress and thereby channel constructively man's essentially destructive instincts, Veblen believed that man's natural endowment that flowered in the neolithic era was not so much smothered as stretched, distended by the process of growth itself.

Veblen was neither clear nor consistent in his descriptions of the nature of man. One hesitates to interpret so elusive and seemingly obscurantist a social scientist. What, for example, are we to make of Veblen's claim that man's instincts are counterpoised and not totally autonomous? The "instinctual proclivities," he tells us, "cross, blend, overlap, neutralize or reinforce one another." Because they cannot be conceived as acting each and several in isolation and independent of one another, "they must therefore incontinently touch, blend, overlap, and interfere." Even the instinct of workmanship, supposedly one of man's deepest drives, is not so "passionate" that it can resist deflection. "It does not, under pressure, tenaciously hold its place as a main interest in competition with the other, more elemental instinctive proclivities; but . . . it rather yields ground somewhat readily, suffers repression and falls into abeyance, only to reassert itself when the pressure of other, urgent interests is relieved." Veblen does not specify what are these "more elemental" proclivities and other "urgent interests." He does mention the "instinct of sportsmanship" to contrast its frivolous activities with those of workmanship; and apparently he assumed that sportsmanship grew out of workmanship as the former's instincts distorted the latter's due to the changes that developed in the circumstances of group life. But if an instinct can be perverted in such a manner one can only wonder if it can be called an instinct; and if man's "instinctual proclivities" can neutralize as well as reinforce one another, we are left in doubt as to which instincts are more generic and which are primary and fundamental.[25]

However imprecise his terminology, Veblen was convinced that the basic instincts of peaceful savage man lose their primal force through the processes of change and growth. Instincts, for example, are teleological impulses toward immediate ends. However, the ways and means to accomplish those ends that the instincts seek are a matter of intelligence, a faculty which is more "extensive" and "elaborate" and can therefore lose sight of the end it is intended to serve. "All instinctive action is teleological, it involves holding to a purpose." Intelligence, on the other hand, can be distracted as change and development drive man farther from the instinctual prompting that gave rise to intelligence. Unlike Kant's "reason," intelligence is only a tool without normative imperatives; it does not impose duty on inclination. Thus the instinct of workmanship can combine with a concern for beauty to produce goods which are both useful and aesthetic; but in a community of pecuniary status it can develop a devotion to technique alone, and the worker's skill and intelligence is frittered away in useless decorative detail. The parental bent is no less corruptible. It may have its origins in altruistic impulses, but it gives way to the "self-regarding sentiments" of a "gerontocracy" as subservience to able-bodied elders gains the upper hand in the increasing predatory and warlike culture that characterizes the late stages of savagery and the early stage of barbarism. Instincts are deflected or distorted as institutions develop, and by institutions Veblen does not mean physical structures—corporations, governments, universities—but "prevalent habits of thought," the ideas, beliefs, and principles by which men order their lives.[26]

Except for Veblen's suggestion that instincts lose their primal quality (or innocence) due to the processes of historical development and the conflicting applications of intelligence resulting from "institutional complications," it is not exactly clear how perverse institutions evolve out of productive instincts. If man is born an amiable savage, why does he become an aggressive barbarian? What indeed is Veblen's image of man?

In *Leisure Class* Veblen referred occasionally to the "predatory instinct." Although he presupposed an initial state of peaceful savagery, he nevertheless conceded that there is no point in cultural evolution "prior to which fighting does not occur," a behavior he attributed to the pervasive "sexual competition," evidence for which could be seen in the "known habits" of primitive groups and anthropoid apes and in our own "well-known promptings of human nature." Yet the point in question is not the possible occasion of combat but the frequent occurrence of "an habitual bellicose frame of mind," the elevation of the fight to a normative institution. This martial state is attained "only when the predatory attitude has become the habitual and accredited spiritual attitude for the members of the group." Thus the predatory instinct is merely potential and only becomes "deeply ingrained in the habits of thought of those peoples who have passed under the discipline of a protracted predatory culture."

When Veblen touched upon the question of human nature in *The Instinct of Workmanship*, he did not presuppose the "natural" goodness of man, thereby assuming what needs to be explained. Nor did his thoroughgoing Darwinism allow him to conceive man as a tragic figure burdened by psychic guilt or original sin. He admitted that in the controversy over man's nature that divided the idealists from the realists the evidence on either side, drawn from anthropology and social theory, "is by no means unequivocal." But he could not accept the position of the nineteenth-century Social Darwinists, who looked to the principle of natural selection as evidence that man is naturally combative and socially competitive. Darwinism showed only that the stronger members of the species have eliminated the weaker. Not only does such a theory suggest that the presently stronger may be deemed unfit and their "instinctual proclivities" useless as evolutionary change continues to take place, but it also suggests that at each previous stage in the evolutionary scheme the extinct species must have been weaker by virtue of being less aggressive, so that at the dawn of history it may well be than man was indeed peaceful.[27]

Veblen knew well that many of the assumptions about man in liberal and conservative social theory were rooted less in Darwinism than in the political philosophy of Thomas Hobbes. In *The Instinct of Workmanship* he therefore digressed in several places to question Hobbes' dictum that the state of nature is a state of permanent war of each against all. Hobbes' account may explain the origins of the Leviathan, but it could hardly explain the biological requirements of survival. How could men exist for a day in a society of acquisitive creatures where everyone's right to everything threatens anyone's right to anything? "It seems antecedently improbable that the domestication of the crop plants and animals could have been effected at all except among people leading a passably peaceable, and presently sedentary life." Not only did the extraordinary length of time for what was achieved in "remote antiquity" speak against Hobbes' view of man as a born predator, but the prevalence of maternal deities among prehistoric communities suggested a culture of fecundity rather than ferocity. As to Hobbes' claim that "fear" haunted the state of nature and hence led to the desire for order, Veblen looked to extant tribal societies and found this to be true among some "warlike" natives in Australia and lower Malaya but not the case among the more peaceable Eskimos and Pueblo Indians. Hobbes had seen sixteenth-century England suddenly plunged into war and revolution, and he and other English political theorists would forever dread a reversion to the state of nature. Veblen's world would also be plunged into chaos and turmoil in the years of World War One, but for him the state of nature would remain not a source of anxiety but of redemption:

> The savage mode of life, which was, and is, in a sense, native to man, would be characterized by a considerable group solidarity within a relatively small group, living very near the soil, and unremittingly dependent for their daily life on the workmanlike efficiency of all the members of the group. The prime requisite for survival under these conditions would be a propensity unselfishly and impersonally to make the most of the material means at hand and a penchant for turning all resources of knowledge and material to account to sustain the life of the group.[28]

The Contamination of the Instincts

Veblen could not avoid the question of humankind's primal alienation if he were to presume an innocent stage of peaceful savagery. In his analysis the condition of alienation does not spring from private property, the historical origins which he regarded as "a hazardous topic of speculation."[29] Much less does it arise with the development of industrial capitalism, which he regarded as merely a continuation of the "barbaric" past, with the modern captain of industry carrying out the role of the archaic chieftain of combat. Nor does it first manifest itself, as it does with Marx, with the appearance of the "alien medium" of money.[30] On the contrary, in human productivity itself may lie the seed of alienation. Aside from the complication and deflection of instincts due to cumulative habit, Veblen observed that "the most obstructive derangement that besets workmanship is what may be called the self-contamination of workmanship itself." This infection arises when primitive man, in order to comprehend the natural world so as to labor upon it and control it, imputes to external objects familiar personal qualities. This tendency toward anthropomorphism or animism leads man to project onto external things his own workmanlike bent. As a result the inert, impersonal phenomena of nature take on personal meaning and human knowledge itself undergoes a basic transformation:

> As all men habitually act under the guidance of instincts, and therefore by force of sentiment instinctively look to some end in all activity, so objects with which the primitive workman has to do are also conceived as acting under impulse of an instinctive kind; and a bent, a teleological or pragmatic nature, is in some degree imputed to them and comes as a matter of course to be accepted as a constitutent element in their apprehended make-up. A putative pragmatic bent innate in external things comes in this way to pass current as observed matter of fact. By force of the sense of workmanship external objects are in great part apperceived in respect of what they will do; and their most substantial characteristic, therefore, their intimate individual nature, in so far as they are conceived as individual entities, is that they will do things.[31]

According to Veblen, in the early savage stage of history the mentalities of "matter of fact and matter of imputation run along side by side" without serious adverse effect on the development of primitive technology. The imputation of anthropomorphic traits to plants and animals, for example, had not hindered tillage, cattle breeding, or domestication, although primitive man's projection of such traits to fire and certain types of rock retarded development of metal working and similar arts. But as the industrial arts grow, they come more and more to rest on objective knowledge, and this leads to the expansion of a scientific milieu which requires impersonal adaptation for its control. Thus although anthropomorphic instincts remain, animism is limited by the demands of practicality. Yet animism is not so much eliminated as sublimated. Knowledge has evolved in a dualistic manner, as a growth in two ranges of apprehension, with animism pitted against facticity. Hence the world is divided into two categories of perception: anthropomorphic and inert. Scientific progress occurred when early man perceived a phenomenon as inert and asked, "What can I do with it?" Similarly, technological understanding is diverted and workmanship "contaminated" when man perceives a phenomenon as animate and asks, "What can it do on its own?" Despite all the advances in industrial and scientific knowledge, modern man has yet to liberate himself from his primitive heritage enough to consider only the first question. The task may be psychologically impossible, Veblen suggests, for the more man works upon the materials of earth the more the animistic qualities "take up a more circumspect, ingenious and idealized form."

> For so alien to mankind, with its instinctive sense of workmanship, is the mutilation of brute creation into mere opaque matter-of-fact, and so indefeasibly does the "consciousness of kind" assert itself, that each successive renunciation of such as imputed bias of workmanship in concrete objects is sought to be redeemed by pushing the imputation farther into the background of observed phenomena and running their putative workmanship bias in more consummately anthropomorphic terms. So an animistic conception of things comes presently to supplement, and in part supplant, the more naive and immediate imputation of workmanship, leading up to farther and more elaborate myth-making; until in the course of elaboration and refinement there may emerge a monotheistic and providential Creator seated in the infinitely remote but ubiquitous space of four dimensions.[32]

Herein lies the dilemma. Marx assumed that through work man would be able to overcome the dualism that separates man from nature because subjective human activity is itself the process of objective activity through which man "humanizes nature."[33] Veblen doubted that this chasm could be bridged, that man could comprehend the world simply by changing it. Whereas Marx believed that man must act in order to know, Veblen believed that man must apprehend before he acts, and what he apprehends may never be the real world as it really is. Man labors upon matter while at the same time never really grasping the natural world; for a disenchanted nature, so necessary to scientific progress, is so chilling to man that he is compelled to impute anthropomorphic interpretations to objects and institutions of his own creation, thereby rendering what is natural and changeable sacred and immutable. Workmanship, then, carries within itself the seeds of its own alienation ("self-contamination"). It often arises only through an animistic identification with the natural world, for primitive man needs first to empathize with that which he must understand. But this process can continue only up to a point, since reality has the capacity to resist false interpretations. Still, the mastery of nature cannot be completely carried out without any illusion of ruling, inherent powers or hidden qualities,[34] and this illusion, Veblen implied, shaped both the "invisible laws" of Adam Smith's world and the "teleology" of Marx's philosophy of history.

Smith and Marx extolled the virtues of labor (albeit for different reasons), but Veblen was careful to point out that workmanship "is peculiarly subject to bias. It does not commonly, or normally, work to an independent, creative end of its own, but is rather concerned with the ways and means whereby instinctively given purposes are to be accomplished."[35] Veblen did not specify what these "instinctively given purposes" are, but he did state that man's regard for his reputation is "a characteristic man always had and will no doubt always have."[36] This tendency is only latent in the sedentary peaceful culture of savagery where men are valued in terms of their industrial efficiency and serviceability. But the "incentive to emulation" is present in communal society even if not pronounced (as modern anthropologists have discovered among the prestige and shame cultures of the Andaman islanders, the Trobrianders, and the Maori fishermen.)[37] Much as Rousseau had intuited that primitive man's development of "conveniences" had produced "the first emotion of pride in him," and that men began to "know what esteem was" when they lost their self-sufficiency with the emergence of group activity,[38] so too did Veblen, drawing upon contemporary ethnological studies, conclude that man's labor activities were bound up with the nature of his social being. "Wherever the circumstances of traditional life lead to an habitual comparison of one person with another in point of efficiency, the instinct of workmanship works out in an emulative or invidious comparison of persons." The upshot is that human labor gives rise to the propensity for emulation, which "with the exception of the instinct of self-preservation . . . is probably the strongest and most alert and persistent of the economic motives proper."[39]

Somehow the conceit of pride wormed itself into the fruit of labor. Ironically, labor produces not so much the substance of property (much less surplus value) as the *idea* of ownership in so far as emulation compels the possession and accumulation of goods as evidence of superior status, and this compulsion serves as an important motive in the transition from the peaceable to the predatory stages of early culture. Thus workmanship, already infected by a "pragmatic bent" which causes the worker to see inert objects and natural phenomena as self-activating, suffers a further contamination by the "canons of invidious distinction" which come to rule a pecuniary culture. Yet the instinct of workmanship never completely atrophies, Veblen noted, and in the early stages of capitalism it may express itself in a dedication to achievement and a repugnance toward waste and futility. Nevertheless, as society modernizes, the instinct becomes perverted and "tends more and more to shape itself into a straining to excel others in pecuniary achievement,"[40] evidence of which is finally demonstrated in a life-style that contradicts the very essence and ethic of workmanship—the life of acquisition and leisure rather than production and labor. In a culture characterized by status emulation, meaning and value are sought not in the processes of production but in the objects of consumption, commodities which have inherited the animistic qualities of power and personal prestige—the sociological dimension of "reification" that is perhaps Veblen's greatest contribution to modern social theory.

Man is flawed in two respects, and herein lies the source of his alienation. The first flaw is the curse of animism, the mind's tendency to mediate matter so that man cannot accept facts simply as objects. There can be no knowledge that is not mediated by prior knowledge, by "prevalent habits of thought." The result of man's anthropomorphic predicament is the resistance of society to rational comprehension. The second flaw is the social snare in workmanship itself. Based on the canons of efficiency and social utility, only to be contaminated by the emulative instinct, workmanship by its very nature can only promote the performance principle at the cost of the pleasure principle (to use Freud's terms). Veblen was convinced that human productivity must be directed toward the interests of the community at large, but he was also convinced that the community's "pecuniary canons of taste" determine what shall be produced. When a product is made to satisfy others it loses its own intrinsic value and the joy of workmanship cannot be an end in itself. And when a product is made solely for the purpose of exchanging it for goods made by others, the laborer now assumes he can realize himself not in production but in consumption, that he can buy his way out of what he had worked himself into. Thus workmanship, an ennobling, altruistic instinct, compels the worker to contribute to his own alienation. He is not so much exploited as socialized by the pressures of "invidious comparison."

The Machine Process and Idle Curiosity

Veblen tried to find a way out of both of these dilemmas, the anthropomorphic predicament and the inversion of workmanship into servitude. In place of man's inevitable animistic propensities Veblen called for the ascendancy of "the machine process." The machine "throws out anthropomorphic habits of thought. It compels the adaptation of the workman to his work, rather than the adaptation of the work to the workman."[41] Men must work with the machine and abide by its processes, for the "discipline" of the machine purges all the anthropomorphic residue in man's nature. The "matter-of-fact" frame of mind is the "cultural incidence" of machine technology. Liberated by the machine, man will be able to see things in terms of cause and effect rather than of good and evil, of "weight, tale and measure" rather than of merit or demerit, of natural processes rather than of established rules of precedent, of impersonal objects rather than of personal forces. Veblen welcomed what Henry Adams and Max Weber dreaded: the disenchantment of the world as a result of the extirpation of animism and supernaturalism. Only then will magic, religion, nationalism, the culture of consumption, the right of property, and the wastefulness and futility of war cease to make sense to a mind no longer capable of alienating itself because it has been freed from the need to mediate experience in human terms.

Surely this is a strange resolution of the human condition: man can recover his pre-alienated wholeness only by divesting himself of his emotional qualities as a man! The obvious ethical dilemmas of such a proposition need hardly be mentioned. The real difficulty is that Veblen's resolution only deepens the paradox of alienation itself. Veblen fails to explain fully why the machine came into existence in the first place, why man, unlike the rest of the animal kingdom, was not content to confine himself to what life objectively requires but instead needed to invent technology. That man did so indicates that he did not become alienated, did not fall from a state of "primitive communism" (Marx) or "peaceful savagery" (Veblen), but that he was already alienated at the center of his being, that the very "instinct of workmanship" that produced the machine estranged man from his essence. For if man's being coincides fully with that of nature, he would be without necessity; his aspirations and his satisfactions would be one and the same, and hence the world would not be alien to him. But the invention of the machine, whether primitive tools or modern technology, suggests "desire," the need for man to become that which originally he is not.

Veblen's technological theory of historical development offers no solution to the very problem of alienation it uncovers. For one thing, it confines man to the role of producer and therefore fails to do justice to the full humanity of the worker. The emphasis on workmanship implies that man is content with the external world of objects, the deterministic plane of nature wherein the meaning of labor is lost in the routine tasks of livelihood and cannot elevate existence above the biological burdens of life. Veblen's concept of man is severely restricted to the *homo faber*, ignoring the whole realm of social relationships and cultural pursuits as all human activity seems reduced to the common denominator of securing the necessities of life. And insofar as the producer, however free, creative, and "happy," moves in a world of things and not of people, it is difficult to see how human personality is developed in Veblen's notion of workmanship. Veblen's Darwinian sense of struggle may have liberated him from the constrictions of orthodox thought, but it also confined him to a naturalism that concerned itself with the brute processes of life and not its human purposes and values. Modern man, like his archaic ancestors, does not work in order to live but lives in order to work, because for Veblen the value of life lies in the activities necessary to carry it on, and nothing more.

Why does man work? It is curious that both Veblen and Marx, while criticizing the capitalist notion that labor reflects necessity, shy away from the deeper implications of man as *animal laborans*.[42] Neither consider that work itself may be alienating insofar as man is driven to exert himself because he is part of nature yet aspires to be more than nature. (Weber attributed this condition to the *Angst* of Protestantism, especially Calvinism; but Ortega y Gasset, writing in a Catholic environment, sees western man in general as "a kind of ontological centaur."[43]) Both Veblen and Marx asked man not to question the meaning of existence but to expand his power over the materials of existence through industry and technology—"the open book of man's essential powers" (Marx).[44] Thus both inadvertently followed the Protestant tradition of urging man to seek in labor what had been lost in life. Moreover, Marx and Veblen were similarly preoccupied with the problem of ideology, with thinking that is unconscious of its motives and with habits of thought that distort the mind's perception of reality. Both believed that genuine liberation begins only when all illusions end. Yet one can only wonder whether the "animism" and "false consciousness" which Veblen and Marx themselves tried to exorcise returned to plague their own thoughts. In the assumptions of both thinkers, work takes on magical qualities; it is the medium whereby Veblen and Marx impute to the processes of the natural world qualities that originate in the human world. The machine is to Veblen what the proletariat is to Marx: the mythic agency through which ideals born of pure desire are realized as objective fact. Primitive man credits sticks and stones of proved efficacy with occult power; in the "modern" minds of Veblen and Marx inanimate processes (i.e., the "discipline of the machine") or metaphysical abstractions (i.e., the "negation of negation") appear to be unconsciously conceived in terms of human values in order to render the external world obedient to their moral wishes.[45]

It might be said, then, that Veblen was not scientific enough in his attempt to formulate an answer to alienation. This is not the position, however, of some of Veblen's best critics. Theodor Adorno, a sympathetic critic who has written the most perceptive essay on the shortcomings of Veblen's social theory, arrives at the opposite conclusion and accuses Veblen of a kind of acquiescent positivism:

> As a positivist who does not acknowledge any other norm but adaptation, he sardonically raises, in one of the most advanced passages of his work, the

question why one should not adjust oneself to the givenness of the principle of waste, futility and ferocity which according to his doctrine form the canon of pecuniary decency: 'But why are apologies needed? If there prevails a body of popular sentiments in favor of sports, why is not that fact a sufficient legitimation? The protracted discipline of prowess to which the race has been subjected under the predatory and quasi-peaceable culture has transmitted to the men of today a temperament that finds gratification in these expressions of ferocity and cunning. So, why not accept these sports as legitimate expressions of a normal and wholesome human nature? What other norm is there . . . ?' Here Veblen's reasoning brings him close to the danger of capitulating before the mere existent, before 'normal barbarism.' His solution is surprising: 'The ulterior norm to which appeal is taken is the instinct of workmanship, which is an instinct more fundamental, of more ancient prescription than the propensity to predatory emulation.' This is the key to his theory of the primitive age. The positivist permits himself to think the potentiality of man only by conjuring it into a given; in other words, conjuring it into the past. He allows no other justification of non-predatory life than that it is supposed to be even more given, more positive, more existent than the hell of existence. The golden age is the positivist's *asylum ignorantiae.*[46]

Veblen is depicted as an empiricist without an ethic; he is searching hopelessly for a mythic norm that is more basic than immediate reality; he wants to establish the validity of an ideal on the basis of its antiquity.

Robert Heilbroner is another sympathetic radical critic who admired Veblen more for the enemies he made than the answers he gave. Heilbroner is disturbed by Veblen's cult of scientism. "It is true that machines make us think coldly, but they may end up by making us think too coldly. Let us not forget that the end of a 'scientific' conduct of production may be the human robot and that while the machine process may exercise our technical judgment, it may stifle and frustrate our imagination and emotions."[47]

Veblen anticipated such criticisms. "For something more than a hundred years," he observed in *Business Enterprise*, "this change in the habits of thought of the workman has been commonly spoken of as a deterioration or numbing of his intelligence."[48] Veblen even conceded at least half the argument on the grounds that certain kinds of intelligence were heightened by technology and other kinds lowered. Perhaps he could acknowledge as much because he himself was ambivalent at the prospect of a totally mechanized society. We already caught a glimpse of his ambivalence in discussing his essay, "The Place of Science in Modern Civilization." His reservations become more pronounced in the final chapter in *The Instinct of Workmanship*. "The limit of tolerance native to the race, physically and spiritually, is short of that unmitigated materialism and unremitting mechanical routine to which the machine technology incontinently drives." Among the various peoples of the Christian world "there is a visible straining against the drift of the machine's teaching, rising at times and in given classes of the population to the pitch of revulsion." Veblen even suggested, with an ironic twist so typical of his conclusions, that though the machine was most successful in bringing man out of the handicraft era, modern man turns away from technology and pines for "the simple life" and a "return to nature." This behavior is particularly true among the "moderately well-to-do, the half-idle classes" which are given to cults and fantasies. "Neither the manner of life imposed by the machine process, nor the manner of thought inculcated by habituation to its logic, will fall in with the free movement of the human spirit, born, as it is, to fit the conditions of savage life. So there comes an irrepressible—in a sense, congenital—recrudescence of magic, occult science, telepathy, spiritualism, vitalism, pragmatism."[49]

Was Veblen prophesying the emergence of the hippies and the flower children of the 1960s, the "new mutants" who turned their back on technology to pursue their quest for pastoral innocence? Or was he expressing his own second thoughts and, as his English admirer R. M. Fox put it, "allowing for the human recoil against mechanization."[50] It is difficult to say for sure, and this is probably how Veblen wanted it. It is also difficult to understand how Veblen could reconcile scientific matter-of-fact knowledge based upon mechanical causation with what he called the "free movement of the human spirit." But it does seem clear that Veblen was searching for something beyond workmanship and the machine process, some epistemological key so precious it could not be corrupted by institutions or turned back against itself by its hidden potential for "self-contamination." Previously it was stated that Veblen had not only an answer to animism but also an answer to the second flaw that besets man, the inversion of workmanship into servitude. If the discipline of technology could help overcome the first flaw, the answer to the second lay in the "instinct of idle curiosity."

Veblen formulated this "instinct" in "The Place of Science in Modern Civilization," where he set out to distinguish genuine empirical inquiry from the pragmatic method of knowledge. "Pragmatism creates nothing but maxims of expedient conduct. Science creates nothing but theories."[51] Scientific knowledge advances only when men think in defiance of immediate interests. Such a procedure requires an "irrelevant attention" to practicality, an indifference to the consequences of ideas in the interests of their total comprehension. The colorless, disembodied epistemology which science aspires to is best approached and systematized under the "canons of curiosity rather than expediency." Only a science that is purely speculative can liberate the imagination sufficiently enough to question its own preconceptions and challenge the given norms of society. Veblen's essay thus attempts to illuminate the limitations of pragmatism as an epistemological proposition. For the philosophy of pragmatism, a product of American culture, could hardly be a resource from which to question the foundations of that culture. Not only does pragmatism tend toward adjustment and adaptation but toward imputation as well. It is no coincidence, Veblen mused, that contemporary American pragmatic philosophers were reading into the nineteenth century doctrine of evolution the eighteenth-century doctrine of progress.

In *The Instinct of Workmanship* Veblen returns to the notion of idle curiosity. He now suggests that workmanship and curiosity may be incompatible. The common man had little capacity for natural wonder, especially in a culture of activism and acquisition, and thus free-floating curiosity remains the peculiar genius of exceptional individuals who are regarded as "dreamers . . . of unsound mind." The quality of idleness, of unconditional reflection, implies a complete absence of utilitarian aim or sentiment, and this explains why it receives such scant attention in America, even though American society benefits from the knowledge and factual information derived from disinterested speculation. Workers labor under the habits and conventions of existing culture, while idle curiosity is "persistently disturbing the body of knowledge on which workmanship draws." But even when that body of knowledge incorporates the new information discovered by the curious dreamers we are no closer to the truth, since workmanship reshapes reality to its own purposes:

> Of the material so offered as knowledge, or fact, workmanship makes use of whatever is available. In ways already indicated this utilisation of ascertained 'facts' is both furthered and hindered by the fact that the information which comes to hand through the restless curiosity of man is reduced to systematic shape, for the most part or wholly, under canons of workmanship. For the large generality of human knowledge this will mean that the raw material of observed fact is selectively worked over, connected up and accumulated on lines of a putative teleological order of things, cast in something like a dramatic form. From which it follows that the knowledge so gained is held and carried over from generation to generation in a form which lends itself with facility to a workmanlike manipulation; it is already digested for assimilation in a scheme of teleology that instinctively commends itself to the workmanlike sense of fitness. But it also follows that in so far as the personalised, teleological, or dramatic order so imputed to the facts does not, by chance, faithfully reflect the causal relations subsisting among these facts, the utilisation of them as technological elements will amount to a borrowing of trouble. So that the concurrence of curiosity and workmanship in the assimilation of facts in this way may, and in early culture must, result in a retardation of technological advance, as contrasted with what might conceivably have been the outcome of this work of the idle curiosity if it had not been congenitally contaminated with the sense of workmanship and thereby lent itself to conceptions of magical efficacy rather than to mechanical efficiency.[52]

We rub our eyes! It is as though Veblen has presented us with an epistemological nightmare. Experience will always be conditioned by animistic traits and hence cannot provide truth; thought will always be distorted in action; and workmanship will never be able to rise above a manipulative concern for using knowledge rather than grasping reality. Only "idle curiosity" can free itself from immediate interests and anthropomorphic illusions and furnish us with knowledge of phenomena by virtue of its superior perception of the phenomenon of knowledge. But even this precious intellectual resource is "contaminated" the moment it is applied, the moment it ceases being idle.

If the problem of society is the problem of knowledge of society, as Karl Mannheim has made us aware, Veblen faced this epistemological issue squarely. He questioned an assumption basic to both the pragmatist and the Marxist, the assumption that through *praxis* the perception of reality can be identified with the nature of reality itself, that the social world can be "known" simply by acting upon it and transforming it. Thus Veblen could offer no solution to human alienation except to invoke the mystique of idle curiosity, a mode of cognition so bereft of functional content that it could not be corrupted by existing institutions, an epistemology so fired by the flame of pure intention that it had no obligation to any cause other than to the canon of curiosity itself.

The idea is noble, but is it plausible? Pragmatists and Marxists alike would maintain that Veblen divorces theory from action, that he wants to meditate on the problems of existence rather than solve them. These criticisms do not go to the heart of the problem of man's alienation. "Idle curiosity" is really a statement of a condition rather than a remedy for it. Curiosity presupposes a state of intellectual void, an attempt to discover in thought what cannot be found in action. It can hardly serve as the means by which one overcomes alienation since it is actually a description of alienation. Veblen would have man know the world before he changed it, but knowing carries the same implication for Veblen as work does for Marx. Knowing begins in doubt just as labor begins in desire. Both activities indicate that man is driven by an impulse to know more than he can learn and to become more than he is. The need to know and the desire to do suggest an emptiness within the nature of man, a craving for self-realization. It is difficult to see how alienation can be overcome through the activities that manifest the very anxiety of alienation itself. Indeed such an assumption may be the illusion of "animism."

6 . . . Reification, Animism, Emulation: The Cultural Hegemony of Capitalism

Capitalism and Its Discontents: Weber, Marx, Veblen

Max Weber, Karl Marx, and Thorstein Veblen, the three great social theorists of industrial capitalism, all assumed that an understanding of the "problem" of modern society must begin in historical inquiry. They also assumed that the future of capitalism could be grasped only by comprehending its historial growth and development; and each believed that the historical dimension of knowledge offers the best perspective for rendering intelligible the present "reality" in which we find ourselves.

These shared aspirations conceal, however, deeper and more fundamental differences. A comparison of Weber, Marx, and Veblen illustrates the number of ways similar historical phenomena can be comprehended from different perspectives. Weber, for example, believed that our human reality can never be known without value-laden "presuppositions," and his skepticism about the possibility of discovering ultimate "factors" or general "laws" led to a tragic vision of history that differs strikingly from Veblen's technological standpoint, to say nothing of Marx's teleological omniscience. Weber's treatment of the rise of capitalism in particular and of modern society in general is subtle, penetrating, and comprehensive in its functional analysis of the interrelationships of ideas and institutions.

Marx's philosophy of history also offers many interesting contrasts when compared to that of Veblen. Marx begins his analysis of the past by assuming that the story of mankind represents a threefold process: an ascent, in which man gains increasing control over nature and its resources through the development of science and technology; a descent, in which man grows ever more alienated from himself and his fellow man; and a synthesis, in which man and history participate in an upward movement of consciousness evolving toward a predetermined end. Veblen, addressing himself to this schema, believed that the "theoretical structure of Marx collapses when these elements are converted into the terms of modern science." To Veblen Marx's approach was "wholly personal" and "teleological": Marx spied a goal at the end of "pre-history" because that is what he wanted to see. In place of the Hegelian-Marxist view, which represented for Veblen the triumph of will over intellect, the American social scientist offered the Darwinian view, which represented the subordination of mind to the mechanical-materialistic dimension of the natural world. The mind's role would not be passive, however; Veblen's Kantianism precluded unilateral materialism or extreme behaviorism, as we saw. Knowledge would be gained through some form of imputation, but the projection would be supposedly more congruent with empirical reality. "In the Darwinian scheme of thought, the continuity sought in and imputed to the facts is a continuity of cause and effect. It is a scheme of blindly cumulative causation in which there is no trend, no final term, no consummation. The sequence is controlled by nothing but the *vis a tergo* of brute causation, and is essentially mechanical. The neo-Hegelian (Marxian) scheme of development is drawn in the image of the struggling ambitious human spirit; that of the Darwinian evolution is of the nature of a mechanical process."[1] Where Marx saw meaning and purpose in history, Veblen saw only movement and process, motion without teleological direction. In Marx the present is a prelude to the future; in Veblen the present is burdened by the past.

Despite these different modes of apprehension, Marx, Veblen, and Weber were equally convinced that the central theoretical problem in historical investigation must be the origins, development, and destiny of capitalism. What is the internal dynamic of the modern system of capitalism? What makes it rise as though it were the demiurge of history, bringing with itself good as well as evil, progress as well as poverty?

In Marx's scenario, capitalism develops directly out of feudalism, the fourth stage of history that succeeds the primitive, communal, and slave modes of production. Marx provided no satisfactory sketch of feudalism; it remained for him a transition stage that saw the transformation of small peasant agriculture involving serfdom to the emergence of urban labor represented by craftsmen and artisans. The disintegration of feudalism is bound up with the rise of the city, the center of both mercantile activity and "free labor" no longer tied to the land. Here, in a period covering the twelfth to the fourteenth centuries, the seeds of capitalism can be discerned in the formation of mercantile and usurer's capital and the increasing alienation of the small producer from the control of his products, the new status of the semi-independent peasant who comes more and more to depend upon the market for the sale of his labor. Although the pattern varies geographically, the full development of capitalism remains hindered by the feudal restrictions of the country, which curb the growth of a credit system, and the guild restrictions of the town, which limit the number of journeymen and apprentices. Thus the new productive forces and the rising new class of merchants are handicapped at each step by the traditional mode of agricultural production and the traditional system of feudal social relations.

Two developments arise to free a nascent capitalism from its feudal shackles. At the end of the fifteenth century new geographical discoveries bring an influx of capital, particularly in the form of gold and silver from America, and at the same time there develops a demand for commodities, the impact of which further undermines existing economic and social arrangements. Even more important in the upheaval of feudalism is the development of the "primary accumulation" of capitalist investment, a development that can only occur, given Marx's labor theory of value, when the owners of money and the means of production encounter directly masses of workers dispossessed of their instruments of production and left with nothing but their labor power, which they must now, out of sheer desperation, sell in exchange for wages. This process occurs in different periods in different countries, and it manifests itself in various ways. Marx concentrates upon the case of England, where the process appears in "classic form." Here it begins in the last third of the fifteenth century, dramatized in the expropriation of the independent farmer, the infamous enclosure movement "written in the annals of mankind in letters of blood and fire." During this period the nobility, impoverished by the great feudal wars, disband their castle retainers and uproot the peasants in order to turn arable land into grazing pastures that can be managed by only a few herdsmen. Whole populations of independent peasants are cast adrift in utter ruin, thrown onto the market as the first "mass of free proletarians." The Reformation contributes a "new and frightful impulse" to the process, through the suppression of monasteries and the distribution of land to royal favorites or speculators who disperse the peasants and consolidate their holdings. The whole enclosure process is a succession of "the most shameless violation of the 'sacred rights of property' and the grossest acts of violence to persons," who are "freed" from the serfdom of the country only to be enslaved by the wage system of the town.

At this stage the seed of capitalism has only been planted. What is necessary for its flowering is the formation of a new class ready to exploit labor. This development begins when manufacturers arise in seaport towns as a result of the accumulation of capital facilitated by overseas discoveries. After the sixteenth century organized production spreads to rural areas, where spinners and weavers can be introduced to collective work habits with little technical training. Thus the capitalist era is not introduced by technical inventions (Veblen's position). The first genuine phase of capitalist production is "manufacture," by which Marx meant hand labor, and this lasts more than two hundred years, from the middle of the sixteenth century to the last third of the eighteenth century. Although a division of labor emerges during this period, manufacture as a mode of production does not represent a radical departure from the medieval handicraft system.[2] What is new is the ascendancy of an emergent class, the bourgeoisie, which comes more and more to control the means of production by virtue of its control of the flow of capital, a new class that represents the movement of capital away from trade and production to the accumulation of capital itself. This class grows considerably in the late sixteenth and seventeenth centuries and expresses its political weight in the English Revolution, the "glorious Revolution" which, Marx writes, "brought into power appropriators of surplus-value," the "bourgeois capitalists" dedicated to promoting free trade in land, extending the domain of modern agriculture on large farm systems, and enlarging their supply of "the free agricultural proletarians ready at hand."[3]

It may be unfortunate that Marx chose England as exemplifying the developing ascendancy of capitalist society in its "most typical form." For here the middle class never rose to assume political domination, at least not in the seventeenth century, and perhaps not even in the nineteenth or twentieth centuries. It is even possible that the "Great Rebellion" in England in the seventeenth century witnessed no fundamental change in the country's social structure. In the most comprehensive study of this issue, Lawrence Stone's *The Crisis of the Aristocracy*, the nobility confronts no serious threat from the rising economic resources and political influence of a mercantile and industrial class of capitalists, whose financial interests, it was traditionally believed, were being thwarted by the privileged positions of a feudal aristocracy. The challenge to the nobility's authority came not from "capitalists or bourgeoisie," writes Stone, "but from solid landowners only one notch further down the social and economic ladder, the squires and greater gentry. As for the real new men, the rich merchants, they were too concerned with scrambling aboard the old status bandwagon to have any wish to scupper it."[4] Stone's emphasis on status aspirations, and his sustained investigation of how the nobility behaved with its wealth and not only how it acquired it, represents a shift from an economic to a sociological interpretation of historical causation that is close to Veblen's analysis of leisure class elites.*

* " 'The essence of social class,' " Stone quotes an anonymous source at the conclusion of his book, " 'is the way a man is treated by his fellows (and, reciprocally, the way he treats them), not the qualities or the possessions which cause the treatment' " (p. 349). In Veblen's analysis, wealth affects behavior, and a person's treatment is influenced by the display of possessions, which serves as a kind of "code" of status relations regulating social communication. Marx was concerned about class, which he viewed as determined by man's relation to the mean of production. Veblen was concerned, as is Stone, with status, which is shaped less by production than by consumption, by specific "styles of life." For an interesting discussion of the status behavior of the seventeenth-century aristocracy, see Stone's chapter on "Conspicuous Expenditure," pp. 249–67.

Veblen and the Stages of Historical Development

In Veblen's scheme of historical development the institution of the leisure class, having antecedents in archaic society, reaches full development in feudal Europe (as well as feudal Japan). The chief characteristics of this development are also social rather than economic, based primarily on the symbolic significance of an individual's occupational role in the social order. This distinction, and not necessarily the individual's position in relation to the mode of production, separates the nobility from the bourgeoisie. The aristocratic code is one of service to the state, especially military service, and of a relaxed life style of pleasure and games, social decorum, and cultural dilettantism. The bourgeoisie, on the other hand, practice a morality of self-improvement, thrift, hard work, and austerity. To Veblen these latter traits represent the revival of the instinct of workmanship, which can be contaminated during various historical episodes but never completely suppressed. These traits, while healthy, also indicate that the members of the new middle class are children of pride, *arrivistes* who have gained a "class feeling" of meritorious reputability because of their entrepreneurial accomplishments. Their pride has little to do with spiritual reassurance in the Weberian sense; it is wholly secular, a matter of mobility rather than anxiety. More important, the appearance of a new economic class presents no threat to the traditional distribution of status; the Protestant ethic (though Veblen does not use this phrase) cannot for long extinguish the aristocratic code, for the "canons of reputability" remain characteristic even during what was for Marx the momentous historical transition from feudalism to capitalism:

> The aristocratic contempt for the tradesman and all his works has not suffered a serious mitigation through all this growth of new methods of bourgeois reputability. The three conventionally recognized classes, upper, middle, and lower, are all and several pecuniary categories; the upper being typically that (aristocratic) class which is possessed of wealth without having worked or bargained for it; while the middle class have come by their holdings through some form of commercial (business) traffic; and the lower class gets what it has by workmanship. It is a gradation of (a) predation, (b) business, (c) industry; the former being disserviceable and gainful, the second gainful, and the third serviceable. And no modernized civilized man is so innocent of the canons of reputability as not to recognise offhand that the first category is meritorious and the last discreditable, whatever his individual prejudices may lead him to think of the second. Aristocracy without unearned wealth, or without predatory antecedents, is a misnomer. When an aristocrat class loses its pecuniary advantage it becomes questionable. A poverty-stricken aristocrat is a 'decayed gentleman'; and the 'nobility of labour' is a disingenuous figure of speech.[5]

The leisure class reemerges in the late Middle Ages, thereby establishing a continuity of cultural habits between a decaying feudalism and a rising capitalism, a legacy of aristocratic values that will continue to hinder the full development of the work instinct. This parasitic class has predecessors deep in the historical past. Veblen derived from his reading of anthropology a scheme of historical evolution. As he saw it, mankind has passed through four main stages: the peaceful savage community of neolithic times; the barbarian economy, in which he detected the origins and relationships of the institutions of private property, war, masculine prowess, and the leisure class; the handicraft economy of the pre-modern era; and the machine technology of the modern industrial age. As we saw earlier, the transition from savagery to barbarism witnessed the passing of peaceful agrarian life and the advent of hunting and fighting as the chief means of livelihood. In such historical transitions Veblen considers the role of religion as well as the mode of production. Hence the emergence of a prestigious and predatory life of exploit also marked the passing of a polytheistic religion of maternal deities, a culture of fertility worship that had sustained what were for Veblen the redeeming propensities of human nature: the instinct of workmanship and the parental bent. Feudalism is the monotheistic expression of the burden of the past; for in the stage of barbarism the very non-productive employments that have come to command the highest prestige are the very professions that enjoyed the most status during the feudal period: "government, war, sports, and devout observers." But Veblen does not see capitalism evolving directly from feudalism, as did Marx, or from Protestantism, as did Weber. Where then did it originate?

It is clear that the origins of capitalism are not to be confused with the beginnings of ownership; not only does private property antedate free enterprise but the conception of the right of possession is meaningless until an inducement to the accumulation of wealth takes place. Veblen surmises that such an inducement may have resulted from the surplus of goods that occurs due to the efficiency of workmanship in the period of late savagery. But the manner, place, and time in which increasing technological mastery transformed the savage plan of free workmanship to the barbarian system of industry under pecuniary control "is perhaps a hazardous topic of speculation." Veblen does not follow Marx in maintaining that technology, like private property and capitalism, simply unfolds according to an "inner dialectic" of development—a *deus ex machina* that relegates to metaphysical philosophy problems that require an explanation on the basis of human psychology. Nor did he suggest that it is man's "desire" or "need" that leads him to change the mode of production in order to produce more goods. Such an assertion would only indicate that man felt a disparity between his aspirations and his satisfactions, that he was, as we noted above, alienated before he became alienated. Instead Veblen argued that man invents technology out of a dedication to efficiency and industry instilled in him by the instinct of workmanship. This formulation by no means resolves the problem of alienation, for even the "instinct" to invent implies that man's true nature is always potential, never actual. But it does broaden the narrow technological rationalism of the Marxist view, which gives to the material instruments of production the central role in human evolution without necessarily explaining why those instruments developed.

As Veblen interpreted existing archaeological and historical evidence, the crude beginnings of technology advanced and became more sophisticated after the passing of the paleolithic age and the semi-development of the neolithic era. In the pre-history of northern European culture, where evidence exists, man begins to employ finished tools, domesticates plants and animals, cultivates soil, and engages in other activities that require the use of instruments of wood and fiber and the expenditure of systematic effort and procedure. This primitive technology in turn creates two untoward consequences. First, it leads to an accumulation of wealth beyond the current necessities of subsistence and even beyond "that slight parcel of personal effects that have no value to anyone but their savage bearer." Second, and perhaps more importantly, the new processes of industry ("crops, fruit trees, live stock, mechanical contrivances") take on a "determinate place and routine" so as to make control of these processes possible for the first time. The material items necessary for the pursuit of industry, which vary with time and place,* become identified with the tangible items of property, so that what was once a means of production becomes a matter of possession. The "strategy of ownership converges" on the industrial arts, and technology, formerly a commonly shared body of knowledge, the "immaterial equipment" of the community, loses its usufruct nature. As technology generates value in productive goods, the laborer no longer has access to the materials of life or the means of production, and thus the "free workmanship" of the neolithic savage era falls under pecuniary control.

Veblen was too astute and catholic a scholar to draw a simple linear development between technology, property, and capitalism. He observed that the Pueblo Indians, for example, could advance materially beyond the simple scheme of savage life without requiring a system of property or pecuniary control over industry; and the Eskimos could

* "The chief subject of ownership may accordingly be the cultivated trees, as in South Sea islands; or the tillable land, as happens in many of the agricultural communities; or fish weirs and their location, as on some of the salmon streams of the American northwest coast; or domestic animals, as is typical of the pastoral culture; or it may be the persons of the workmen, as happens under divers circumstances both in pastoral and in agricultural communities; or, with an advance in technology of such a nature as to place the mechanical appliances of industry in a peculiarly advantaged position for engrossing the roundabout processes of production, as in the latterday machine industry, these mechanical appliances may become the typical category of industrial wealth and so come to be accounted 'productive goods' in some eminent sense." Veblen, *IOW*, 151.

still live communally while going far beyond neolithic man to develop boats, sleds, dogs harnessed and domesticated, fishing nets, harpoons and spears, and other elaborate appliances "embodying a minutely standardized technique." Veblen would not dismiss these cases as merely examples of "cultural retardation" without searching for the missing factors that brought the institution of private property into being. He wondered whether the presence of an "inchoate priestly class" (shamans, medicine men, angekut) who get their living in part "by their wits," and who come to acquire special claim to things by the value of their ministrations, had anything to do with the development of the pecuniary obligations between productive servants and the idle masters. Veblen also suggested that with the accumulation of wealth there develops an "inducement to aggression." Yet Veblen, with his awareness of the pitfalls of causal explanations, realized that this formulation still leaves us wondering whether "property provokes predation or predation initiates ownership."[6]

Moving forward to the period of early modern Europe, Veblen discusses the relationship of religious movements to the development of capitalism. Here he considers, without once mentioning the source, Weber's *The Protestant Ethic and the Spirit of Capitalism*, which had been published in Germany about the same time as Veblen began writing *The Instinct of Workmanship*. Veblen notes that the tenets of modern faith had been "revised and reconstituted" in terms of a morality of "self-help and autonomy" more consonant with the ideals of workmanship that reemerged in the Protestant era; and he observes that in the Catholic countries of southern Europe commercial enterprise had been checked, a situation also true in less pronounced fashion for the peoples of central Europe. The development of capitalism does indeed seem to follow a pattern, with industry arising among those people who have shed the archaic superstitions and cults of ancient orthodoxy and have adopted the milder piety of modern faith. The Reformation may have issued in the dissent and individualism necessary for the mentality of capitalism. "This concomitance between technological mastery and religious dissent is doubtless susceptible of a good and serviceable explanation at the hands of religious experts." But Veblen discusses the thesis only to dismiss it. He could not, as we shall see, accept Weber's argument that capitalism represented the "spiritual" extension of Christianity, an argument that seemed to both pervert the meaning of primitive Christianity and to ignore the role of modern science. As to why capitalism developed in Europe in the Protestant North and not in the Catholic South, Veblen suggested, "without prejudice," that the factor differentiating the two regions may have been racial rather than religious!*

* With characteristic aplomb Veblen writes in a footnote: "In this connection it is worth noting, for what it may be worth, that there is a similarly rough concomitance between the diffusion of the blond racial stock in Europe and the modern forms of

In contrast to both Marx and Weber, Veblen remained convinced that capitalism had its origins in the "era of handicraft," the period succeeding two phases of Barbarism that are roughly equivalent, in European history, to the Dark Ages and feudalism. He conceived the handicraft era as the revitalization of man's instinctual heritage that had been deflected but not destroyed by the servile condition of labor under feudalism. Veblen derived much of his information from the research of Werner Sombart and Karl Bücher, sources he acknowledged in *The Instinct of Workmanship*. And like Sombart, Veblen believed that an inducement to the accumulation of wealth was a prerequisite to the rise of capitalism. But it is to the rhapsodic description of Lewis Mumford, Veblen's greatest anthropological disciple, that we should turn to understand why Veblen would feel that this period of handicraft represented the finest, and perhaps the last, flowering of the human instincts:

> Wherever tools and muscle power were freely used, at the command of the workers themselves, their labors were varied, rhythmic, and often deeply satisfying, in the way that any purposeful ritual is satisfying. Increase of skill brought immediate subjective satisfaction, and this sense of mastery was confirmed by the created product. The main reward of the craftsman's working day was not wages but the work itself, performed in a social setting. In this archaic economy there was a time to toil and a time to relax: a time to fast and a time to feast: a time for disciplined effort, and a time for irresponsible play. In identifying himself with his work and seeking to make it perfect, the worker remolded his character.
>
> All the praise of tool-making and tool-using that has been mistakenly applied to early man's development becomes justified from neolithic times onward, and should even be magnified in evaluating the later achievements of handicraft. The maker and the object reacted one upon the other. Until modern times, apart from the esoteric knowledge of the priests, philosophers, and astronomers, the greater part of human thought and imagination flowed through the hands.[7]

This happy era of handicraft was not to last. The discipline of various crafts inculcates an apprehension of more and more efficient ways of workmanship, and soon mechanical appliances are contrived to abridge manual labor. These developments Veblen welcomes, for machine technology would, if uncontaminated, sustain a healthy matter-of-fact frame of mind. But mercantile activity developed side by side with craftsmanship, and herein arises the irony.

In the early stages of the handicraft era the craftsman enjoys an honored status and tends to retain a residue of animism and construe facts in anthropomorphic terms, interpreting his products not as objective

protestantism and religious heresy. Whether this fact strengthens or weakens any argument that may be drawn from the concomitance of heresy and industry cited above may perhaps be left an open question." Veblen, *IOW*, 268.

creations but as personal contributions subject to external appraisal. And insofar as the occupation of craftsmanship is confined to a certain social strata, a sense of "class consciousness" develops by which workers continually rate their serviceable efforts in the eyes of the community, contrasting themselves unfavorably with other orders of society who are not engaged in the production of things serviceable for human use. While the worker feels the sting of aristocratic disdain, the petty merchant, in contrast, can afford to be indifferent to community sentiment because he responds only to the objective fluctuation of the emerging market relations. By a strange twist of human evolution, it is the proto-capitalist who in the early stage of handicraft comes to take up the scientific habit of mind so central to a rational comprehension of society. The chief technique of this new apprehension is "accountancy," the exact quantification of all things, the impersonal and objective rating of all phenomena on the single criterion of price. Bookkeeping, ledgers, tables, rudimentary statistics—these are the commercial artifacts of the great breakthrough in physical science and mathematics; and Veblen was quite willing, as was Sombart, to credit capitalism for first translating empirical concepts into economic categories and for seeing science rather than religion as the handmaiden of the entrepreneurial revolution that marked the late stages of the handicraft era.[8] Moreover, the crucial factor of material science explains why capitalism could not have arisen directly out of feudalism, an age of faith characterized by a "cult of fearsome subjection and arbitrary authority" that all but killed the critical, empirical spirit. That spirit reemerges not in workmanship, still "contaminated" by the habits of social custom, but in capitalism, the one institution that best imitates science in its quest for power through the abstract reasoning of quantification. "Even the day-dreams of the pecuniary day-dreamer," wrote Veblen, "take shape as a calculus of profit and loss computed in standard units of impersonal magnitude."[9] The substitution of money values for human values was only one of the many results of capitalism's appropriation of science by way of the account book. As Mumford neatly puts it: "The power that was science and the power that was money were, in the final analysis, the same kind of power: the power of abstraction, measurement, quantification."[10]

The technology of capitalism may be scientific, but technique itself does not make a capitalist society, nor is the capitalist dedicated to pure science alone. Veblen was interested primarily in the "cultural consequences" of modern technology being put to use by a new entrepreneurial class. He was concerned with what Marxists would call the "hegemonic" status of capitalism, or in Veblen's terms, how the "pecuniary culture" of a part of society comes to dominate all of it. This culture comes into existence when the handicraft era passes over into the business era and then to the stage of machine technology. A business culture is characterized by (a) a price system based on property and contract; (b) competition based on the money unit and market relations that are at first accountable to the canons of efficiency in production; (c) a technology that systematizes the processes of output; (d) consumption habits that also become more standardized; (e) and eventual growth and consolidation of industries based upon private ownership. But these consequences do not necessarily "contradict" or "negate" the previous era of handicraft. Many elements of business principles, Veblen notes, are of the same nature as that "sentimental impulse to self-aggrandizement that lies at the root of predatory culture and so makes the substantial core of all pecuniary civilizations." Indeed even the craftsman of the handicraft era was as much a trader as a technician. He stood in close proximity to the market; and, with the coming of a wider and more extensively differentiated technological scheme, and with wider and more remote market relations due to increased transportation facilities, he was absorbed up into the entire commercial system and culture of modern capitalism.

If the worker was absorbed, the businessman was aborted. As industry develops into larger productive units, the businessman loses touch with the affairs of technology, for which he has come to display a "trained incapacity." In the modern era it is the engineers who take over the functions assigned in orthodox economic theory to the "entrepreneur," and the "efficiency engineer" now assumes the scientific frame of mind that had once characterized the salutary merchant mentality in the handicraft era. In the age of modern industry businessmen are wholly absorbed in banking, underwriting, insurance, activities that have nothing to do with the material equipment of technology or the tangible performance of industry. The more removed the businessman is from the matter-of-fact processes of industry, the more caught up he becomes in an animstic projection of powers external to himself. The final "inversion" comes when businessmen turn to salesmanship and public relations as a medium of power, thereby submitting themselves to the whims of consumer demands. The capitalist, like the worker, becomes the creature of his own creation—industrial society.

Veblen does not bemoan the fate of the businessman, whose pecuniary inclinations had been pronounced from the beginning of his appearance in early modern history. But the worker is victim of a double irony. In the era of handicraft, artisans and guildsmen enjoyed a considerable measure of autonomy. Craft workers were the "masterless men" who broke the last bonds of feudalism, undermined the power of the landed interests, bravely challenged the arbitrary authority of the nobility, and tenaciously asserted the personal rights which they had won for themselves. In doing so the workers assumed the habits of initiative, self-help, and individualism, thereby shedding the guild solidarity they possessed when struggling against the remnants of feudalism. It was in this period that John Locke came forward to propound a theory of "natural rights" as an answer to the scheme of experience embodied in the system of handicraft, in which the individual workman, laboring for a livelihood by use of his own personal force and skill, became the source and creator of value. Veblen quotes Locke's *Second Treatise:*

> Though the earth and all inferior creatures be common to all men, yet every man has a property in his own person; this nobody has a right to but himself. The labour of his body and the work of his hands we may say are properly his. Whatsoever, then, he removes out of the state that Nature hath provided and left it in, he hath mixed his labour with, and joined to it something that is his own, and thereby makes it his property.

As a philosophy of liberty based on the ethic of workmanship, Lockeanism was a broad and generous statement. But it was also superfluous. By the time it had become a creed of Enlightenment liberalism, the inalienable right *of* property had been alienated by the economic changes that precluded the worker from the right *to* property. The philosophy of Locke, as Hegel said of philosophy in general, arrived too late.

There is another aspect of Locke which, though Veblen fails to mention it, may serve as a transition to the discussion that follows. Convinced that government must rest on private property, Locke maintained that property was a natural and inalienable right which entitled man to the "labor of his body and the work of his hands," a dictum which located ownership in the creative workmanship of the original possessor. Man owns what he makes, and "everyone had a right . . . to as much as he could use." Although man may appropriate by his labor everything that is useful for his self-preservation, man produces more than he can consume, and hence the value of his work is threatened to the extent that the fruit of his labor may rot and decay. "Thus came in the use of money—some lasting thing that men might keep without spoiling, and that by mutual consent men would take in exchange for the truly useful but perishable supports of life." With the invention of money labor is no longer a sufficient entitlement to property. The way is now open for everyone to acquire and dispose as he sees fit. Currency prevents the spoilage of value and stimulates "larger possessions and the right to them"; man may now "rightfully and without injury, possess more than he himself can make use of."[11] From Veblen's perspective, Locke liberated man from feudalism and delivered him to the acquisitive society of capitalism.

According to Locke, the invention of money brought man closer to the realization of one of his natural entitlements, the right to "happiness." Marx rejected completely this view, dismissing liberalism as a great illusion, another figment of "false consciousness." To Veblen the illusion was precisely the problem, for it was more real than Marx imagined

Money, the "Mystery" of Commodities, and Reification

Locke maintained that money frees value from the fixed nature of property, gives durability to the objects of workmanship, and hence liberates man from the economic bondage of traditional society. Marx insisted that money represents the "alienated ability of mankind"; it is the "veil" within which true value is lost from sight. Money frees man from feudalism only to imprison him in the universe of fetishism. Veblen could agree with Marx, but only up to a point.

The issue of alienation which Marx had explored in his *Economic and Philosophic Manuscripts* of 1844 becomes, in Volume One of *Capital*, an aspect of "reification." This term, first coined by Georg Lukacs in 1923,[12] implies that products made by man come to assume in capitalist society an existence independent of man, "the erection of an objective world of things" *(Vergegenständlichung)*. In *Capital* and in the *Grundrisse* Marx's primary concern is the "mystery" of commodities, their ability to command human beings because of some inner "laws of motion," which inheres in their behavior and governs their exchange. Marx attempted to demystify the "fetishism of commodities" by distinguishing use value from exchange value in order to show how all products in capitalist society lose their former quality when they come under the medium of exchange and the sphere of the "universal commodity"—money. In bourgeois society men persist in obscuring the extent to which the value of commodities resides in the amount of socially necessary labor expended in their production. It could be said, as Michel Foucault has observed, that Marx, for all his dialectical skill in analyzing the phenomenal form of commodities, did little more than provide an "exegesis" of value mired in nineteenth-century assumptions.[13] An equally telling problem in Marx's analysis of reification is the assumption that this phenomenon as expressed in the commodity fetish takes place with the historical development of capitalism. Marx was certain that exchange relations emerge in fully developed form only when the idea of ownership emerges sufficiently enough to render objects private and therefore alienable:

> Objects in themselves are external to man, and consequently alienable by him. In order that this alienation may be reciprocal, it is only necessary for men, by a tacit understanding, to treat each other as private owners of those alienable objects, and by implication as independent individuals. But such a state of reciprocal independence has no existence in a primitive society based on property in common, whether such property takes the form of a patriarchal family, an ancient Indian community, or a Peruvian Inca State.[14]

Must objects become "external to man" in order to be "alienable"? Veblen once began an essay by quoting M. G. De Lapouge: "Anthropology is destined to revolutionize the political and social sciences as radically as bacteriology has revolutionized the science of medicine."[15] It was from the research of Franz Boas that Veblen became familiar with the custom of potlatch, and he perceived in the high society of modern culture what ethnologists had discovered among Indians and natives. "Costly entertainments, such as the potlatch or ball, are peculiarly adapted to serve this end [ostentation]. The competitor with whom the entertainer wishes to institute a comparison is, by this method, made to serve as a means to an end. He consumes vicariously for his host at the same time that he is a witness to the consumption of that excess of good things which his host is unable to dispose of singlehanded, and he is also made to witness his host's facility in etiquette."[16]

The French sociologist Marcell Mauss, Durkheim's successor who came to admire Veblen as the only American sociologist of consequence, explored the many implications of similar rituals in *Essai sur le don*.[17] Among Boas's Kwakiutl potlatch and Malinowski's Trobriand kula, Mauss developed a theory of the "structure" of reciprocity, and he found traces of similar practices in Greek, Roman, and old Germanic cultures. Although the idea of ownership is implicit in the custom, potlatch itself does not depend on a well-defined system of private property and has little to do with commodity relations in the Marxist sense of the term. "This is not the ordinary world of toil and care, the calculations of advantage or the acquisition of useful goods," writes Johan Huizinga in *Homo Ludens*. It is a world of fantastic, lavish ritual that functions to distribute goods and even to destroy them, a system by which mutual relations and obligations are expressed in haughty challenges of personal esteem and dramatic contests of conspicuous waste, a custom in which gift-objects seem inseparable from the "spirit" of those who bear them. Huizinga believed that potlatch was another expression of the "play" element in human culture. More recently anthropologists of different ideological persuasions have attempted to offer a political meaning of the phenomenon. The French Marxist Maurice Godelier views potlatch and similar rituals as an early expression of the "alienation" of the donor in the mystic rites of exchange, while Marshall Sahlins believes that these festive rituals of primitive exchange provide the basis for "alliance, solidarity, communion—in brief, peace, the great virtue that earlier philosophers, Hobbes notably, had discovered in the State."[18]

Interpreting such rituals as potlatch has led to a controversy, in the anthropological scholarship of economic institutions, between the "formalists" and the "substantivists," between those who see tribal economies as formal economic models based on a "market mentality," and those who insist that exchanges in archaic communities are social "prestations," obligatory gifts without considerations of profit.[19] To Veblen, however, the absence of profit calculations is merely further evidence that economic behavior, primitive as well as modern, must be understood in broader sociological terms, the result of the deeper motives of prestige and power. Hence he viewed potlatch as a form of strategic power moves dramatizing the relationship of domination to subordination. However one interprets the phenomenon, the upshot is that the "gift-ritual" compromises as well as complicates the dichotomy between use value and exchange value that is so central to Marx's theory of reification. Anthropologists have discovered among Indian tribes, especially those of the northwest coast of America, that the central feature of wealth is its display value. Wealth may be found in consumable goods, but the more desired symbolic wealth derives from prestige goods of non-utilitarian worth—strings of dentalium shell, woodpecker scalps, and large ceremonial obsidian blades.[20] These objects serve to maintain, either through display or donation, the prestige and status of the owner. Such tribal customs would seem to indicate that Marx's categories of value are obscured in the continuum of reciprocity that characterizes primitive exchange and stresses the predominance of social functions over economic transactions. All this only goes to suggest that anthropology and ethnology provide ample evidence that the earliest human societies were alive with rituals, magic, and myths that can only be described as reifications.

Veblen was not the first social scientist to be aware of the far-reaching implications of such rituals. But he was the first American scholar to use such anthropological data to demonstrate a point that would be articulated a half-century later by European philosophers like Jean Braudrillard and Jurgen Habermas: Marx's analysis of alienation and reification is too narrowly restricted to a discourse on production alone. When man is regarded as primarily a producer there can be no comprehension of the "structure of symbolic interaction" between mind and culture. The real focus of reification should be semiology, the study of commodities as "signs," non-human objects that transmit meanings to human subjects.[21]

Translated into more familiar language, we might say that commercial advertisers are the great dream merchants of semiology. Madison Avenue peddles not only the reality of the product but its image, not the technical performance of a commodity like an automobile but its cultural promise as a symbol. In advertising truth is replaced by credibility and what the commodity signifies is the only reality. The beautiful model next to the bottle of Clairol suggests that the contents of the bottle will produce beautiful hair. In the world of signification we are a long way from the "rationalist" world of Marx, where ideas corresponded to reality, words to things, and use values to human needs. We are in the outlandish world of Veblen, who perceived the cultural implications of semiology to point out that we consume not only to satisfy basic needs but to situate ourselves in an hierarchical social system.

Mediation, not production, is the key. If the labor theory of value cannot be applied to pre-capitalist formations, where use value does not take the form of commodities, neither can labor still be regarded as the dominant sphere of man's activity in modern society. Veblen suggests why in industrial society the ultimate problem is not production but consumption, not how goods come to be made but how they take on meaning. The role of meaning as a feature of the mediating tendencies of mind needs to be explored in relation to the "root of all evil"—money.

In his 1844 notebooks Marx regarded money as an "alien medium" because it concealed the true value of labor and, as a vehicle of exchange, took on qualities external to man. With the prevalence of money man's slavery reaches its climax since all that represented human effort has been "transmitted" to an external agency that becomes an end in itself. In the *Grundrisse* Marx further insists that money is so abstracted from tangible wealth that it cannot even be regarded as part of reality. "As a general form of wealth money is confronted by the entire world of real valuables. Money is the pure abstraction of the same—pure fantasy. Where wealth appears to exist in complete material, palpable form as such, money only has its existence in my head, as a pure figment of my mind." Ultimately money is for Marx a disease of the mind, an imaginary, hallucinatory power that generates the illusion of personal alchemy. "I am ugly, but I can buy the *most beautiful* woman. Therefore I am not ugly, for the effect of ugliness, its power of repulsion, is destroyed by money."[22]

Marx's writings on money bear a striking resemblance to the protests of seventeenth-century Puritans against the sins of covetousness. Both were convinced that "filthy lucre" would destroy all hope for human regeneration, and both recognized the Midas complex and its Faustian paradox: he who craves everything can enjoy nothing. The ancients were also aware, as were Rousseau, Thoreau, and other moderns, that wisdom begins with the cessation of desire; Aristotle observed that acquisitiveness, having no aim, has no limits. But such moral injunctions hardly exhaust the topic. Another way of approaching the problem might be called the "sociology of money." Today French scholars like Baudrillard and Roland Barthes are exploring the meaning of money, wealth, and commodities through the study of semiology, viewing their various manifestations as a kind of sign language.[23] Actually this mode of analysis had been anticipated a half-century ago by the American sociologist George Herbert Mead. "Money," wrote Mead,

> is a symbol for something that is wanted by individuals who are in the attitude of willingness to exchange; and the forms of exchange are then the methods of conversation, and the media of exchange become gestures which enable us to carry out at vast distances this process of passing over something one does not want, to get something he does, by means of bringing himself into the attitude of the other person. The media of these tokens of

wealth are, then, in this process of exchange just such gestures or symbols as language is in other fields.[24]

The problem that so deeply troubled Marx, the "mystification" of money and commodities, scarcely bothered Veblen, at least not in the same way. Money he could cheerfully dismiss as "the exact science of making change,"[25] a form of communication which, like language and gesture, suggests not the "objectification" of human relations and hence man's increasing privatization but his integration and socialization. With Marx he could agree that the money economy had something to do with the rise of surplus, but this development led not so much to the curse of exchange value in capitalism as the logic of irrational superfluities, the drive toward conspicuous consumption that begins with archaic man. Men desire money simply because they desire goods. As a common denominator of exchange, money is nothing but the reification of the power of goods to command men's desires. Why then do men desire goods? We come again to the "fetishism of commodities."

Although Marx recognized that all economic relations are social phenomena, he seemed to be indifferent to the cultural significance of commodities. Not only did he deny that commodities are "symbols" and that money is a form of "language,"[26] he precluded from his investigations any concern for the human "wants" which commodities satisfy and perhaps the deeper and more complex motivations which they reflect.[27] If it was difficult for Veblen to accept Hegel's view that physical things are alienated mental activity dramatizing the false separation of subject and object, it was equally difficult for him to accept Marx's view that commodities are alienated social activity that dramatize the creations of men that have become independent of men. Veblen saw commodities as they may have first appeared in primitive form, as "organic extensions of personality" whose meaning is shaped by the animistic mind.[28] Now a Marxist might grant that Veblen was correct about the status of objects in archaic society. With the advent of bourgeois capitalism, however, the "alien medium" of money comes between man and his objects and human relations are now externalized by exchange value, a relation that relates only "thing to thing." It is precisely here that Veblen reverses the entire theoretical scheme of Marx's explanation of reification. The development of capitalism is not so deanimizing that total "objectification" takes place and the worker becomes a "slave" to a world of fetishized objects he can neither comprehend nor control. On the contrary, the psychological bond between subject and object, between person and thing, is never completely dissolved. Indeed, if commodities become so abstract and depersonalized in their seemingly autonomous existence under capitalism, what explains the nature of their "fetishism"? Why are men so attracted to that which is apparently so alien to their being?

For Veblen, who had been influenced by Kant and had studied under Charles Sanders Peirce,[29] and who sensed the mediation of mind in every act of observation, the answer is obvious: commodities retain a strong personal sign-character which enables man to impute to them human qualities which he can recognize. Man is not "mystified" by the cold, disembodied status of objects as mere objects. Rather he is awed by the commodity object as a symbol expressing the forceful and superior character of the person who possesses it. Ownership itself originates in bold feats of hunting and fighting, conquest and plunder. In the mind of primitive man living in the predatory stage of barbarism a connection is thus formed between possession and strength, ownership and power, a prodigious display of commodities and a superior position of status. This meaning connection becomes more developed in the feudal era, when brute valor is raised to the level of noble virtue and booty and trophies come to be prized as evidence of "preeminent force."[30] Veblen leaves no doubt that this primitive mentality is alive in the modern mind:

> With the primitive barbarian, before the simple content of the notion has been obscured by its own ramifications and by a secondary growth of cognate ideas, 'honorable' seems to connote nothing else than assertion of superior force. 'Honorable' is 'formidable'; 'worthy' is 'prepotent.' An honorific act is in the last analysis little if anything else than a recognized successful act of aggression; and where aggression means conflict with men and beasts, the activity which comes to be especially and primarily honorable is the assertion of the strong hand. The naive, archaic habit of construing all manifestations of force in terms of personality or 'will power' greatly fortifies this conventional exaltation of the strong hand. Honorific epithets, in vogue among barbarian tribes as well as among people of a more advanced culture, commonly bear the stamp of this unsophisticated sense of honor. Epithets and titles used in addressing chieftains, and in the propitiation of kings and gods, very commonly impute a propensity for overbearing violence and an irresistible devastating force to the person who is to be propitiated. This holds true to an extent also in the more civilized communities of the present day. The predilection shown for heraldic devices for the more rapacious beasts and birds of prey goes to enforce the same view.
>
> Under this common-sense barbarian appreciation of worth and honor, the taking of life—the killing of formidable competitors, whether brute or human—is honorable in the highest degree. And this office of slaughter, as an expression of the slayer's prepotence, casts a glamor of worth over every act of slaughter and over all the tools and accessories of the act. Arms are honorable, and the use of them, even in seeking the life of the meanest creatures of the fields, becomes an honorific employment. At the same time, employment in industry becomes correspondingly odious, and, in the common-sense apprehension, the handling of the tools and implements of industry falls beneath the dignity of able-bodied men. Labor becomes irksome.[31]

There is, of course, an excess of hyperbole in this passage from *Leisure Class*. Yet it serves to indicate that man does not look upon external objects as reified things but as symbols representing something else. The fetishism of commodities lies in their prestige value, in their ability as "signs" to command respect, authority, deference. In a world governed by symbols and sign values, it suffices that one can *appear* to be powerful and successful by acquiring the commodities that convey those human attributes. It is precisely because commodities radiate a "quasi-personal fringe" that Veblen cannot regard them as Marx's disembodied abstractions. Commodities are rich with human meaning, but that meaning exists solely in the mind of the interpreter. What is alienating, then, is not the fetishism in commodities but the animism in man which compels him to impute personal and individual qualities to observed phenomena.

Veblen was convinced that this behavior, rather than being peculiar to modern capitalism alone, had its origins in primitive communities where perception is a matter of "folk-psychology, not of mechanical fact." This anthropomorphic habit of conceiving phenomena in personal terms also impels the mind to project will onto matter. "All obvious manifestations of force are apprehended as expressions of conation—effort put forth for a purpose by some agency similar to the human will. The point of view of the archaic culture is that of forceful, pervading personality, whose unfolding life is the substantial fact held in view in every relation into which men or things enter." The tendency to see inanimate things in animate terms, to endow inert matter with anthropomorphic qualities, prevails "pretty much universally" in archaic cultures, and it reinforces "the apprehension of phenomenon in terms generically identical with the terms of personality and individuality."[32]

In Veblen's analysis reification could not possibly reflect the lifeless state of commodities, their chilling "thinghood" which renders their behavior seemingly autonomous and beyond man's grasp. Rather, reification occurs when "external objects are in great part apperceived in respect of what they will do; and their most substantial characteristic therefore, their intimate individual nature, in so far as they are conceived as individual entities, is that they will do things."[33] That the commodity, whether it be a captured canoe or a purchased Cadillac, "will do things" for man that he cannot do for himself, that it will give him the power and prestige that society denies him, that it will enable him to become that which he is not—this pathos is for Veblen the psychological meaning of reification.

It should now be clear that Marx's commodity fetish and Veblen's animism are two aspects of the same behavior, the difference being that the former was determined to locate the origins of reification in the "laws" of political economy, while the latter perceived reification as characteristic of the collective mentality of predatory society in general. But Veblen also perceived another aspect of reification in the stratification of society based upon the possession of prestige symbols, and in the phenomenon of "emulation" he discovered why the commodity fetish, instead of alienating man and producing social conflict, integrates man and produces social cohesion.

Emulation and the Hegemony of Capitalism

Veblen viewed emulation as an innate characteristic of man, but the nature and expression of that ambiguous natural endowment changes in the course of history. In the early primitive cultures of small peaceable communities, there is little competitiveness and social discrimination, and what emulative spirit exists is directed toward those productive workers who contribute to the life of the community. But with the advance of tools, including weapons, some men can devote themselves to hunting large game and taking part in raids upon neighboring tribes. Now the activities of men came more and more to take on the character of exploit, and an "invidious comparison" between the hunter-warrior and others grows continually easier and more habitual as the predators bring home tangible evidence of their superior prowess. Thus arises the distinction between "honorific employments" involving exploit and "humiliating employments" involving activities serviceable to the community.

The accumulation of articles of wealth by methods other than toil represents man's attempt to identify with the superior class by possessing its symbols. Wealth has little to do with use value, and even the consumption of goods is not directed toward the satisfaction of basic needs and comforts. The incentive to wealth, the familiar "profit motive" of political economy, is more a cultural trait than an economic truth. "The motive that lies at the root of ownership is emulation; and the same motive of emulation continues active in the further development of the institutions to which it has given rise and in the development of all those features of the social structure which this institution of ownership touches. The possession of wealth confers honor; it is an invidious distinction."[34] This motive increases as society becomes larger and more diffuse and mobile, creating a situation where it is difficult to appraise a person except by some external valuation, such as fancy dress, cultivated manners, or extravagant possessions. The irony is that emulation, though a primitive trait, does not vanish with the march of progress. For the greater advance in industry the greater will be the opportunity for comparison, and hence the more intense will be the craving after the economic signs of social respectability. Moreover, status discrimination based on an "invidious comparison of persons in respect to worth, value, and potency" is, as in the case of inherited wealth and vested rights, "transmitted by descent from honorable antecedents." Thus economic success as a measure of approbation is an impression that grows stronger with each generation that inherits the belief.[35]

Veblen's theories of human behavior may have been outrageous in Victorian America, but they were not alien to the thinkers of the seventeenth and eighteenth centuries. Rousseau observed how "esteem" functions as the social motive for wealth, and in *Rameau's Nephew* Diderot offered perhaps the finest literary treatment of emulation and status anxiety as a form of alienation so acute as to disturb even Hegel from his metaphysical daydreams.[36] British social philosophers were no less keen on the relation of social pressures to economic behavior. Adam Smith advised that "the great secret of education is to direct vanity to proper objects," Bernard de Mandeville argued that "pride" was the particular "vice" from which flowed "public benefit," and even Hobbes realized that power could not be translated into authority without a modicum of social conscience among the citizenry. "There is no greater vexation of mind" than "scorn and contempt," wrote Hobbes, who was certain that "most men would rather lose their lives . . . than suffer slander."[37] Perhaps the document in English political philosophy that most resembles Veblen's analysis is John Millar's *The Origin of the Distinction of Rank* (1779), a discourse on the manners and customs of different stages of civilization that stresses the sociological determinants of wealth and consumption. The men of the Enlightenment, however, tended to view their contemporary society as transitory and artificial, an "unnatural" phenomenon whose illusions and distortions would yield to the power of reason (Locke), compassion (Rousseau), or philosophy itself (Hegel). Veblen doubted the redemptive capacities of mind or heart. Indeed his own mind seemed almost burdened with knowledge of archaic society. Looking backward, he was the first modern scholar to give economic behavior not only a sociological content but an anthropological basis, and in so doing he discovered two related problems in contemporary industrial civilization that remain with us like a post-Marxist incubus—the cultural hegemony of capitalism and the social stigma of labor.

Veblen arrived at this discovery by viewing modern capitalism as a sociological phenomenon with anthropological precedents. As a result he wanted to broaden traditional economic investigation in order to comprehend behavior as a function of the social situation with roots in earlier cultures. In modern society, as in primitive communities, the concern for status can become such an obsession that the "pleasure-pain" assumptions of political economy seem rational in the extreme. Is the profit margin more important than the motives of pride, or even self-preservation more essential than status aspiration? Veblen, of course, did not state the case in such bald terms, but he could not resist refuting a serious principle by means of a satirical portrait:

In persons of delicate sensibility, who have long been habituated to gentle manners, the sense of shamefulness of manual labor may become so strong that, at a critical juncture, it will even set aside the instinct of self-preservation. So, for instance, we are told of certain Polynesian chiefs, who, under the stress of good form, preferred to starve rather than carry their food to their mouths with their own hands. It is true, this conduct may have been due, at least in part, to an excessive sanctity or tabu attaching to the chief's person. The tabu would have been communicated by the contact of his hands, and so would have made anything touched by him unfit for human food. But the tabu is itself a derivative of the unworthiness or moral incompatibility of labor; so that even when construed in this sense the conduct of the Polynesian chiefs is truer to the canon of honorific leisure than would at first appear. A better illustration, or at least a more unmistakable one, is afforded by a certain king of France, who is said to have lost his life through an excess of moral stamina in the observance of good form. In the absence of the functionary whose office it was to shift his master's seat, the king sat uncomplaining before the fire and suffered his royal person to be toasted beyond recovery. But in so doing he saved his Most Christian Majesty from menial contamination.

Summum crede nefas animam praeferre pudori,
Et propter vitam vivendi perdere causas.[38]

Veblen's humor should not distract us from the theoretical import of this passage. Veblen proved to be an early student of what came to be known in sociology as "role playing." That men would carry out the social function of their class regardless of consequences only indicates the extent to which that function shapes man's thoughts and actions. The completely socialized man whose entire life is absorbed by his social role is another example of how human consciousness can be lost to forces outside of itself, only now reification is not associated with commodities but with society itself. Reification operates in society by endowing social roles with ontological status.[39] Man's identity, personality, and selfhood are achieved through the fulfillment of a role that is detached from human intentionality, preformed by institutions, class systems, and cultural habits. Men in society do not have lives, they have only social functions and their functions are lived out through mere mimetic repetitions of the prototypical actions embodied in the roles. "Manners," wrote Veblen, ". . . are in part an elaboration of gesture, and in part they are symbolic and conventionalized survivals representing former acts of dominion or of personal service or of personal contact. In large part they are an expression of the relation of status—a symbolic pantomime of mastery on the one hand and subservience on the other."[40]

Veblen's sensitivity to the social determinants of economic behavior may also be seen in his grasp of what Robert Merton would later call the "latent functions" of manifest conduct.[41] Veblen observed that while education is a means to enlightenment, the leisure class studies ancient languages and fine arts, not out of any prompting of "idle curiosity" but to dramatize how far removed it is from immediate industrial concerns. Similarly, in our time the automobile is a means of transportation, but the upper class purchases Cadillacs to indicate it occupies a position superior to that of the Chevrolet owner. Because of his perceptions of the social foundations of behavior Veblen was alert to conduct and mannerisms designed less to satisfy needs than to improve status. Moreover, he could readily perceive how supposedly radical "counterculture" styles are easily appropriated by the leisure class. Although he admired John Ruskin and William Morris as critics of the waste and ugliness of capitalism, he doubted that their aesthetic call for a return to arts and crafts and household industry offered a real alternative. Veblen himself, ironically, was a practitioner of Ruskin's and Morris' economy of simplicity, making his own furniture out of the rawest of materials. But he saw that the finely handwrought crafts and the artistic book making of Morris would be far more expensive than the industrial methods of mass production, and thus the superior excellence imputed to "antique and obsolete processes" would have less to do with artistic beauty than with the snob appeal of precious articles beyond the reach of the masses. The canons of taste can also be "contaminated," and the buyer of rare art, manifestly a connoisseur, is also enhancing his prestige as a "latent" status seeker.[42]

That even new artistic forms and cultural styles originating in social protest can be appropriated by the upper class suggests an even more important sociological aspect of Veblen's theory of emulation—its conservative implications. As pecuniary standards pervade the community existing institutions exercise a normative restraining force and readily deflect or absorb all challenges. Institutions are perpetuated by emulation, which is always directed upwards as the mass of men continually adapt themselves to the culture and life-style of the classes immediately above them. Thus individuals "internalize" the norms of the social order:

> The institution of a leisure class has an effect not only upon social structure but also upon the individual character of the members of society. So soon as a given proclivity or a given point of view has won acceptance as an authoritative standard or norm of life it will react upon the character of the members of a society which has accepted it as a norm. It will to some extent shape their habits or thought and will exercise a selective surveillance over the development of men's aptitudes and inclinations.[43]

Because of the human propensity of emulation, the upper class is in a position to set a "prescriptive example of conspicuous waste" and to provide an "imperative example" of how the "canons of reputability" are established. Thus the norms that organize and provide cohesion to a society's value system originate at the top of the class structure and permeate downward, affecting (or "contaminating") the populations of the various strata below. It is for this reason that Veblen could not dismiss the "superstructure" of society—that layer which stands at the top of the social pyramid and represents all the false ideologies of religion, nationalism, and capitalism—as a mere "reflection" of society's structural "base" that has its dynamic in the mode of production. The ideas of the leisure class may be as false as they are pernicious, but its power is as real as its influence is ubiquitous.

In treating reigning cultural ideas as the unconscious foundations of social life, Veblen was anticipating an issue in social theory that would later be discovered by Antonio Gramsci—the phenomenon of hegemony. The problem of hegemony lies in explaining how a whole of society can come to be dominated by the values of a part, and why man therefore consents to his own domination by others, a phenomenon made all the more perplexing because it involves man's subjugation to ideas rather than to power and coercion. In short, how does the ruling class legitimate itself if not by force? Veblen sensed that in a mass society the phenomenon of power, the ability to command by threat of coercion, gives way to the phenomenon of influence, the ability to persuade by the tendency of emulation. Veblen's shrewd analysis of the social determinants of economic behavior enabled him to see how emulation functioned to cushion the effects of alienation and exploitation, thereby integrating the worker into the culture of capitalism.

Status Deprivation and the Integration of the Working Class

Veblen addresed himself to the issue of the working class in "Some Neglected Points in the Theory of Socialism," published in 1892. The essay was written partly in response to the labor unrest of the early 1890s and partly in answer to Herbert Spencer's severe criticisms of the socialist movement in America. Spencer had denounced socialism as a threat to competition and the system of free contract that allegedly had done so much to promote economic progress. Veblen, who had respected Spencer since his undergraduate days, assumed the role of the analyst as a way of countering the alarmist. Before fretting over the presumed dire consequences of socialism, advised Veblen, one should plumb the depths of the "chronic feeling of dissatisfaction" plaguing the laboring classes. Spencer's claim that the source of discontent lay in a feeling of "ennui" on the part of the workers may be one cause, Veblen acknowledged, but it is not the sufficient cause. Even less convincing was the Populist-Progressive contention that the economic system functioned to make the rich richer and the poor poorer, a sentiment that had, Veblen observed by noting the economic gains made by labor, only "the fascination of an epigram." If the source of labor unrest lay neither in boredom nor in desperation, where may the cause of discontent be found?

Veblen answered this question by introducing an idea that would be developed more than a half-century later by social scientists, the idea of *relative deprivation*. "The existing system has not made, and does not tend to make, the industrious poor poorer as measured absolutely in means of livelihood; but it does tend to make them relatively poorer, in their own eyes, as measured in terms of comparative economic importance, and, curious as it may seem at first sight, this is what seems to count." What workers feel is not physical but emotional privation, and this takes the "ignoble form of emulation," of striving after a "good name" and a reputable standing in the community. Suffering from status anxieties, workers direct their resentment toward the owners of private property "whose possessions rise above a certain rather indefinite average. This feeling of injured injustice is not always distinguished from envy; but it is, at any rate, a factor that works toward a leveling policy. With it goes a feeling of slighted manhood, which works in the same direction."[44]

In Veblen's writings the American social order emerges as a class society without a class conflict. Without a well-developed sense of class consciousness, the worker came to envy and eventually adopt the life-style of the leisure class, believing that the meaning and value of life would not be found in production, as Marx and Veblen had hoped, but in consumption according to the "pecuniary canons of taste." Desiring to climb up into the middle class, and influenced by the acquisitive and relatively idle culture of the *nouveaux riches*, the industrial worker suffered the indignity of "slighted manhood" the more he sought the elusive respect of those above him. Here we might find a clue to the problem that had troubled disenchanted Marxists: the seemingly willing collaboration of the working class in its own subordination. To the extent that the industrial worker compared himself to his image of people in a higher class, the worker conceded the right of that class to judge him.

Was this behavior peculiar to only Veblen's American society? Perhaps. Yet such behavior may take on larger significance as the rest of the industrialized world becomes "Americanized." Dramatic cases in point are Abudada, Kuwait, and other oil-producing countries of the Mideast, where one of the most important social and cultural consequences of instantaneous prosperity is the immediate importation of foreign workers. With sudden affluence productive work becomes more stigmatized than ever, and as the Cadillac replaces the camel, commodities take on the status of social icons. If the "barbarian status" of women remains the same, everyman becomes a sheik.

Whatever the validity of Veblen's ideas for the rest of the world, studies by social historians of nineteenth- and twentieth-century America tend to confirm his observations, making him a prescient anatomist of what later would be called "the hidden wounds of class." That the American worker failed to become a radical social force cannot be explained simply by pointing to prosperity and social mobility. The American worker was materially no better off than the German worker before World War One; and, as historians have discovered, while a measure of low-level mobility existed for the industrial workers, the social structure did not offer a widespread "rags-to riches" ladder to success, the Alger myth so dear to business elites.[45] Yet it is exceedingly difficult, given the paucity of historical data, to discover whether the worker believed in the myth of individualism because the modicum of social mobility did allow many workers to rise from the bottom of the ladder, even though not very far. Since workers' attitudes on this question are so crucial we are compelled to speculate. If, on the one hand, the workers remained skeptical of the myth, why did they fail to develop a radical class-conscious *élan* as a means of penetrating the false ideology? On the other hand, if they believed in the capitalist ideology of opportunity and mobility and yet failed to rise in occupation, income, and status, did they allow themselves to become integrated into the social order by turning their resentment against themselves, viewing their failure in terms of personal inadequacy rather than social inequity and thereby suffering individual guilt?

Although data from the nineteenth century are silent on these questions, we do have evidence from the mid-twentieth century to indicate that as opportunity and mobility increase workers' attitudes become heavy with injured dignity and self-reproach. Whatever the source of this sentiment—religious, ethnic, psychological, etc.—the attitudes of workers are expressed in two curiously distinct ways. One sentiment, which was uncovered by Richard Sennet and Jonathan Cobb, shows the worker admiring the culture and character of the upper class, not so much because of its wealth as its superior inner resources. In contrast to the harsh, brutal, and often wild milieu of working-class life, marred by drunken brawls and family quarrels, upper-class life appears tame, quiet, genteel, "civilized" by a higher capacity for self-control. Even though the worker might despise the white-collar occupations of the banker and the salesman, he looks to their domestic culture as a "prestige model" that he wishes he and his family could emulate.[46] We might call this a Weberian sentiment, inasmuch as the worker imputes superior qualities of inner restraint to the upper class. But there is another sentiment shared by the lower class that is closer to Veblen's observations. This attitude turns up in Studs Terkel's inverviews with workers from all walks of life. The following statement, by a Chicago steel worker, suggests Veblen's thesis about the degradation of manual labor in the eyes of the workers and their envy of the leisure class's freedoms and hedonistic life-styles:

> If I were to put you in front of a dock and I pulled up a skid in front of you with fifty-pound sacks of potatoes and there are fifty more skids just like it, and this is what you're gonna do all day, what would you think about—potatoes? Unless a guy's a nut, he never thinks about work or talks about it. Maybe about baseball or about getting drunk the other night or he got laid or didn't get laid. I'd say one out of a hundred will actually get excited about work.
>
> Why is it that the communists always say they're for the workingman, and as soon as they set up a country, you got guys singing to tractors? They're singing about how they love the factory. That's where I couldn't buy communism. It's the intellectuals' utopia, not mine. I cannot picture myself singing to a tractor. I just can't. (Laughs.) Or singing to steel. (Singsongs.) Oh whoop-dee-do, I'm at the bonderizer, oh how I love this heavy steel. No thanks. Never hoppen.
>
> Oh yeah, I daydream. I fantasize about a sexy blonde in Miami who's got my union dues. (Laughs.) I think of the head of the union the way I think of the head of my company. Living it up. I think of February in Miami. Warm weather, a place to lay in. When I hear a college kid say, 'I'm oppressed,' I don't believe him. You know what I'd like to do for one year? Live like a college kid. Just for one year. I'd love to. Wow! (Whispers) Wow! Sports car! Marijuana! (Laughs.) Wild, sexy broads. I'd love that, hell yes, I would.[47]

When comparing the studies of Sennet and Cobb on the one hand and Terkel on the other, we find that workers seem to entertain two differing views of the upper class. Some regard the wealthy as morally superior, others regard them as sensually freer. However one might explain this dual attitude—and doubtless a Freudian could—the undeniable reality is that the American working class possesses little cultural autonomy. It looks outside of its own milieu, and generally above it, for discrete models of behavior. This is true not only for the culture of conduct but for the culture of work itself. One of the striking features of the nineteenth-century American labor force was that many of its members were immigrants who arrived with little comprehension of and even less attraction to the imperatives and ethos of industrial labor. Yet peasants, farmers, skilled artisans, and casual day laborers were soon harnessed to new punctual and rigorous work habits, an effort that required considerable propaganda on the part of the business elites.[48] The success of American business leaders in disciplining a potentially recalcitrant and unruly work force is further evidence not only of the power of capitalism but of its cultural hegemony.

Lenin was perhaps the first Marxist theoretician to sense that the working class was ill-equipped to penetrate the ideology of the ruling class; hence the "spontaneity" of the proletariat must be triggered by the "consciousness" of the party. Yet it was the Italian Gramsci who first appreciated fully the power of ideas as a creative and, more importantly for our purposes, a conservative force. Veblen, too, understood the stabilizing function of ideas in a capitalist society. In Veblen's analysis, the animistic and anthropomorphic elements in ideas prevent the population from thinking objectively and apprehending the real causal sequence of natural phenomena. It is characteristic of the ruling class to appeal to ideals rather than to facts, and these "devout proprieties" have the effect of "inducing and conserving a certain habitual recognition of the relation to a superior, and so stiffening the current sense of status and allegiance."[49]

For Marx the hegemony of the capitalist class was merely a historical stage that would be overcome by working-class struggle and class consciousness; for Veblen it was a more complex matter that suggested both the survival of archaic traits and the inability of modern scientific thought to take hold of the mind of the masses. Yet there is an entirely different perspective that needs to be considered. Was the deference enjoyed by the capitalist classes based solely on power and propaganda, or did it derive from a genuinely distinct moral character which the masses may have actually recognized? Veblen depicted capitalism as an oligarchy of power and an orgy of waste. Max Weber, in contrast, perceived in early capitalism elements of a timocracy, a form of rule based upon the principles of honor, duty, and probity. On the one hand we have a portrait of the capitalist as a hedonistic creature of endless desires, on the other as a heroic character of restrained passions. Weber's study of capitalism needs to be examined, not only because his historical analysis provides an interesting contrast to Veblen's treatment, but also because Veblen's solution to the problem of capitalist hegemony may be better seen, from Weber's perspective, as merely an extension and magnification of the problem itself.

7 . . . Veblen, Weber, and the "Spirit of Capitalism"

No two social theorists could be more intellectually and temperamentally opposed than Thorstein Veblen and Max Weber. Between the radical empiricism of the American and the conservative humanism of the German ran an ideological fault that was as wide as it was deep. Neither scholar had any influence on the other,[1] and in tone and thesis their works are so widely different as to invite little basis for comparison. Why then compare them?

The reason for comparing them is simply that both were preoccupied—one is tempted to say "obsessed"—with the historical meaning of contemporary industrial society. They were also certain, as we saw earlier, that the future of modern capitalism could be grasped only by comprehending its growth and development; and to do so Weber turned to America as the historical embodiment of the "Protestant ethic," the country in which Veblen grew up, to discover that capitalism was neither basically ethical nor essentially Christian.

A comparison of Veblen and Weber deserves our attention for other reasons. As contemporaries who reached the height of their intellectual powers in the years before World War One, they responded to many of the same historical experiences: economic growth and industrial expansion at the turn of the century, the transformation of bourgeois capitalism into bureaucratic, corporate forms of management, and the crisis of the First World War and the Bolshevik Revolution. Responding to these unsettling events, they addressed themselves to strikingly similar problems. In the early 1890s Weber and Veblen wrote articles on agriculture, the stock market, the credit system, and finance capitalism. Weber's *Protestant Ethic and the Spirit of Capitalism* appeared in essay form in 1904–1905, five years after the publication of Veblen's *Theory of the Leisure Class,* and five years later Veblen offered his own interpretation of religion and capitalism in "Christian Morals and the Competitive System." In 1915, when Weber was anxiously pondering and writing about the fate of Hohenzollern Germany, Veblen published *Imperial Germany and the Indus-*

trial Revolution; in 1918, the same year that Weber registered his eloquent protest against the suppression of academic freedom and wrote his important essay on the mission of education, "Science as a Vocation," Veblen published a similar statement in *The Higher Learning in America*. During this war period Veblen and Weber also worked for their respective governments, and each wrote provocative articles on the Russian Revolution, though taking decidedly different views. And after their respective deaths (Weber in 1920, Veblen in 1929), their richly stimulating articles that had remained buried in scholarly journals were published as books by their admiring students.

Their publications followed the course of historical events in large part because both authors shared the same theoretical concerns. Although living in different political cultures, Weber and Veblen were deeply interested in the issues of power, authority, legitimacy, and the personalized hegemony manifested in the phenomenon of "charismatic leadership" and of "captains of industry." They were similarly interested in the methodological issues of scientific objectivity and the crucial role of technological expertise in modern society, and both were highly critical of the Marxist interpretation of history. Finally, Weber, no less than Veblen and Marx, probed deeply into the origins of capitalism, only he arrived at strikingly different conclusions about the problems of alienation, reification, hegemony, and the ultimate fate of the "spirit of capitalism" in the modern world.

Aside from these intellectual parallels, an even more compelling reason for comparing Weber and Veblen is the eclipse of the latter by the eminence of the former in American social theory. In part this eclipse was due to the influential scholarship of Talcott Parsons and the school of sociology known as "structural functionalism" (more on this later). Not only did Parsons, as we saw, liken Veblen's "instinct of workmanship" to Weber's idea of "the calling," thereby equating a biological endowment with a religious imperative, he went so far as to claim that Veblen's social theory is "essentially very simple" and that a "quite adequate comprehension of all Veblen's real contributions can be found in Weber's work."[2] Parsons' claim mistakes resemblance for similarity. If an analogy is to be found, it might be in Weber's ideas of Protestant filial duty and Veblen's notion of the "parental bent," but even that parallel may be too superficial to suggest an "adequate comprehension of all Veblen's real contributions."

Max Weber and the Rise of Capitalism

Veblen, as we noted, traced the rise of capitalism to the handicraft era of the fifteenth and sixteenth centuries, while Marx maintained that capitalism arose out of the collapse of the feudal synthesis of landed wealth and hereditary power. Weber rejected both the technological and the materialist interpretation of history. Neither

Veblen's description of predation and consumption nor Marx's theory of exploitation and surplus value are for Weber the primary characteristics of capitalism. Instead Weber sees capitalism as a product of a unique type of personality that appears on the historical scene at the time of the Reformation. What made the capitalist so peculiarly different? It was not his egoism and avarice, human traits found in precapitalist societies and personified in the rapacious activities of the Spanish conquistadores and the English pirates, as well as the Roman aristocrats and the Chinese mandarins. The unique feature of the capitalist personality is the strenuous moral discipline involved in his attitude toward work as a spiritual obligation and a social duty. Weber sees capitalism as less a pleasurable acquisitive drive than a joyless devotion to hard work as a responsibility that carries its own intrinsic reward. He identifies the principles of modern capitalism as follows:

> The earning of more and more money, combined with the strict avoidance of all spontaneous enjoyment of life, is . . . thought of so purely as an end in itself, that from the point of view of the happiness of, or utility to, the single individual, it appears entirely transcendental and absolutely irrational. Man is dominated by the making of money, by acquisition as the ultimate purpose of his life. Economic acquisition is no longer subordinated to man as the means for the satisfaction of his material needs. This reversal of what we should call the natural relationship, so irrational from a naive point of view, is evidently as definitely a leading principle of capitalism as it is foreign to all peoples not under capitalistic influence.[3]

Weber and Veblen were in agreement in at least one respect (no doubt because they both drew upon Sombart): that the capitalist "spirit" found expression in the efficient and rational reorganization of production on the basis of "rigorous calculation" (Weber) and "systematic accountancy" (Veblen). Modern capitalism, in contrast to the "adventurous capitalism" of previous eras, is based on the rational pursuit of economic gain by way of long-range investments, organized exchanges for commodities and securities, continuous administration of political bodies, and business enterprises sanctioned by contract and other legal forms. Veblen had recognized many of these features in the handicraft era, especially the technological improvements in the modes of production. But Veblen, imbued with the idea of science as the harbinger of progress, and disposed to see in history more continuity than change, explored neither the psychology behind the movement toward rationalization nor the meaning of man's new attitudes toward work and wealth, a reorientation of values that involved nothing less than a cultural revolution. It was Weber's great achievement to locate this change in a source where neither Veblen nor Marx had looked—in religion.[4]

Weber suggested that the new attitude toward work that emerged in the sixteenth century was connected with the Lutheran doctrine of the calling. In contrast to the monastic ideals of medieval Catholicism, the Lutheran doctrine called upon man to serve God and test his moral character in the day-to-day life of worldly affairs. Yet though the idea of the calling, so foreign to the Middle Ages and antiquity, gave spiritual and moral meaning to mundane pursuits, the doctrine itself could not explain the intensity and even "anxiety" with which those pursuits were carried out. Thus Weber turned to the creeds of Calvinism, and he found not only an "ascetic" expression of Protestantism but a theology of terror that seemed to account for the activistic itch of modern capitalist man. With Calvinism it is difficult to regard religion as an "opiate" that offers the comfort of an illusion. The teachings of the Calvinists exalted God's infinite wisdom and mercy and assigned man's condition to a state of infinite depravity. Man could never comprehend the mysterious ways of God, an inscrutable Being whose motives of anger and wrath remained impenetrable. Even more horrifying was the Calvinist doctrine of predestination, according to which each individual's state of grace had been irrevocably foreordained at the moment of creation. These doctrines, Weber argued, must have produced in man an "unprecedented inner loneliness." Before God man stood alone; neither the sacraments of the Church nor the prayers of the priest could intercede with God to assist his salvation. But this inner isolation of the individual found an outlet in the doctrine of work. Examining the pastoral writings of the Puritan divines, Weber discovered that Calvinism, despite its priority of faith over works, had in fact encouraged unremitting worldly effort as a means of easing human anxiety. Even though theoretically no outward sign of grace was possible to observe, doubts about one's spiritual condition could easily be interpreted as evidence of imperfect faith; therefore the individual could assume himself one of the chosen and engage in "intense worldly activity" to sustain the necessary self-confidence. Economic striving would not help man attain salvation but it would help him relieve his doubts about his moral standing. Man, in other words, could not be saved by work but he could be saved *to* work as a way of life ordained by God. "You may labor to be rich for God," Weber quotes one Puritan divine, "though not for the flesh and sin." As long as it involved ceaseless effort and absence of indulgence, and one worked for God rather than for oneself, the successful pursuit of gain was the duty of the Christian and the businessman alike.[5]

Weber's thesis posed a serious challenge to Veblen's entire analysis of capitalism. The contrasting perspectives need to be juxtaposed even at the risk of simplification. Where Veblen delved into the technical developments of the handicraft era, Weber stressed spiritual rather than material factors as crucial to the development of modern capitalism. Where Veblen saw capitalism as a continuation of barbarian habits of exploit, Weber regarded the capitalist "ethic" as a heroic moral discipline that represented, at least in its origins, a decisive break with the predatory behavior of men living in the pre-capitalist stages of history. And where Veblen depicted the capitalist as a status-seeking creature of comfort and even a schemer of industrial sabotage, Weber emphasized the primacy of individual conscience and the Protestant admonition against idleness, leisure, and indulgent consumption as sinful and spiritually damnable. Veblen and Weber differed, then, over the origin, nature, and ethical meaning of capitalism. It is misleading to regard these differences as basically political, with Veblen the radical bard of technocracy and Weber the conservative sage of bureaucracy. There is more to it than an ideological analysis would ever reveal.

For one thing, the American and the German social theorist were separated by curiously ironic ethical stances. Veblen, a satirist who could somehow also believe in determinism and scientific objectivity, chastized the capitalist in the most severe moral terms, as though the hapless creature could be held responsible for what he had wrought. Weber, an anguished humanist who deeply valued freedom and regarded the mind of the individual as the ultimate focus of investigation, offered an account of capitalism which depicted the capitalist as unaware of the consequences of his own actions—while trying to create an ethical religiosity he produced an entrepreneurial society. Moreover, Weber came to be recognized as one of the greatest sociologists of the modern age, yet he wrote an interpretation of the rise of capitalism that minimizes the role of social forces and stresses transcendent spiritual concerns; while Veblen, an economist trained in philosophy and steeped in anthropology, wrote an interpretation of capitalism as a sociological phenemenon susceptible to a structural functional analysis of its cultural components. No less ironic are their respective attitudes toward work. Veblen regarded "workmanship" as a healthy natural "instinct" that promotes the ends of life, whereas Weber regarded work as an "irrational" compulsive activity that may very well distract one's attention from the pains of existence.[6] This final irony is compounded by the fact that it reflects two entirely different personalities. Veblen could rhapsodize about work because he avoided the boring tasks of physical labor, appeared uniquely (and marvelously!) lacking in academic ambition, and was in fact, according to contemporaries, actually sluggish and lazy. Weber, in contrast, seemed to regard his scholarly work almost as a matter of personal salvation, as though the "Protestant ethic" sprang darkly from his own German *Angst*. When once asked what his strenuous academic labors meant to him, he replied: "I want to see how much I can endure."[7] Small wonder that Weber felt compelled to give capitalism a moral significance it had not received even in the quite visible hands of Adam Smith.

Although Veblen's interpretation of the evolution of capitalism has gone virtually unnoticed by historians, the Weberian thesis has been the focal point of controversy for three-quarters of a century. Some critical scholars maintain that capitalism is actually older than Protestantism; others question Weber's alleged characterization of Calvinism as a static creed; still others point to areas like Holland and the Rhineland as examples that disprove the causal primacy of the Protestant ethic in the genesis of capitalism.[8] More recently, the political scientists Michael Walzer and Sheldon Wolin have argued that Weber tried to reconcile two incompatible temperaments, the "repressed" Calvinist and the liberated capitalist, and that he tried to translate spiritual anxiety into economic activity, when in reality that troubled condition was sublimated into political reformation as the Puritans attempted nothing less than the total regeneration of man through secular means.[9]

Perhaps the most significant reappraisal, at least from the perspective of Veblen's argument, was that offered by Werner Sombart. In *Luxury and Capitalism* (1913) Sombart revised his earlier thesis about the religious background of the capitalist "spirit," spelled out in the classic work that influenced Weber and Veblen, *Der Moderne Kapitalismus* (1902), and he now argued that capitalism represents the transition of an economy of needs into an economy of acquisition. The impetus for this development came from the *nouveaux riches* whose fortunes burgeoned in France and England from 1600 to 1800. These new social elements altered the moral climate of the age by forming alliances with the impecunious nobility, whose status they aspired to by means of purchasing the expensive appurtenances of social standing. Veblen, who often cited Sombart, could readily agree that the notion of acquiring money as a means of moving out of one's class was foreign to the earlier feudal corporate theory and even to Calvinist theology. He could also agree that capitalism resulted not only from technical developments but from the "contamination" of acquisitive habits that originated among the *arrivistes* who aped the idle rich and then spread rapidly through the rest of society. Both Sombart and Veblen thus minimized the Marxist emphasis on production, for once class lines are weakened, the energies of society are directed toward an ever-increasing horizon of consumption. In this sense capitalist society represents the unleashing of acquisitive tendencies in an economy where wealth tends to be regarded not as a fixed quantity but as a resource capable of infinite expansion. Despite these shared viewpoints, however, Sombart and Veblen disagreed on one essential premise: as an economist Sombart saw capitalist behavior as "modern," as an anthropologist Veblen saw it as archaic. Economic surplus and even affluence were not foreign to some primitive communities, Veblen could have pointed out, while modern capitalist societies, though endowed with abundance, dedicate their economic theories to the proposition of scarcity.[10]

Veblen could acknowledge his indebtedness to Sombart, as did

Weber. But the American social scientist could learn little from Weber's peculiar interpretation of capitalism. The incompatibility of the two writers involves more than the employment of different definitions of capitalism. Their contrapositions can best be illuminated by discussing American history.

Ben Franklin and John Adams

In the field of American history Weber's systematic thesis must be weighed against Veblen's unsystematic impressions. This is only proper, for Weber regarded America as the country where the "spirit of capitalism . . . was present before the capitalist order";[11] and it is of course out of the American context that Veblen formed his attitudes and perceptions. It should be mentioned at once, however, that Weber's sense of the outcome of American capitalism by no means contradicts Veblen's caustic portrait of the same development. Weber acknowledged that while religion provided the vision of the world that shaped capitalist activity, capitalism itself, once established, is sustained by its own momentum as religion ceases to be a movement and becomes an institution. Indeed one finds in a concluding passage of the *Protestant Ethic* a rather Veblenesque observation that American capitalism has been transformed from a fervent ethic of salvation into a frivolous energy of "sport":

> Since asceticism undertook to remodel the world and to work out its ideals in the world, material goods have gained an increasing and finally inexorable power over the lives of men as at no previous period in history. Today the spirit of religious asceticism—whether finally, who knows?—has escaped from the cage. But victorious capitalism, since it rests on mechanical foundations, needs its support no longer. The rosy blush of its laughing heir, the Enlightenment, seems also to be irretrievably fading, and the idea of duty in one's calling prowls about in our lives like the ghost of dead religious beliefs. Where the fulfilment of the calling cannot directly be related to the highest spiritual and cultural values, or when, on the other hand, it need not be felt simply as an economic compulsion, the individual generally abandons the attempt to justify it at all. In the field of its highest development, in the United States, the pursuit of wealth, stripped of its religious and ethical meaning, tends to become associated with purely mundane passions, which often actually give it the character of sport.[12]

Weber's interpretation of late "victorious" capitalism may reflect a "disenchantment with the world" that corresponds to Veblen's melancholy detachment, a disillusionment with modern history that became more complete with Weber's visit to the United States in 1904.[13] But Weber's uncritical treatment of early American history, of New England Puritanism in particular, has not fared well among historical scholars. Although Edmund Morgan finds traces of a "Protestant ethic" among the Puritan ministers who looked to a war for independence from England as a means of arresting a deeply felt moral retrogression among the populace,[14] other colonial scholars find Weber's thesis either entirely unacceptable or at least subject to modification. Intellectual historians have noted that the Puritans were steeped in a "medieval" theology which restricted economic activity and that they aspired to a communal social ethic in which the chief legacy of man's sinful nature was individualism itself.[15] Economic historians find colonial New England closer to a state-administered mercantilist system than to Weber's "ideal type" of capitalism as an enterprise working toward unlimited profit and functioning according to rational calculation.[16] And social historians, following Weber's methodological advice and choosing a colony as a case study in "specification," tend to reinforce the view of intellectual historians by showing that Puritans not only thought but behaved in a manner more concerned with "the inward, spiritual life of the community than with the colony's complex commercial and trading business."[17] Yet whatever their specialty, historians critical of Weber have not been able to offer an alternative explanation of the rise of capitalism in America; nor have they been able to offer an alternative answer to the question that Weber bravely set out to explain in the *Protestant Ethic:* Why does modern western man work so hard?

It seems clear that although New England Puritanism did not altogether kill the "spirit of capitalism," neither did it nourish it. There was, as Bernard Bailyn has noted, a "delicate balance of tensions in the life of the pious merchant," a psychic equilibrium divided between a medieval ethic which condemned profit making and a Protestant "worldly asceticism" that sanctioned it; and the growth of capitalist society could take place only when that balance had collapsed.[18] Granted that capitalism could flourish only with the demise of the Puritan mission, it is still unclear why capitalism did flourish. Historians speak of "economic ambition" and the "temptation" of "worldly success" as undermining the communal ethos of Puritanism.[19] Still, one wants to know what the Puritan, or for that matter man in general, is ambitious about, and why he can be tempted by the idea of "success," itself an ambiguous term that assumes more than it explains. Even if we grant that the erosion of Puritan hegemony liberated man from the burden of guilt and stimulated the profit motive, we still must face the fact that we really know almost nothing about the motive as such. Profit may be pursued for a variety of motives, and a variety of ambitions may be aspired to by a single motive. Did the budding American capitalist conceive wealth as an end in itself, or was material acquisition only a means of gaining something else? Weber sought to resolve this dilemma of the apparent pluralism of intentionality. In an attempt to move beyond explanation to comprehension, for him the highest level of understanding, Weber became deeply interested in the structural motivations behind historical events. He wanted to discover the subjective meaning of the actions of historical figures even though those figures may not have been aware of the motives for their actions. And when he studied the origins of the "spirit" of American capitalism he focused on the ideas and values of Ben Franklin. Weber's encounter with Franklin represents a case of a scholar finding the right man and discovering the wrong meaning.

It is tempting to chide Weber for seizing upon Franklin's *Advice to a Young Tradesman* as "the characteristic document of the capitalist spirit."[20] No doubt Weber took Franklin's smug maxims more seriously than did Franklin himself. And clearly Weber would scarcely be able to reconcile with his idea of Protestant asceticism the Franklin who indulged in sports, theatre, rich cuisine, fine liqueurs, and beautiful young women (in reverse order with the passing of age). The unfortunate thing, however, is that Weber appears to have been unfamiliar with Franklin's *Dissertation on Liberty and Necessity, Pleasure and Pain* (1725). Here Weber might have found ample evidence of the psychologically anxious young man who would take up the life of unrelenting activity to ameliorate the dread of existence. "Uneasiness," wrote Franklin at the age of 19, was "the first Spring and Cause of all Action," and man should work and strive as the means of gaining freedom from the pangs of disquietude. Pleasure and pain are psychologically linked in Franklin's analysis: the attainment of pleasure simply consists in the elimination of pain. "Pleasure is wholly caus'd by *Pain*. . . . The *highest Pleasure* is only Consciousness of Freedom from the *deepest Pain*. . . ." In these somber reflections Weber may have found not only the nervous restlessness of the busy entrepreneur but a historical connection with the primacy of pain mentality that operates as a central premise in the classical economics of Adam Smith and Jeremy Bentham.[21]

Let us now turn Veblen on Franklin. It is fruitful to speculate on such an intellectual encounter, not only to suggest that Veblen would certainly have seen basic attitudes and values in Franklin that Weber had missed, but to expand an interpretation of early American history beyond the political, economic, and religious spheres to include a neglected sociological dimension.

Reading Franklin's essays and theoretical reflections, Veblen may have first thought he had discovered an early intellectual comrade. The Veblen who had been so convinced that private property was not created by labor but seized in conquest could certainly sympathize with Franklin's theory of wealth. "There seems to be but three ways for a nation to acquire wealth," wrote Franklin. "The first was by *war*, as the Romans did, in plundering their conquered neighbors. This is *robbery*. The second by *commerce*, which is generally *cheating*. The third by *agriculture*, the only *honest* way."[22] The third way, alas, would appear to Veblen as a conceit of Physiocratic theory. Veblen wrote on farm life in the early 1920s. Witnessing the transformation of modern American agriculture from the supposed delights of husbandry to the political demands for parity, Veblen dismissed farming along with finance capitalism as another attempt to "get something for nothing." Long before the historian Richard Hofstadter uncovered the bourgeois roots of Populism, Veblen played his own role in exposing the "agrarian myth."[23]

Skeptical of Franklin's economic theories, Veblen would also be ambivalent about Franklin as a model of the scientific intellect. Franklin's inventive mind, his marvelous powers of observation, his experiments with heat and electricity and bifocal lenses, his tinkering with gadgets and his probing into the mechanical laws of natural phenomena would certainly impress Veblen. Indeed Franklin's career could even be regarded as the embodiment of the combination of technological activity and social duty that characterized the new mode of thinking in the handicraft era, which for Veblen represented the historical period when modern capitalism first took root as a mechanical frame of mind. But Franklin's determination to turn all theoretical reflection into practical application would violate Veblen's principle of "idle curiosity," which demands an "irrelevant attention" to the immediate uses of scientific knowledge. Franklin's inability to engage in disinterested inquiry would be, for Veblen, evidence of the "contamination" of the workmanship instinct by a bourgeois culture from which he could not free himself. One can well imagine Veblen dubbing Franklin with the epitaph that Van Wyck Brooks laid on Mark Twain: a potential genius and an actual failure.

Weber had regarded Franklin's Quaker-founded Pennsylvania as imbued with the "capitalist spirit," whereas areas like Virginia were established strictly as a business proposition by "capitalist adventurers" rather than by religious sects. Weber also saw in Franklin's ethical philosophy the "Alpha and Omega" of the doctrine of the calling, "which his strict Calvinist father had drummed into him again and again in his youth," and Weber maintained that these ideas and values in Franklin's writings could be found "in all his works without exception."[24] Weber overstates the case for Franklin as exemplifying the energy of piety in the service of capitalism, and he misses completely what Veblen surely would have discovered—the social as contrasted to the spiritual basis of Franklin's behavior.

In Franklin's most candid work, his *Autobiography* (1791), we find no trace of the religious anxiety that Weber assumed led man to sublimate his inner isolation by means of entering the life of business. Nor do we find in this mature work any trace of the metaphysical doubts that led the young author of the dissertation on pleasure and pain to see happiness and suffering as logically connected. Indeed Franklin's instrumentalist approach to religion, in which the consequences and social uses of a doctrine take precedence over every other criteria of truth, is so bleached of all theological content as to render Franklin closer to a cheery pragmatism than to a morbid Calvinism.

There are remnants of Protestant morality in Franklin's thought and behavior, to be sure. But it is revealing that Franklin applied Weber's notion of "rational calculation" not only in pursuit of work but in pursuit of women. His witty "Advice on Choosing a Mistress" reads like Bentham's notebooks on sampling a brothel, the "felicific calculus" applied to feminine "limbs," "torsoes," and other physiological objects upon which falls the empirical eye. (Two centuries later Hugh Hefner showed his deep sense of history by publishing Franklin's essay in *Playboy*.) Franklin could be excessively rational, but he used reason to give play to the emotions, not to repress them. Weber argued that the Protestant ethic, as exemplified in Franklin, combined the making of more and more money with "the strict avoidance of all spontaneous enjoyment of life, [and] is above all completely devoid of any eudaemonistic, not to say hedonistic, admixture."[25] When Franklin made a list of virtues he enumerated them, in a style that befits a Weberian Protestant, one after the other with mathematical precision. But chastity was number 12 in a list of 13, and Franklin admitted he was better at adhering to that virtue during the day than during the evening.

Not only does Franklin's behavior as a calculating sensualist play havoc with Weber's notion of asceticism, but one finds in Franklin no evidence of the Quaker's refusal to kneel or bow before secular authority on the grounds that veneration belongs to God alone. Franklin can scarcely be regarded as the epitome of the "heroic" bourgeois individualism that Weber discerned in Protestant capitalism. With God pretty much reduced to a vague first cause by deism, Franklin did in fact respect the secular manifestations of authority, particularly in the form of public opinion. He would never offend the sensibilities of others. "I made it a rule to forebear all direct contradiction to the sentiment of others and all positive assertion of my own."[26] Franklin was quite willing to subordinate private conscience to public convenience. Perhaps this behavior illustrates one of the many tensions in the Puritan legacy. Franklin's dedication to the ideal of public service bears some resemblance to the Puritan ideal of stewardship yet at the same time violates Calvinist theology. Secular humanitarianism requires that virtuous acts be judged in light of social utility, while Calvinism judges the spiritual intent of the actor, the condition of the heart, and God's plan for the world. In Franklin's thought individual moral judgment, the Puritan realm of ethical inwardness, is externalized and collectivized and in the process equated with popular consensus.

If Franklin's successful career had its basis neither in simple profit seeking nor in internal spiritual torment, wherein lies the causal explanation of his actions? Fortunately the *Autobiography* offers, even with its irony and self-parody, an extraordinary inner analysis of the drives that inspired Franklin's diverse activities. Now many scholars have noticed the "Puritan" motives in Franklin's behavior, such traits as frugality, industry, and self-scrutiny; while others have discovered that he "was no great lover of toil" and that, while he opposed the import of European luxuries, he desired to multiply the comforts of American life.[27] But the overriding drive in Franklin, so strong as to cause him to add to his list of virtues the principle of "humility" to counteract it, is the distinctly un-Christian idea of pride. "In reality there is perhaps no one of our natural passions so hard to subdue as *pride;* disguise it, struggle with it, beat it down, stifle it, mortify it as much as one pleases, it is still alive and will every now and then peep out and show itself." Despite his protestations, Franklin is actually gratified to be endowed with so strong an ego, and he even goes so far as to thank his Creator for blessing him with such a practical passion. "Most people dislike vanity in others . . . but I give it fair quarter wherever I meet with it, being persuaded that it is often productive of good to the possessor. . . . And therefore . . . it would not be altogether absurd if a man were to thank God for his vanity among the other comforts of life." Such thoughts may have indeed seemed "absurd" to Jonathan Edwards. But the important thing is that Franklin's passion of pride expressed itself not in an arrogant assertion of superiority but in a sensitive instinct for comformity. "In order to secure my credit and character as a tradesman, I took care not only to be in reality industrious and frugal, but to avoid all appearances to the contrary." It was socially important, Franklin tells us, not to be seen carrying books and to avoid going fishing or shooting, "debauched" activities that would indicate he was not hard at work. He desired to be "esteemed an industrious, thriving, young man," and he was willing to manipulate appearances accordingly, realizing the necessity of keeping up a respectable image and adjusting his behavior to the expectations of the community. Thus the secondary traits he ascribed to human motives, avarice and ambition, give way to the primary drive toward status and prestige. To Franklin pride meant self-esteem and the desire for praise and admiration. And feeling this instinct so deep in his bones, he believed it was universally characteristic. "Almost every Man has a strong natural desire of being valued and esteemed by the rest of his Species."[28]

Franklin's reflections on pride and the desire for approbation are hardly unique to Enlightenment thought and indeed represent a main intellectual current in the American Revolution itself. The founding fathers believed strongly in the powerful role that status plays in the social order, and although they recognized that the revolution would change the flow of political power, they assumed that social authority, in the form of deferential leadership, would remain characteristic. Even the doctrine of equality carried no implications of social leveling. In the new republic the revolutionists had no intention of destroying the gradations of social hierarchy, and many regarded these gradations as part of an inevitable social structure that reflected the "natural" distinctions among men.[29]

Although Veblen would find such distinctions a matter of convention, and not of nature, he would also find much to agree with in the thoughts of the founding fathers. Any Veblenian interpretation of early American history must begin with John Adams, the statesman and philosopher who most keenly appreciated the extent to which the "passion for distinction" governed human actions. The austere Adams, who regarded Franklin's escapades in Paris as an example of "continuous discipation [sic],"[30] may also be considered a more authentic embodiment of the Puritan legacy.

In *Discourses on Davila* (1792), a rumination on social psychology that presages *Leisure Class,* Adams argued that "the great leading passion of the soul" is "emulation," which he variously called "the love of praise" and the "desire of the attention, consideration, and congratulation of others." Adams gives emulation a status as fundamental as Freud's sex instinct. "The desire of esteem is as real a want of nature as hunger; and the neglect and contempt of the world as severe a pain as gout and stone." Emulative approbativeness is the hidden wish of everyman "to be observed, considered, esteemed, praised, beloved, and admired by his fellows." It is manifested in several ways. One form is merely the desire for "attention" by any means, the Veblenian attainment of status through even flagrant vices and crimes, the celebrity of bold deeds. "The greater number, however,"

> search for distinction neither by vices nor by virtues; but the means which common sense and every day's experience shows, are most likely to obtain it; by riches, by family records, by play, and other frivolous personal accomplishments. But there are few, and God knows, but few, who aim at something more. They aim at approbation as well as attention; at esteem as well as consideration; and at admiration and gratitude, as well as congratulation. Admiration is, indeed, the complete idea of approbation, congratulation, and wonder, united.[31]

Although Adams and Veblen shared a similar psychology of motivation, they scarcely could agree on the political and ethical implications of man's tendency to emulation and desire for approbation. Veblen believed that both traits had their origins in archaic man's labor activity that generated the compulsion of "invidious comparison," an alienating mentality which in turn sanctioned the advent of private property and class stratification. Adams could never conceive the "instinct of workmanship" as a natural endowment, and thus he looked to emulation as a necessary, civilizing force. "Indolence is the natural character of man," wrote Adams, "to such a degree that nothing but the necessities of hunger, thirst, and other wants equally pressing, can stimulate him to action, until education is introduced in civilized societies, and the strongest motives of ambition to excel in arts, trades, and professions, are established in the minds of all men. Until this emulation is introduced, the lazy savage holds property in too little estimation to give himself trouble for the preservation or acquisition of it. . . ."[32] Adams, however, was closer to Veblen than to Hamilton in his conviction that an aristocracy was not to be trusted since wealth, rather than enlighten and elevate, only corrupts the poor away from the ethic of work and saving, labor and capital, and ushers in a life of leisure and luxury. In Adams we have a post-Calvinist skeptic who realized that the "Protestant ethic" could no longer be relied upon in building political institutions. Unable to believe in man's capacity for self-denial, Adams fully shared the *Federalist* premise that democracy cannot prevent tyranny unless all classes, rich and poor alike, are restrained by external checks.

Adams would also share Veblen's conviction that man is something more than a *homo economicus*. Indeed the idea of *homo sociologicus* permeated much of Enlightenment thought, particularly in documents like Franklin's *Autobiography*, wherein the elusive author deliberately created, in typical eighteenth-century fashion, a multifaceted self. The egotism and vanity of man preoccupied such *philosophes* as Rousseau and Diderot, and, as we have seen, British writers like Locke, Hobbes, Adam Smith and John Millar traced ambition and avarice to man's social nature. In the face of this body of intellectual history, it is surprising that the concepts of "status," "social role," and "reference group"—to use contemporary terminology—seldom appeared in nineteenth-century economic thought and today are accorded little importance by Marxist scholars. The political philosopher C. B. Macpherson, for example, has argued that it was the growth of the market economy that emancipated man from traditional communal bonds and thereby introduced the compulsion of social ambition and "possessive individualism" into modern life. Yet, as Veblen well knew, a sensitivity to reputation and a "propensity" to possess characterized older forms of society. Indeed, as Albert Hirschman has recently shown, the various political arguments that gave rise to capitalist ideology promised nothing more than to "tame" the older aristocratic "passions"—honor, glory, the love of power, etc.—by making them responsive to the more reasonable and harmless province of economic interests.[33] In Veblen's terms, "invidious comparison" underscored the contention for "honor" in the feudal ages; and if "emulation" is the ultimate aim of avarice, as Adam Smith observed, the social need for approbation psychologically ties bourgeois man to his archaic forebears. In a word, pride comes before capitalism.

Rousseau believed that pride separated the innocent savages who were "strangers to vanity" from civilized man, *l'homme sociable* who becomes obsessed with *amour-propre*. Veblen could accept this distinction, although he would disagree with its presumed genesis: Rousseau saw pride arising from man's tendency to compare himself to others *("la fureur de se distinguer")* the moment he forsakes his isolation and comes to depend economically upon others, whereas Veblen saw "invidious distinctions" emerging not from communal effort but from the division of labor and leisure that marks the transition from peaceable savagery to the barbarian stage of exploit and predation. However social theorists might try to explain the "original sin" of pride without recourse to Christian paradox, it was John Adams who sensed so shrewdly its implications for a democratic society.

In his debates with Jefferson over equality and aristocracy, Adams spelled out further the various meanings and political significance of emulation. Jefferson had agreed with Adams that an aristocracy could be founded, even in America, on the basis of Adams' definition of an aristocrat as a person who has the ability to "command or influence two votes, one besides his own." But Jefferson argued that for an aristocracy to be "natural" the aristocrat's power must derive from either talents or virtue. To this Enlightenment fantasy Adams simply replied that "Education, Wealth, Strength, Beauty, Stature, Birth, Marriage, graceful Attributes and Motions, Gait, Air, Complexion, Physiognomy" were also talents, and some more "natural" than Jefferson's regard for conventional virtue. The key to Adams' concept of aristocracy was "influence," and some people possessed it far more than others regardless of whether they morally or intellectually deserved it.[34]

It is their common interest in the role of influence that makes a comparison between Adams and Veblen so fruitful. Both sensed that in either a republic or a democratic society the phenomenon of power would yield to the phenomenon of influence, the ability to persuade by the tendency of emulation. Adams was convinced that the ability to win the respect of others and thereby influence their attitudes was due to a variety of earned qualities and even unearned genetic accidents or environmental fortunes among men. He was also convinced that emulation stimulated men to aspire to positions of status, for the individual is driven by a basic need to feel himself, to show himself, and to be recognized as, if not superior to others, at least equal to others. But in Adams' era, in contrast to Veblen's, one could presume that this desire for social power would be realized by certain qualities, attributes, or talents possessed by the individual himself. By mid-nineteenth century, the era of Marx and socialism, the characteristics that Adams had listed seemed to be reduced to a single criterion as the United States passed from a quasi-aristocratic republic to a mass democracy. Some men could still enjoy the status of an aristocrat as defined by Adams; now, however, the commanding power lay solely in money, not as an end in itself, but as an instrument of emulation, a means by which one can impose his will through the act of purchase and achieve status by means of economics. Money can buy what Jefferson once hoped that only virtue and talent could command. Both Adams and Jefferson died two decades before Marx wrote his *Economic and Philosophical Manuscripts,* but one can imagine them sharing Marx's protest against the corrupting impact of money on social life:

> That which *money* can create for me, that for which I can pay (i.e., what money can buy)—that *I*, the possessor of the money, am. The extent of the power of money is the extent of my power. The properties of money are the properties and essential powers of me—its possessor. Thus what I *am* and what I *am capable of* is in no way determined by my individuality. I am ugly, but I can buy the *most beautiful* woman. Therefore I am not *ugly*, for the effect of *ugliness*, its power of repulsion, is destroyed by money. I—according to my individual nature—am lame, but money gives me twenty legs, therefore I am not lame. I am a wicked, dishonest, unscrupulous, stupid man; but people honor money, and therefore also its possessor. Money is the highest good, therefore its possessor is good. Besides, money saves me the trouble of being dishonest; therefore I am presumed to be honest. I am stupid, but money is the real mind of all things; how can its possessor lack mind?[35]

People honor money, and therefore its possessor. Marx believed that such attitudes of "false consciousness" will yield to the inexorable power of history. Veblen saw the worship of money as a form of social alienation deeply rooted in the emulative nature of man, a phenomenon that had its origins in primitive man's respect for power and success. Tocqueville discerned another dimension in the phenomenon, and his reflections on Jacksonian America suggest why the "spirit" of capitalism died before it was born.

Tocqueville: Wealth and Envy in Jacksonian America

Daniel Bell, in discussing the role that Veblen had assigned to the engineers, suggests that Veblen should be ranked with "elitist" theoreticians like Saint-Simon, technocrats who would give power only to those directly connected with the production of goods.[36] This judgment needs to be qualified. If Veblen's prescriptions imply a radical elitism, they also suggest a liberal and perhaps even a conservative egalitarianism. For the more one examines Veblen's distinction between industrial and pecuniary employments, the more one is drawn back into the great social conflicts of Jacksonian America. In America, President Jackson announced in his ringing bank veto message, the "real people," those engaged in "the sober pursuit of honest industry," are the true conservatives. Jackson specified the planters and farmers, mechanics and laborers as "the bone and sinew of the country," the "common men" who are at the mercy of the "money power."[37] As Jacksonian ideology indicates, Veblen's own complaint against wealth without work had roots deep in the American value system. That value basis was itself threatened early in the nineteenth century, when America entered the era of small-scale manufacturing and banking after the War of 1812, and then proceeded to full-scale industrialization after the Civil War. The political alignments reflect the fate of the moral philosophy of labor in America. The Jeffersonian ideology of workmanship and husbandry found a platform first in the Republican Party and then in Jacksonian Democracy, both of which were either absorbed into or ultimately defeated by the Whig party and commercial capitalism in the election of 1840. With the triumph of Whiggery, Lockeanism became the central ideology of American political life.[38] And Locke, as we noted, made money the touchstone of value, the vehicle that could preserve the worth of commodities even at the cost of the value of labor.

The argument of *The Protestant Ethic* rests on the assumption that a wholly new personality, inspired by the "methodological character of worldly ascesticism," forged the rise of capitalism as an unintended consequence of religious striving for salvation.[39] This assumption only deepens the paradox. For in the money economy of capitalism, as Georg Simmel pointed out in *Philosophie des Geldes*, and as Weber himself implicitly recognized, there is no longer any direct relationship between the moral personality of those who earn money and those who merely come to possess it, between the ethic of work and the status of wealth.[40] It could be said that Weber was attempting to explain the formation of capitalism, and not its function, and that he would agree with Veblen (and Simmel) that after capitalism comes into existence it is the social milieu, and not religion, that governs the economic behavior of individuals. Yet this explanation cannot apply to America since, as we have seen, capitalism emerged only after the collapse of Puritanism. What needs to be explained is not so much the rise of the capitalist "spirit" but the hegemony of capitalist society, the permeation of a whole culture with the values of opportunity and enterprise. Our discussion must move forward from Puritanism, Franklin, and Adams to the buoyant era of Jacksonian democracy.

That "honored" status of money which Marx saw as the fraudulent characteristic of nineteenth-century bourgeois society in general was for Tocqueville what it became for Veblen—the frantic characteristic of American society in particular. Disturbed by his own observations, Tocqueville asked the same question of Jacksonian man that Weber had asked of capitalist man: "Why the Americans Are So Restless in the Midst of Their Prosperity" is the title of one of Tocqueville's chapters in *Democracy in America*. Tocqueville and a host of other European travelers in the United States saw Americans as obsessed by a feverish pursuit of wealth, "the shortest cut to happiness." But the pursuit took its price in psychic turmoil. "In no other country are the faces of the people furrowed with harder lines of care," wrote a British traveler; "work and worry eat out the hearts of the people." Tocqueville did not perceive this "secret disquietude" arising from the people's inner loneliness and spiritual anxiety that Weber regarded as the restless drive of the capitalist personality. On the contrary, Tocqueville located the source of acquisitive hunger in the proposition of equality itself, a proposition of mass society which, as Durkheim would also stress a half-century later, renders human desires infinite and sets man off on a joyless quest for happiness. But Americans, unlike the French, Tocqueville notes in a curious anticipation of Durkheim's thesis, do not commit "suicide" as a result of the dissatisfaction that is bound to follow the mere physical gratification of consumption. They continue to chase after the dream of social equality through economic means, innocent of the fact that "even if they unhappily attained that absolute and complete equality of position, the inequality of minds would still remain which, coming directly from God, will forever escape the laws of man." Tocqueville's observations are as poignant as they are prophetic:

> Among democratic nations, men easily attain a certain equality of condition, but they can never attain as much as they desire. It perpetually retires from before them, yet without hiding itself from their sight, and in retiring draws them on. At every moment they think they are about to grasp it; it escapes at every moment from their hold. They are near enough to see its charms, but too far off to enjoy them; and before they have fully tasted its delights, they die.[41]

The illusions of equality were, for Tocqueville, the direct result of America's social structure. A fluid, amorphous society creates competition for achievement and, just as important, for the symbols of social position and economic success. Paradoxically, the openness of the social order, rather than nourish diversity and individuality, maximizes competition among the people and thereby, as Thoreau and the Transcendentalists well knew, intensifies the uncertainties of status and the pressures of conformity. Tocqueville discerned the same inner loneliness of the individual in capitalist society as did Weber, but the condition signified a social rather than a spiritual isolation:

> When the inhabitant of a democratic country compares himself individually with all those about him, he feels with pride that he is the equal of any one of them; but when he comes to survey the totality of his fellows and to place himself in contrast with so huge a body, he is instantly overwhelmed by the sense of his own insignificance and weakness. The same equality that renders him independent of each of his fellow citizens, taken severally, exposes him alone and unprotected by the influence of the greater number. The public, therefore, among a democratic people, has a singular power, which aristocratic nations cannot conceive; for it does not persuade others to its

benefits, but it imposes them and makes them permeate the thinking of everyone by a sort of enormous pressure of the mind of all upon the individual intelligence.[42]

Tocqueville's argument that society shapes and moulds the individual leaves unanswered what forces shape society itself. It is understandable that he would fail to find an aristocracy functioning in America the way it had in the old world. Tocqueville was, after all, writing about America and the promises of freedom while thinking about France and the tyrannies of the *ancien regime*.[43] If we regard aristocracy in Adams' and Veblen's sense of the term, as the ability to command attention and exercise influence, we can observe a strong aristocratic element functioning in the United States as a plutocracy long before the rise of full-scale industrial capitalism.[44] Social historians are presently discovering the enormous concentrations of wealth in the hands of a nucleus of families, cultural elites which enjoyed social hegemony in Jacksonian America, and one scholar has even interpreted the institution of slavery as a form of "conspicuous consumption."[45] These elites in the "age of the common man" indulged in a life-style of semi-leisure, extravagant town houses, fashionable operas and cotillions, well-dressed servants and well-shined carriages, "country quarters," personal libraries, the lavish hospitality of a *fête champêtre*, and other extravagant expenditures that one wealthy Philadelphian described as the "millionairism of money aristocracy."[46] Numerous contemporary social critics, some as politically diverse as James Fenimore Cooper and Orestes Brownson, complained of the deleterious influence that America's new "aristocracy" exercised, and moral reformers wrote of the perils of "Wealth and Envy."[47] William Gouge, an editor, political economist, and leading theoretician of the Jacksonian Democrats, described the lust for money in terms that Adams and Veblen could understand:

> With some men, the love of wealth seems to be a blind passion. The magpie, in hiding silver spoons in its nest, appears to act with as much reflection as they do, in piling money-bag on money-bag. They have no object in view beyond accumulation. But with most men, the desire for great wealth appears subordinate to the love of great power and distinction. This is the end, that the means. They love fine houses, splendid equipages, and large possessions, less for any physical gratification they impart, than for the distinction they confer, and the power they bestow. It is with some, as much an object of ambition to be ranked with the richest men, as it is with others to be ranked with the greatest warriors, poets, or philosophers.[48]

Neither Weber, Tocqueville, nor Veblen would find this passage difficult to interpret. For these three sociologists shared a common insight that separates them from Marx and from the whole socialist tradition. All three saw bourgeois man as possessed by an unquiet spirit or temperament; and each recognized that the dynamism of capitalism had penetrated almost the whole of society, whose members are driven by acquisitive dreams and arrested by possessive fears. Weber attributed this development to the inner uncertainties of religious salvation, Tocqueville to the phantom creed of equality. Veblen, however, saw man's restlessness as deriving from the phenomenon of status itself. It is necessary to stress this point, for present-day Marxist scholars argue that the behavior of men under capitalism is due to a competitive "ethic" that was historically conditioned by the fact of economic scarcity in pre-industrial society. With the advent of abundance man need no longer be a nervous striver in an atomized social order. Even Freudianism, writes Herbert Marcuse, can now be reinterpreted in affluent America as the theoretical basis for the liberation of man from all repressions and the realization, at last, for the hitherto buried "pleasure principle."[49] The problem here is that for Weber, Tocqueville, and Veblen (and for Sombart, Durkheim, and Simmel) economic progress perpetuates the problem of alienation instead of solving it. Weber denies that man can find religious salvation through the secular means of economics (or politics); Tocqueville observes that the desire for equality becomes more intense in proportion as equality is more complete; and Veblen stresses that aspiration to status, honor, and deference is insatiable and cannot be realized since emulation itself is inherently self-contradictory.[50] The human craving for wealth as a sign of "invidious distinction" can never be satisfied; since it is not for any particular sum of goods, but always for *more* of the conspicuous possessions than others have, the craving is as ceaseless and as compulsive as Weber's work ethic:

> In the nature of the case, the desire for wealth can scarcely be satiated in any individual instance, and evidently a satiation of the average or general desire for wealth is out of the question. However widely, or equally, or 'fairly,' it may be distributed, no general increase of the community's wealth can make any approach to satiating this need, the ground of which is the desire for everyone to excell everyone else in the accumulation of goods. If, as is sometimes assumed, the incentive to accumulation were the want of subsistence or of physical comfort, then the aggregate economic wants of a community might conceivably be satisfied at some point in the advance of industrial efficiency; but since the struggle is substantially a race for reputability on the basis of an invidious comparison, no approach to a definitive attainment is possible.[51]

In one sense Veblen's views of capitalism and those of Weber are compatible and mutually illuminating. Both thinkers perceived bourgeois man as driven by vaguely understood, if not totally unconscious, motives: Veblen's capitalists attempt to find status security through pecuniary striving, Weber's capitalists seek spiritual reassurance through unrelenting labor. The connection between capitalism as the reflection of inner torment and capitalism as the reification of social *Angst* did not go unnoticed among a few sagacious nineteenth-century American intellectuals: Brownson, George Ripley, Emerson, Thoreau, William Ellery Channing, the favorite author of Weber's pious mother, and Melville, who treated commercial enterprise itself as a parable of Christian self-alienation. "Every age," wrote Emerson, "like every human body has its own distemper. . . . Our forefathers walked in the world and went to their graves, tormented with the fear of Sin, and the Terror of the Day of Judgment. These terrors have lost their force, and our torment is unbelief, the uncertainty as to what to do."[52] Transcendentalist intellectuals broke with their Unitarian religious heritage because it left man with a restless spiritual hunger that could be fulfilled only through economic and social institutions. They perceived what would remain implicit in Weber's analysis: Christianity carried in the doctrine of the calling the seeds of its own destruction. In the very act of realizing this doctrine, capitalism undermined the theology on which it had been founded. The calling turned man away from the majesty of Providence to the conceit of pride, and pride expressed itself in a desire for approbation that issued in a servility to mass opinion and to the values of the market place—hence Thoreau's repudiation of the western work ethic and his conversion to the contemplative "wisdom" of eastern philosophy. As men felt more and more that they must prove themselves, not privately in the eyes of God, but socially in the eyes of Tocqueville's tyrannical public, the "spirit of capitalism" killed the very substance of Protestantism. Nietzsche, an admirer of Emerson, arrived at the same conclusion about the "death" of God at the hands of man. The Transcendentalist indictment of the "corpse-cold" institution of religion in America raises a question that may be put to Weber's thesis: if capitalism is successful, is Christianity possible?

Religion, Science, and Rationalization

Thorstein Veblen posed a similar question in an important essay written in 1910. That question, involving Veblen's understanding of the true nature of Christianity, and also his attitude toward the role of science in the reformation of society, are the central issues which radically separate him from Max Weber. These two issues, religion and science, suggest why Weber's realism can be brightened by Veblen's idealism and why, conversely, Veblen's technological daydreams must be tempered by Weber's bureaucratic nightmares.

Veblen's essay, "Christian Morals and the Competitive System," can be read as an answer to Weber's thesis on Protestantism. Although Veblen characteristically fails to mention Weber, he does refer in general terms to the widespread impression that "Christian morality" and "pecuniary competition" are "intimately involved in the occidental scheme of life."[53] Veblen begins by asking: "Do they further and fortify one another? Do they work together without mutual help or hindrance? Or do they mutually inhibit and defeat each other?" The questions are crucial, Veblen states, since the popular impression is that Christianity and capitalism are so closely linked that modern civilization could not survive if one or the other of these institutions disappeared.

Examining the historical foundations of Christianity, Veblen finds that original, non-institutional Christianity was based on two principles: brotherly love in the form of mutual service, and humility in the form of non-resistance. The first principle actually antedates Christianity and represents the "savage spiritual heritage" that "springs eternal" throughout history. As evidence Veblen points to the amazing receptivity to the Christian idea of love during the Roman era, a response to a "revolutionary moral principle" that can only indicate that the converts must have been predisposed to such a "spiritual attitude" by the habits of their own daily life and conduct. The second principle, non-resistance, is not so firmly rooted among free peoples. It arose among people subject to Roman rule who had no basic rights with which to defend themselves against the "sway of the Caesars." The lower classes, experiencing "Roman devastation and punishment-at-large," lost all class distinctions and differential rights and were left "naked and unashamed and free to follow the promptings of hereditary savage human nature which makes for fellowship and Christian charity." The Roman masses were reduced to a "passably homogeneous state of subjection, in which one class or individual had little to gain at the cost of another, and in which, also, each and all palpably needed the succor of all the rest." Thus non-resistance emerged to reinforce the more basic traits of mutuality and brotherhood. It is notable, Veblen pointed out, that Christianity tends to spread in proportion to the experience of defeat and subjugation, and hence it is in its origins seldom a doctrine of the "master classes."

The institution of capitalism, however, is of an entirely different heritage. Modern capitalism had its doctrinal origins in the seventeenth-century principle of natural rights, which in turn represents the culmination of the ideas of egotism, self-interest, and individualism that gradually assumed dominance during and after the transition from medieval to modern times. Although of relatively recent origin, capitalism as a pecuniary scheme of life, that is, capitalist society, developed slowly. In the handicraft era, the right of ownership could support both equality and humanity since the mode of production was so elemental that the creative relation of the worker's efforts to the community could be appreciated by everyone. But under modern corporate organization and machine technology, there is no longer such a "close and visible touch between the workman and his product, as would persuade men that the product belongs to him by force of an extension of his personality." The alienation of man from the fruit of his labor also signals the divorce of modern acquisitive business from the canons of Christian serviceability. Thus Christian morals and business principles are "institutional by-products" of two different cultural situations, and they are incompatible in so far as they reflect two distinct habits of mind. The principles of Christianity inculcate humility, brotherly love, and mutual succor, those of capitalism inculcate self-assertion, competition, emulation, and "a valuation of men, things, and events in pecuniary terms."

Veblen believed, or perhaps desperately hoped, that the "instincts" of natural Christianity would prevail over the institutions of capitalism. In the past a Christian revulsion against materialism expressed itself in abnegation and renunciation. Yet modern Christianity may reassert its ancient traits of mutual aid and brotherhood and come to serve as a criterion against which business ethics will be exposed in all their spiritual emptiness. The Christian, as well as the scientist, is intellectually equipped to see that there is "little in the current situation to keep the natural right of pecuniary discretion in touch with the impulsive bias of brotherly love, and there is in the spiritual discipline of this situation much that makes for an effectual discrepancy between the two." Reinterpreted in the light of ancient truths, Christianity can become the death-conscience of modern capitalism. "Particularly is this true," added Veblen as though he were asking Weber to update his thesis, "since business has taken on the character of an impersonal, dispassionate, not to say graceless, investment for profit."[54]

Veblen had simply redefined Christianity to distinguish its early principles from its modern practices, its primitive communal ethos from its present competitive ethic. Whatever might have been the response of Weber, who knew more about world religions than Veblen or any contemporary social theorist cared to learn, our response must be one of astonishment. "Christian Morals and the Competitive System" is Veblen's most desperate and inconsistent essay. Not only does his treatment of Christianity contradict his earlier argument that competitive exploit develops with the passing of polytheistic and matriarchal forms of worship, but Veblen never makes it clear whether the masses of Roman converts were communalists because they were Christian or whether they were Christian because they were communalists. However he approached the matter, he would have to concede that an "animistic" inspired principle of love and brotherhood is preferable to a technologically inspired principle of heartless calculation that would imbue the "spirit of capitalism." Veblen's sudden discovery of the value of primitive Christianity as a weapon with which to attack modern Protestant morality raises another embarrassing problem: how to reconcile the "instinct of workmanship" with the Judeo-Christian tradition of regarding labor as a punishment imposed on humanity by God because of man's original sin?

We thus come to what is, from the Weberian point of view, the most serious weakness in Veblen's solution to the "problem" of capitalism. Veblen may have vaguely hoped for a revitalization of the ideals of primitive Christianity, but his own "faith" rested solidly on the evolution of empirical progress. It will be recalled that Veblen assumed that science, technology, and the "machine process" would offer man a new, objective mode of apprehension that would eliminate anthropomorphic mental tendencies and eventually extirpate the world of animism. This assumption rested on the hope that the industrial method of knowledge, based on the canons of workmanship, efficiency, and productivity, would come to absorb the business habit of mind based on pecuniary exploit. The cruel irony, however, is that the opposite seems to have occurred. For modern capitalism itself developed out of a system of rationally calculated, routinized production methods that had as its aim not only profit but scientific precision. The very attributes that Veblen had assigned to the engineers came to characterize the mentality of the managerialists of capitalism as well. Veblen seemed to realize this when he would refer to the "impersonal, dispassionate" nature of modern business. Other contemporaries celebrated what Veblen only conceded. Walter Lippmann, for example, believed that the liberal Progressives could look to the new managerialists since the leadership of industry had passed to "the hands of men interested in production as a creative art instead of as brute exploitation." "That subtle fact," wrote Lippmann in 1913, "the change of business motives, the demonstration that business can be conducted as medicine is—may civilize the whole class conflict."[55]

Veblen, along with Lippmann, Herbert Croly, Lincoln Steffens and a number of other liberal writers who welcomed various forms of managerial rule, failed to comprehend what Weber called the phenomenon of "rationalization." There is no evidence in Veblen's writings that he foresaw that increasing scientific rationality of the techniques of production would be extended to absorb almost all phases of life. In Weber's writings, on the other hand, rationalization is perceived as the prevalent form of control in modern industrial society. Bureaucracy, the flower of scientific management ("Taylorism"), brings into existence a new form of power: domination by administration. Moreover, "formal rationality" orients human action to abstract, systematized rules and norms, to an impersonal order in which calculations can be made "without regard for persons." The capitalist's orientation to the impersonal market, the bureaucrat's to impersonal rules, and even the scientist's to impersonal data are all aspects of rationalization that have left the world "disenchanted," rid of every vestige of animism, as Veblen had wished, but also rid of the groundsprings of human action and the values of mind that are beyond scientific calculation.[56] It is, Weber insists, the scientific enterprise of elevating means to the status of ends that has brought about the devaluation of man, certainly the most grotesque of the unintended, irrational consequences of rationalization.

Weber's comprehension of the meaning of rationalization suggests the weakness of Veblen's analysis of modern capitalism. Where Veblen saw technology as liberating man from the domination of leisure-class values, Weber saw technology as a new institutionalized form of domination that would reduce the scope of freedom; and where Veblen believed that science would enable man to apprehend social phenomena more objectively, Weber saw that science, by regarding man as an extension of nature, gave sanction to those in power to treat man as nature. Weber opposed the Bolshevik Revolution, and he clearly would have agreed with D. H. Lawrence's remark that all modern society is "a steady sort of Bolshevism; just killing the human thing and worshipping the mechanical thing."[57] Veblen enthusiastically supported Bolshevism, as we shall see; yet he would have to confront Weber before he could free Lenin from the "iron cage" of bureaucracy.

Weber's brilliant insights into the many implications of rationalization also suggest why Veblen's determination to separate industry and business must prove futile. Both the "habits" of productive technique and those of commercial enterprise had become so functionally assimilated by culture and science that the "machine process" could not undo what the machine itself had joined together. Veblen's dilemma reminds one of the indictment that Allen Tate and the conservative "Southern Agrarians" levelled at the communists in the 1930s: they wanted capitalism without the capitalists. For Veblen's dream of a society run solely by engineers comes near to the predicament of communist leaders today who want to borrow the rational techniques of capitalism. Those techniques are an outcome of the calculating, quantitative bias of modern rationalism that is itself an expression of the "spirit" of capitalism that Veblen wanted to see purged from industrial society.

Veblen's faith in the engineering profession to carry out the role of extirpation can only be regarded as desperately fanciful as Marx's faith in the proletariat to fulfill its historical mission of class conscious revolution. If the proletariat could not rise to this challenge, as Lenin recognized, the engineers have indeed risen as a leading profession only to become one of the most conservative political forces in upper middle-class American life. The integration of the engineering profession into the fabric of American society could be interpreted by Weber as a case study in rationalization. Absorbed by bureaucratic procedure, engineers cannot lead, innovate, strike out in bold new directions; enamoured of the equation of scientific truth with objectivity, they cannot question the rationalized world but merely accept it as it appears. Only the "charisma" of the great man can challenge the routinization of the industrial processes. Veblen's dilemma goes even deeper than Weber's theory of bureaucratic domination. The idea of the engineer as a leader is a fundamental misconception. Just because technology can do everything, to be an engineer and nothing but an engineer means, as Ortega y Gasset has noted, "to be potentially everything and actually nothing."[58] Science cannot define the purpose of existence, and the engineer cannot help man realize the meaning and value of life. Far from questioning or criticizing the values of his society, the engineer endeavors to preserve them or adjust to them. He may set into motion orderly mechanisms of change, but he is bounded by the goals of the institution whose tasks he performs. It may even be said—and Veblen would appreciate the irony—that the engineers have become the new aristocrats, specialists with titles, diplomas, esoteric language and knowledge symbols beyond the comprehension and possibly the control of the masses. "The engineer," wrote Veblen in 1923, "is something new under the sun."[59] Veblen did not have in mind a new elite that would continue the hegemonic function of the captains of industry.

Yet the final irony is even more bitter. In America the first professionally trained engineer to reach the pinnacle of political power was Herbert Hoover, the complete embodiment of both the capitalist values of individualism and opportunity, and the technician's values of efficiency and productivity. As the last great spokesman for the Protestant ethic,* Hoover symbolized both Weber's "spirit of capitalism" and Veblen's "instinct of workmanship." Hoover was sworn into office as President of the United States on March 4, 1929; Veblen died on August 3, 1929.

* While President Jimmy Carter's commitment to the welfare state bears little resemblance to Hoover's philosophy of individualism, the present Chief Executive displays no difficulty in combining what for Veblen should be two incompatible mentalities: rigorous training in nuclear engineering and a devout belief in Protestant theology.

Part Three . . .

INSIDE THE WHALE

8 . . . The Barbarian Status of Women

In many contemporary feminist studies the name Thorstein Veblen receives hardly more than a passing mention or citation. One finds no sustained analysis of his books, essays, and treatises (nine volumes in all). Even in Alice S. Rossi's otherwise excellent and comprehensive anthology, *The Feminist Papers: From Adams to de Beauvoir*, Veblen is conspicuous by his absence. This neglect is regrettable, for there was a time when Veblen came to be regarded as the major cultural critic of the world of masculine domination, the thorn in the side of chauvinism as well as capitalism. To the Greenwich Village left he emerged as a sardonic castigator of class distinctions and macho pretensions alike. To other generations Veblen was appreciated more as a ponderous scholar than as a mordant satirist. Likening Veblen to Ibsen, the German emigré T. W. Adorno praised the American economist as "one of the last significant philosophers who dares to take the woman question seriously."[1]

This chapter continues our analysis of Veblen from the perspective of comparative social theory, contrasting his views with those of other commentators on the women question, including the liberal John Stuart Mill, the Marxist Friedrich Engels, the feminist Charlotte Perkins Gilman, and the conservative H. L. Mencken, the nemesis of both Veblen and women's liberation. We need to consider other points of view, not only because such an exercise better enables us to understand that a given historical and social phenomenon can be interpreted in more ways than one, but also because we are then in a better position to understand the unique strengths as well as the peculiar deficiencies in Veblen's standpoint and mode of analysis. Veblen came closer, I am convinced, than most other theorists in grasping the contemporary significance of the historical origins of women's oppressed status in modern society. As in the case of alienation and reification, however, he uncovered a problem he could explain better than he could resolve.

John Stuart Mill and Veblen: Liberalism and Naturalism

Veblen's grasp of the problem of women's oppression can perhaps best be appreciated by contrasting it with John Stuart Mill's approach to the same question. In *The Subjection of Women* (1869), Mill argued that the goal of feminine equality remained the unfinished political commitment of liberalism itself, a commitment that could be fulfilled when women are granted the political rights that have been available to men in the progress of history. Although he recognized that the struggle for women's emancipation would be long and arduous, Mill remained convinced that he could demonstrate that contemporary attitudes about women's "natural" inferior status had not been founded historically on willful consent or on any social ideas conducive to the benefit of humanity or the good of society. Conceding that established folkways were mired in ancient prejudices, he accepted the challenge of changing popular sentiment by means of exposing its fallacious premises and base origins. "I consent," wrote Mill in reference to common attitudes about women, "that established custom, and the general feeling, should be deemed conclusive against me, unless that custom and feeling from age to age can be shown to have owed their existence to other causes than their soundness, and to have derived their power from the worse rather than the better parts of human nature."[2]

Bravely Mill was waging an uphill battle against "untaught" feelings and customs, the Burkean "prejudices" that give society its organic cohesion and historical stability. Yet it remains questionable whether Mill succeeded in what he set out to do—demonstrate the "unsound" historical causes of women's status in contemporary society. His argument, though cogently reasoned and lucidly expressed, was limited to showing how far history had left women behind as men advanced from a society of prescription and inherited status to the modern society of free contract and open competition. But Mill was unconcerned about the origins of women's oppression in early primitive society, and he was too skeptical of the idea that there may be "natural" differences between the sexes to see that the issue of equality could indeed be irrelevant to the larger issue of women's political freedom and personal autonomy. Similarly, Mill questioned the institution of marriage on the grounds of legal equity, showing how it functions to the disadvantage of women in respect to property, servitude, and even physical safety. But the origins of that institution beyond its contractual formulation is a subject that Mill did not feel it necessary to explore. In effect, Mill was attempting to bring up to date all the institutions that touched on women's existence, and to do so he drew moral distinctions between traditional and modern society that made sexual equality less an empirical fact than a normative ideal. As an ethical argument, Mill's treatise is a ringing statement; as an analytical explanation of the reasons for women's subjected status, it is a rhetorical document that inspires more than it illuminates. Mill seemed to feel that women were suffering from something like historical backwardness, victims of progress whose unkind fate must be redressed before the conscience can rest. This formulation confuses the answer with the question. Granted that women of the last century had been denied political rights, we must still ask why it is that women continue to find themselves oppressed in those societies where they have won the very rights that Mill had advocated, namely suffrage and liberalized divorce laws. It may be that modern democratic society has eliminated the obvious but perpetuated the more subtle reasons for women's subjected status throughout the ages. Perhaps we have come so far only to know so little about those reasons.

To Thorstein Veblen, the naturalist who tried to explain "higher" phenomena by "lower" ones, the reason for women's oppression stemmed less from the absence of political rights than from the presence of social rituals. Veblen's preoccupation with the survival of archaic traits in the modern age afforded him a unique perspective on the woman question of the late nineteenth century. Where Mill saw women's emancipation almost as an article of political faith, the inevitable result of democratic progress and social change, Veblen saw women's continued oppression as an anthropological artifact, a residue that reflected the persistence of custom and the continuity of habit. Veblen elaborated his argument in "The Barbarian Status of Women," published in the *American Journal of Sociology* in 1899, 30 years after the appearance of Mill's *The Subjection of Women*. This article followed a previous one in the same journal on "The Beginnings of Ownership." Another essay, on "The Economic Theory of Woman's Dress," appeared five years earlier in the *Popular Science Monthly*.[3] These analytical discussions comprised the scholarly material that Veblen drew upon, and condensed and livened with flashes of wit and satire, for his first and most popular book, *The Theory of the Leisure Class*.

A Darwinist of science, Veblen was also an ironist of progress, a unique combination that enabled him to see in human evolution the descent of women as well as the ascent of man. In the initial stage of history, the era of "peaceable savagery," there exists neither a well-defined division of labor nor a division among sexes along occupational lines. But when the use of tools and the technical command of material forces reach a certain degree of efficiency, distinctions between sexes gradually develop according to respective economic activities. Two types of employment emerge: the honorific, which involves masculine strength; and the humiliating, which calls for feminine diligence. An appreciable advance in the use of tools must precede the differentiation of employments, for tools provide the weapons with which man can contend with ferocious beasts. Tools also supply food sufficient to support more dense populations which are then able to make hostile contact with one another in a new life of warlike prowess and plunder based on the advent of surplus. Moreover, in the era of savagery the work of getting a livelihood is too exacting to allow for any portion of the community to be exempt from vulgar labor. Tools free life from the demands of subsistence economics and make possible the existence of a well-defined leisure class. Henceforth the standards of merit rest on an "invidious distinction" between those who are capable of fighting and those who are not. To men goes the honor of defending the tribe, conquering the enemy, and plundering his possession—the activities of predation and exploit. To women falls the onus of engaging in the "uneventful everyday work" of the primitive community—the activities of industry and drudgery. Women may contribute to the welfare of the community by their productive efforts, but it is the men who, as warriors and hunters, produce nothing and enjoy everything. When the predatory scheme of life becomes settled upon tribal groups or hordes by long habituation, the ostracism of womanly occupations is complete:

> One of the early consequences of this depreciation of infirmity is a tabu on women and women's employments. In the apprehension of the archaic, animistic barbarian, infirmity is infectious. The infection may work its mischievous effect both by sympathetic influence and by transfusion. Therefore it is well for the able-bodied man who is mindful of his virility to shun all undue contact and conversation with the weaker sex and to avoid all contamination with the employments that are characteristic of the sex. Even the habitual food of women should not be eaten by men, lest their force be thereby impaired. The injunction against womanly employments and foods and against intercourse with women applies with especial rigor during the season of preparation for any work of manly exploit, such as a great hunt or warlike raid, or induction into some manly dignity or society or mystery. Illustrations of this seasonal tabu abound in the early history of all peoples that have had a warlike or barbarian past. The women, their occupations, their food and clothing, their habitual place in the house or village, and in extreme cases even their speech, become ceremonially unclean to the men. This imputation of ceremonial uncleaninless on the ground of their infirmity has lasted on in the later culture as a sense of the unworthiness or Levitical inadequacy of women; so that even now we feel the impropriety of women taking rank with men, or representing the community in any relation that calls for dignity and ritual competency; as, for instance, in priestly or diplomatic offices, or even in representative civil offices, and likewise, and for like reason, in such offices of domestic and body servants as are of a seriously ceremonial character—footmen, butlers, etc.[1]

The stigma of womanly employments is connected with the institution of ownership itself. As we saw, Veblen traced the origins of property to the capture of persons, especially non-combatant women who come to be sought not only for their labor but prized also as "trophies" symbolizing the laurels of masculine prowess. The relationship of male domination to female subordination results from man's "use and abuse over an object" that belongs neither to the community nor organically to the "quasi personal fringe" of the capturer. The earliest form of possession is an "ownership of the women by the able-bodied men of the community." Moreover, the habit of appropriating captured women hardens into a custom which gives rise to a "conveniently recognized marriage relation" that receives the sanction of the community. The "coercive ownership-marriage" system is the basis of private property and the patriarchal family. The growing predilection for mastery and coercion as a manly trait, together with the "growing moral and aesthetic approbation of marriage on a basis of coercion and ownership," shapes the popular tastes of the community, including the tastes of women. Thus the institution of marriage, like the institution of property, is both founded on exploit and sustained by emulation. "Through the precept and example of those who make the vogue, and through selective repression of those who are unable to accept it, the institution of ownership-marriage makes its way into definitive acceptance as the only beautiful and virtuous form of the relation. As the conviction of its legitimacy grows stronger in each succeeding generation, it comes to be appreciated unreflectingly as a deliverance of common-sense and enlightened reason that the good and the beautiful attitude of the man toward the woman is an attitude of coercion. 'None but the brave deserve the fair.' "[5]

Once it has been established that possession of women serves the same status function as ownership of property, the independent, "masterless" women lose caste, other possible forms of the marriage relation "fall under a polite odium," and now all men seek to attach "some woman or women to themselves by the honorable bonds of seizure." But as the group increases in size it becomes difficult to obtain a wife by this method, and thus a remedy is sought in a "mimic or ceremonial capture" of the free women and their assimilation into the "acceptable class of women" who are already attached to some master. The "probable motive" for this assimilation is to preserve the status of men of high standing who might otherwise be tempted to seek sexual relations outside of the marriage. The marriage ceremony is "by no means looked upon as a fatuous make-believe." The paraphernalia of magic and religious rites is testimony that the marriage is a reenactment of the original deed of marriage by capture. Ultimately marriage can be seen as another aspect of animism and reification, an institution whose brutal human origins have been lost sight of as it takes on seemingly innocent ceremonial functions, thus assuring that women's servitude is sustained by symbolic action:

> As seen in the light of this animistic preconception, any process is substantially teleological, and the propensity imputed to it will not be thwarted of its legitimate end after the course of events in which it expresses itself has once fallen into shape or got under way. It follows logically, as a matter of course, that, if once the motions leading to a desired consummation have been rehearsed in the accredited form and sequence, the same substantial result will be attained as that produced by the process imitated. This is the ground of whatever efficiency is imputed to ceremonial observances on all

planes of culture, and it is especially the chief element in formal adoption and initiation. Hence, probably, the practice of mock-seizure or mock-capture, and hence the formal profession of fealty and submission on the part of the woman in the marriage rites of peoples among whom the household with a male head prevails. This form of the household is almost always associated with some survival or reminiscence of wife-capture. In all such cases, marriage is, by derivation, a ritual of initiation into servitude. In the words of the formula, even after it has been appreciably softened under the latter-day decay of the sense of status, it is the woman's place to love, honor, and obey.[6]

As an outgrowth of emulation between the members of a warlike community, the patriarchal household is a "predatory institution." Veblen recognized that maternal forms of household also existed throughout history, and he wondered whether such institutions, which he called "the household of the unattached woman," may have developed after a considerable period of peaceful and industrious life. Many North American Indian tribes, he noted, seem to incorporate traces of both systems of relationship; and where a mixture of the two systems is found, the lower class seems to partake of the maternal household and the upper the paternal. Veblen also noted that the patriarchal system had been considerably weakened in western countries, where the disintegration of the traditional scheme of male status resulted from new modes of economic life "on the lines of industrial freedom." Since the patriarchal form has no basis in earliest primitive life and is increasingly out of place in modern industrial life, it may be breaking down at present. Are there then any grounds for thinking that the institution of property will erode with the institution of marriage? "That is perhaps a question of speculative curiosity rather than of urgent theoretical interest."[7]

Veblen's attitude toward women was of course part of his critique of the orthodox economic theory of the day. In view of his hostility toward capitalist theory, which equated value with market relations, it was natural for Veblen to develop a distinction between female and male occupations as a way of dramatizing what was for him the true source of value—productivity and serviceability. In its extreme formulation the difference between women and men is the difference between the worker and the capitalist, between those who make goods through socially useful labor and those who make wealth through non-productive exploit. Thus when Veblen attacked the mystique of "economic man" he did so in the most literal sense, pointing out that the notion distorts understanding of early economic life not only because of its individualist premise but also because of its masculine bias. Responding to John B. Clark's *The Essentials of Economic Theory*, Veblen showed why the study of economics was too important to be left to male scholars:

In the primitive economic situation—that is to say, in savagery and the lower barbarism—there is, of course no 'solitary hunter,' living either in a

> cave or otherwise, and there is no man who 'makes by his own labor all the goods that he uses,' etc. It is, in effect, a highly meretricious misrepresentation to speak in this connection of 'the economy of a man who works only for himself,' and say that 'the inherent productive power of labor and capital is of vital concern to him,' because such a presentation of the matter overlooks the main facts in the case in order to put the emphasis on a feature which is of negligible consequence. There is no reasonable doubt but that, at least since mankind reached the human plane, the economic unit has been not a 'solitary hunter,' but a community of some kind; in which, by the way, women seem in the early stages to have been the most consequential factor instead of the man who works for himself. The 'capital' possessed by such a community—as, e.g., a band of California 'Digger' Indians—was a negligible quantity, more valuable to a collector of curios than to anyone else, and the loss of which to the 'Digger' squaws would mean very little. What was of 'vital concern' to them, indeed, what the life of the group depended on absolutely, was the accumulated wisdom of the squaws, the technology of their economic situation. The loss of the basket, digging-stick, and mortar, simply as physical objects, would have signified little, but the conceivable loss of the squaw's knowledge of the soil and seasons, of food and fiber plants, and of mechanical expedients, would have meant the present dispersal and starvation of the community.[5]

In some respects Veblen's distinction between early female and male occupations resembles the Marxist distinction between labor and capital. But it would be difficult to assimilate Veblen's analysis of the reasons for women's oppressed condition with the analysis that derives from the Marxist tradition. An examination of Engels' account of the plight of women, as outlined in *The Origin of the Family, Private Property, and the State,* may help to show the difficulties in establishing such a synthesis.

From Engels to Lévi-Strauss

Engels begins his study by positing a scheme of early human development that, as with Veblen's analysis, distinguishes sharply between the savage ("primitive communism") and the barbarian stages of history. He also sees the deterioration of women's position in early history as taking place with the passing of the savage and the advent of barbarian society; and he discerns a similar connection between the degraded image of physical and domestic work and the emergence of slavery and the division of labor. There the comparison between Engels and Veblen ends. What separates the two theorists is not only the Marxist preconceptions of the former but their different views of the causal sequence of historical phenomena.

According to Engels, the beginnings of women's oppression is to be found in the institution of private property, and the development of both phenomena is bound up with the emergence of the patriarchal family. The problem that confronted Engels was to explain how the family transformed itself from the maternal clan system of savage society, a wholesome, equitable unit that functioned mainly for the purpose of procreation, into the father-dominated family of civilized society. Engels made use of the anthropologist Lewis H. Morgan's theory of different family forms to account for the transformation. But whether describing the "pairing," "panuluar," or the "consanguine" family, it is always the economic mode of production that gives Engels' analysis its explanatory power. When the mode of production is communal, as in savage society, the family does not exist as an economic institution composed of single pairs; property and tools are shared; and women's household work is esteemed as much as man's labor. But the development of productive resources shatters this communal harmony by introducing private property, which is first manifested in domesticated animals and cultivated land, resources that replenish themselves beyond subsistence needs. Although Engels may have failed, as we saw earlier, to explain satisfactorily the origins of property, he was nevertheless certain that it had transformed relations between men and women. Private property brings wealth, which somehow "strengthened" the position of the father, who proceeds to challenge the traditional order of inheritance against the clan in favor of his own children and to overthrow the mother's traditional right to retain her female lineage within the family. "The overthrow of mother right was the *world-historical defeat of the female sex.*" The family is now based on the supremacy of the man, who simultaneously introduces the principle of monogamy and his own right to conjugal infidelity. Women lose not only sexual freedom but political, economic, and social freedom as well. As production for exchange replaces production for use, ownership of things passes to those who work outside the household; and as the males amass greater wealth and power the status of the women sinks, domestic labor loses esteem, and the female is reduced to servitude and bondage. The term "family" itself, noted Engels in reference to Marx's observation, derives from the Latin word *familia*, which originally signified the totality of household slaves belonging to one individual. No less than Marx was Engels convinced that the family constituted the "embryo" of class society and contained "all the antagonisms which later develop on a wide scale within society and its state."[9]

There are several difficulties with the Engels-Marx analysis of the historical origins of women's oppression. In the first place, there is sufficient anthropological evidence to indicate that women do not always enjoy the equal status of men in older societies with neither private property, a class system, nor a well-defined state; and there are modern capitalist societies where women not only inherit property but are entitled to such legal rights as divorce, alimony, and child support that are enforced by the state.[10] John Stuart Mill would applaud this data as evidence of progress in women's rights, but Veblen approached the problem of women's oppression from neither a liberal nor a Marxist point of view. The real issue that separates Engels and Veblen may be seen in the following passage from *The Origin of the Family:*

> How and when the herds and flocks were converted from the common property of the tribe or gens into the property of the individual heads of families we do not know to this day; but it must have occurred, in the main, at this stage. The herds and the other new objects of wealth brought about a revolution in the family. Gaining a livelihood had always been the business of the man; he produced and owned the means therefor. The herds were the new means of gaining a livelihood, and their original domestication and subsequent tending was his work. Hence, he owned the cattle, and the commodities and slaves obtained in exchange for them. All the surplus now resulting from production fell to the man; the woman shared in consuming it, but she had no share in owning it. The 'savage' warrior and hunter had been content to occupy second place in the house and give precedence to the woman. The 'gentler' shepherd, presuming upon his wealth, pushed forward to first place and forced the woman into second place. And she could not complain. Division of labour in the family had regulated the distribution of property between man and wife. This division of labour remained unchanged, and yet it now put the former domestic relationship topsy-turvy simply because the division of labour outside the family had changed. The very cause that had formerly made the woman supreme in the house, namely, her being confined to domestic work, now assured supremacy in the house for the man: the woman's housework lost its significance compared with the man's work in obtaining a livelihood; the latter was everything, the former an insignificant contribution. Here we see already that the emancipation of women and their equality with men are impossible and must remain so as long as women are excluded from socially productive work and restricted to housework, which is private. The emancipation of women becomes possible only when women are enabled to take part in production on a large, social scale, and when domestic duties require their attention only to a minor degree. And this has become possible only as a result of modern large-scale industry, which not only permits of the participation of women in production in large numbers, but actually calls for it and, moreover, strives to convert private domestic work also into a public industry.[11]

Veblen would definitely agree with Engels' solution—the massive entry of women into public industry. But he would have found odd Engels' desire to see domestic duties reduced to "a minor degree," an attitude that indicates that Engels himself inherited the impression that different kinds of labor are either meaningful and honorable or dull and undignified. This attitude, originating with barbarian man, is carried forward by modern bourgeois man and indeed constitutes the psychological premise of the value theory in classical economics. To Veblen the "irksomeness of labor" is a cultural imputation rather than an actual observation, a socially conditioned impression that is imposed on the act of work, domestic or otherwise, and not necessarily inherent in it.

The real question is why women's work suffered a loss of esteem. Engels has no convincing answer to this question. He tells us that "gaining a livelihood had always been the business of the man" and that the " 'savage' warrior and hunter had been content to occupy second place in the house and give precedence to the woman." This state of sexual egalitarianism is corrupted by wealth, which causes even the " 'gentler' shepherd" to push himself forward to take over the woman's position and to force her into a servile condition. Private property, exchange relations, and the division of labor, the productive forces that create wealth, serve to overthrow the equal and possibly superior position of women in early society. In Veblen's analysis of the *déclassé* process of women, it is not the rich shepherd who does the pushing around; it is the warrior and hunter, the brutes of stealth and strength. It is not the mere possession of wealth that overthrows women but the manner in which it comes to be possessed, and the technique of seizing wealth by "force and fraud" is peculiarly masculine and comes to be accepted as evidence of superior power and skill.

Veblen would also deny that gaining a livelihood "had always been" the man's function in early society. On the contrary, it was the women who possessed a peculiarly intimate sense of the rhythms of growth and fertility. Referring to the animate world of crops and animals as the "speechless others," Veblen maintained that the scheme of this world is one of "fecundity, growth and nature, and all these matters are natural to women rather than to men; and so in the early stages of culture the consciousness of kind and congruity has made it plain to all the parties in interest that the care of crops and animals belongs in the fitness of things to women. Indeed there is such a spiritual (magical) community between women and the fecundity of animate things that any intrusion of the men in the affairs of growth and fertility may by force of contrast come to be viewed with the liveliest apprehension."[12] In *The Instinct of Workmanship* Veblen attributes to women the two basic propensities that are the lifeblood of society: workmanship and the parental bent. Veblen was unwilling, as other nineteenth-century anthropologists were almost too willing, to claim that the earliest societies were organized by the principle of matriarchy. He realized that such a claim was only "conjectural history." Nevertheless, Veblen remained convinced that in primitive society women, possibly because of their capacities for motherhood, were better endowed to apprehend intuitively what was necessary for the care of crops, flocks, and soil. "It is all the more evident that communion with these wordless others should fall to the women, since the like wordless communion with their own young is perhaps the most notable and engaging trait of their own motherhood." Moreover, since the rest of the tribe tends to attribute magical and anthropomorphic traits to what is essentially women's technological role, women come to occupy the central place in the earliest schemes of economic life. And, ironically, while women who labor upon the materials of earth are actually extirpating animism, they come to be worshipped as wonder-workers who can master nature because they can sympathize with the objective world and thus appear to make it respond to human desire. This curious relationship between the naturalization of the world that women bring about as workers, and the animism that is being generated by their image as life-giving producers, is sustained by the primitive's imitation of superior powers. "The sense of imitative propriety, as well as the recognized constraining force exercised by example and mimetic representation through the impulse of imitation, will have guided workmanship shrewdly to play up womankind and motherhood in an ever-growing scheme of magical observances designed to further the natural increase of flocks and crops."[13] At one time in remote history, Veblen maintained, the true doers and makers were properly honored.

In Veblen's analysis, the sexual division of labor occurs not with the rise of property but with the predatory raids of man which themselves give rise to the institutions of ownership. In the seizure of women lies the original claim to individual possession. Female captives, it will be recalled, are the first manifestation of ownership in archaic societies because they are regarded neither as items essential for the survival of the conquering tribe nor as objects that belong a priori to the possessor by virtue of their being an "organic extension of his personality." From these speculations Veblen derived his theory of marriage as a form of subjugation that originates in conquest and is sustained by the symbolic ceremony of coercion, an institution in which women cannot be said to have lost the right to share property since they are, in the eyes of barbarian man, the first expression of property as a "trophy." Against Engels' almost one-dimensional economic interpretation, Veblen offered an interpretation that combined an anthropological sensitivity to ritual and a social-psychological sensitivity to motivation—marriage by capture originates less from the scarcity of women than from the vanity of men.

Engels would have rejected what could only seem a rude, Darwinian interpretation of the origins of women's oppression. He scoffed at the notion, prevalent in late nineteenth-century anthropology, of the origin of exogamy, of "marriage by abduction" by tribes which seized wives outside of their own group; and he cited Morgan's *Ancient Society* to show that exogamous and endogamous communities are actually part of a larger "gens" unit in which the distinction between the two types of marriage practices collapses. To a large extent Engels and Veblen had different views toward marriage and the subjection of women because they proceeded from different assumptions about original human nature. Engels denied that there existed in the state of early communal society any evidence of personal envy, sexual jealousy, and even the incest taboo (which for Freud and most anthropologists is as universal as it is eternal); and he maintained that in primitive society "modern individual sex love [was] previously unknown to the whole world."[14] Veblen, on the other hand, was perhaps closer to Freud in his assumptions about man's "instincts," "drives," and "propensities," believing that "sexual competition" played a role in stimulating the primal combative tendencies in man (though it was the development of economic surplus that brought into existence "an habitual bellicose frame of mind").[15] And while he may have agreed with Engels that modern romantic sex love was unknown to the primitive world, he would have stressed that individual self-love, the desire for esteem and approbation, was more than latent and increasingly expressed itself in deeds of "emulation" and "invidious comparison."

Veblen's analysis may seem ultimately crude, suggesting as it does a kind of Darwinian view of women's subjugation based on the authority which the strong acquire over the weak. But in Veblen's eyes women are deficient in only one attribute: ferocity. Indeed Veblen wanted to show, in his anthropological digressions as well as his economic studies, that women were the true workers, the actual producers of food, clothes, and shelter, while the male warriors and chieftains divided their time between occasional plunder and frequent idleness. This distinction between those who create value through socially useful labor and those who thrive and command status on the basis of non-productive exploit plays no role in Engel's analysis of the oppression of women. The absence of a sociological sensitivity to status distinctions may suggest why Engels' solution to women's oppression is fraught with difficulties. Engels assumed that the opportunity for women to liberate themselves by engaging in socially meaningful work would be possible "only as a result of modern large scale industry." There is a grim irony in this assumption. For the growth of industrialization has not only meant the creation of new social and occupational classes—the "technostructure" that Veblen perceived long before Daniel Bell or John Kenneth Galbraith—it has also meant the deliberate exclusion of educated, talented women from the professional working force. In Veblen's analysis it is necessary to understand the sociological, and not only the economic, reasons for that systematic exclusion, and to do so one cannot look to industrialization to solve the problem of sexual discrimination that may have had its origins in preindustrial society. Indeed from a Marxist analysis sexual discrimination as a historical phenomenon encounters the same explanatory difficulties as "alienation": if both these developments were the result of the "productive forces" of history, how can those same forces also serve as their historical solution?[16]

A Marxist, it is true, would doubtless stress the "contradictions" that arise historically from the "productive forces." This perspective remained closed to Veblen. A Darwinist more interested in the naturalistic descent of man than in the presumed upward movement of human consciousness, a former student of Kantian philosophy, hence sensitive to the limitations of ultimate metaphysical knowledge, Veblen had no sympathy for Hegel and the omniscient claims of dialectical reasoning. He chose instead to go back to the beginning, to the origins of things, and search for a "genetic explanation" of modern social relationships. Veblen focused on the emergence of the hunting mode of activity and the advent of tribal warfare, developments that resulted from material surplus and elevated feats of male prowess to cultural dominance by virtue of their "preeminent force." Henceforth the position of women deteriorates as she is forced to labor relentlessly in digging roots, drawing water, gathering wood, milking cattle, dressing victuals, and rearing children—the domestic activities that seem to men so "ceremoniously unclean." These early status distinctions based on the sexual division of labor persist as habits and customs in our modern age. In Victorian America of the late nineteenth century, it was not a little outrageous for Veblen to describe women as having been reduced to a "chattel," and to maintain as well that property originates not in the ownership of things but of human beings, and that captive women were the first manifestations of slavery out of which evolved the institution of "ownership-marriage." Yet Veblen's observations were not entirely alien to the world of nineteenth-century anthropology, and even to eighteenth-century English political theory.[17] Indeed one may find some resemblance to Veblen's ideas in the work of the contemporary anthropologist Claude Lévi-Strauss, who also sees women as the first form of "currency." Both Veblen and Lévi-Strauss are interested in the strategy of marriage alliances; both believe that economic systems, like kinship systems and authority systems and authority relations in general, may be regarded as a kind of "language" of social communication; both concentrate on status distinctions, and not necessarily the mode of production, as the means by which men have come to dominate women; and both assume that the capture and exchange of women preceded the acquisition and exchange of goods in primitive communities. "In human society," writes Lévi-Strauss, "it is the men who exchange the women, and not vice versa."[18]

The theories of Lévi-Strauss, however, are as unverifiable as the speculations of Veblen. Anthropologists have uncovered enough evidence to suggest that women's status, although virtually inferior to that of men in almost every society, may vary with respective feminine social roles in different times and in different places. Among the Toda community in the South Seas, for example, Margaret Mead found domestic work "too sacred" for women, while Carol P. Hoffer's study of the Kpa Mende of the Sierra Leone offers a case study of women obtaining effective political rule through the manipulation of marriage arrangements.[19] And among the Eskimos, as Veblen well knew, the wife could be regarded as a form of "gift-exchange" even though private property remained a dormant concept and pecuniary exploit an unfamiliar behavior. Nevertheless, anthropologists are in agreement about a fact of life that feminists have been aware of for centuries: that whatever the cause, biological constraint or social conditioning, the female is burdened with a subordinate status that seems to grow heavier as women's consciousness is "raised" to the pitch of social passion. Women anthropologists are plunging into this problem on a grand scale of scholarly industry, and understandably they are puzzled by a riddle that seems to defy both the evolutionist and the diffusionist modes of analysis. Thus the pertinent questions raised by Michelle Zimbalist Rosaldo and Louise Lamphere: "Although it seems likely that the developments of big-game hunting and warfare promoted an ethic of male dominance, it is difficult to see why biases associated with man's earliest adaptations should remain with us today. The question then becomes: why, if our social worlds are so different from those of our ancestors, has the relation of the sexes continued to be asymmetrical, and how is it that social groups, which change radically through time, continue to produce and reproduce a social order dominated by men?"[20]

Is our scheme of culture so different from that of our ancestors? This question, one that Mill had also failed to consider fully, Veblen most certainly would put to the contemporary social theorist. His central aim, though often couched in irony and hyperbole, was to show how the "modern survivals of prowess" and the "conservation of archaic traits" function in contemporary society to perpetuate sexual discrimination and to exclude women from the industrial work force. The ancient leisure-class scheme of life affects almost all sections of society, including the contemporary wives and daughters of the men who have fallen under the sway of the prevalent canons of reputability. Modern industrial work, like earlier agricultural and manual labor, is thus seen as degrading, and professional employment related to the useful production of goods and services is worse than degrading; it is "vulgar" and hence "un-womanly." Married women especially dare not challenge this canon of decency for fear of jeopardizing their husbands' reputation. "It is still felt that woman's life, in its civil, economic, and social bearing, is essentially and normally a vicarious life, the merit or demerit of which is, in the nature of things, to be imputed to some other individual who stands in some relation of ownership or tutelage to the woman. So, for instance, any action on the part of a woman which traverses an injunction of the accepted schedule of proprieties is felt to reflect immediately upon the honor of the man whose woman she is."[21] In modern society, Veblen suggests, the status of the wife remains almost what it had been when her forebear had been seized and abducted; she still remains the appendage of the husband, whose interests she serves and whose image of the good life she replicates. Nowhere is this residue better seen than in the dress habits of the modern women.

The Economic Psychology of Women's Dress

Veblen believed that the patriarchal household was experiencing a decline due to modern industrial life. Yet one remaining artifact indicating the survival of masculine domination could be seen in the feminine mode of dress. Veblen recognized that dress had its origins in the principle of adornment as well as the physical need for protection and comfort. But decoration of the body represents only the "*naive* aesthetic sense" of dress which is of slight importance in modern apparel. The evolution of dress proceeds from the simple forms of adornment and ornamentation to a mixture of aesthetics and economic accessions, a line of development that extends from pigments and trinkets to what is presently understood by apparel. Primitive decoration is not necessarily an economic expression, nor are the durable items of adornment that may reflect mythical or religious meanings. What constitutes dress as an economic factor is its function as an index of the wealth of the wearer—nay, of its owner, for in patriarchal society the wearer and the owner are not necessarily the same person. Women's dress symbolizes the wealth of the "economic unit" that the wearer represents. And the more extravagant the garment the more is the wearer to be considered as "something in the nature of a chattel," a captive who advertises the pecuniary strength of her husband by allowing him, either by custom or coercion, to spend lavishly upon her. The practice has many precedents in the behavior of archaic men and women, and its purpose is the same always and everywhere—to display wasteful expenditure:

> The extra portion of butter, or other unguent, with which wives of the magnates of the African interior anoint their persons, beyond what comfort requires, is a form of this kind of expenditure lying on the border between primitive personal embellishment and incipient dress. So also the brass-wire bracelets, anklets, etc., at times aggregating some thirty pounds in weight, worn by the same class of persons, as well as, to a less extent, by the male population of the same countries. So also the pelt of the arctic fur seal, which the women of civilised countries prefer to fabrics that are preferable to it in all respects but expense. So also the ostrich plumes and the many curious effigies of plants and animals that are dealt in by the milliners. The list is inexhaustible, for there is scarcely an article of apparel of male or female, civilised or uncivilised, that does not partake largely of this element, and very many may be said, in point of economic principle, to consist of virtually nothing else.[22]

Veblen offered three principles of modern women's apparel: expensiveness, novelty, and ineptitude. The first principle serves to dramatize the "conspicuously unproductive consumption of goods," the wife's ability to squander wealth as a means of social distinction. But when the mode of a particular style becomes popular, and producers thus seek to lower its price, that style is now within the reach of a sufficient number of buyers to undermine its function as a symbol of leisure-class status. Hence the curious rise of novelty in fashion: women's apparel must show *prima facie* evidence of having been worn but for a comparatively brief time, perhaps even once, like the delicate evening gown. Where cultural historians seem almost to be at a loss to explain the sudden fluctuations in dress styles,[23] Veblen presumed to know why vogues change after a short period of stabilization: imitators must never be allowed to catch up, even, and especially, at the right fashionable moment. In the world of fashion the status of the leisure class is never endangered; the matrons can defend themselves against all threats even in a prosperous, affluent society. When a growing number of upper middle-class women begin to emulate leisure-class economic behavior, they only reveal a crude wastefulness which demonstrates that their means of display had been recently acquired. The imitators still lack knowledge and habit of good form in dress and manners, affectations that require such prolonged, deliberate cultivation that they can be afforded only by those who can waste time and effort. What is wasteful is reputable.

Veblen's third principle of apparel—ineptitude—illustrated the social rationality behind the economic irrationality of women's dress styles in the late nineteenth century. Leisure-class wives display the same disdain for work in their social lives as their husbands display in their economic activities. The "conspicuous abstention" from all labor is symbolized in the woman's long hair, dangerously high "French heel," and bulky ankle-length skirt, which hampers the movement of the wearer and disables her for any useful occupation. Even women who must earn their living perpetuate the impression through their cumbersome dress that they are more disposed to leisurely consumption than meaningful production. Observing the "voluntarily accepted physical incapacity" on the part of women who are bent on showing that they are both expensive and useless, Veblen believed it almost futile to attempt to reform dress in the direction of convenience, comfort, or health. The most obvious violence to health may be seen in the corset, which does to western women what the "abortive foot" did to their "Chinese sisters": deforms the natural body for the sake of the male's idea of feminine beauty as a combination of fragility and infirmity. "Both of these are mutilations of unquestioned repulsiveness to the untrained sense. It requires habituation to become reconciled to them. Yet there is no room to question their attractiveness to men into whose scheme of life they fit as honorific items sanctioned by the requirements of pecuniary reputability. They are items of pecuniary and cultural beauty which have come to do duty as elements of the ideal of womanliness."[24]

Veblen noted that the corset and the long skirt had been recently passing out of vogue as a new desire for comfort seemed to determine women's preferences. Yet the shift in tastes from socially compelled habits to rationally analyzed consumption may be more apparent than real. The cult of personal comfort "seems to have been due to a ramification of the sentimental athleticism (flesh-worship) that has been dominant of late; and now that the crest of this wave of sentiment has passed, this alien motive in dress is also receding."[25] With the decline of sports dress may again return to the cultural dictates of expensiveness and novelty. Yet dress as an expression of conspicuous waste need not always follow the canons of novelty. It may be archaic, as in the case of the dress of domestic servants, whose awkward garments of lace are designed to suggest the long-established family heritage of their employers. The archaic compulsion is also characteristic of uniforms worn at young girls' "finishing" schools, where juvenile fashion is resisted and plain simplicity becomes itself an indicator of superior social position. Whatever the mode of dress, the strategy is always that of self-display, and the vicissitudes of fashion point up the element of class emulation in social life.

Fashion, as J. C. Flugel has remarked, may be the "mysterious goddess" whose decrees are easier to obey than to understand.[26] Veblen understood the phenomenon perhaps too well, and as a result we are offered a somewhat one-sided interpretation of the meaning of dress styles. For one thing, he exaggerated the continuity between primitive and modern patterns of behavior. In archaic societies, where the savage is afraid of novelty and strangeness, dress remains stable and serves a socializing function. In modern cultures, where the individual is afraid of absorption and obliteration, dress styles continually change and serve a segregating function. And the discriminating role of modern dress could well suggest, as Georg Simmel noted,[27] that woman is the staunchest adherent to fashion, not only because she is an appendage of the husband, but primarily because the weakness of her social position engenders in her a strict regard for custom, which in turn, ironically, gives her the strength to desire "individualization and personal conspicuousness" in dress, to be assertive rather than submissive in the one sphere that compensates for her lack of position in a masculine culture based on a calling or profession. Women find freedom in fashion, even if it is only the freedom of an illusion.

In Veblen's writings one also finds no suggestion that dress may be understood in light of the psychology of individual egotism as well as the sociology of class emulation. Women and men may exploit fashion as a means of enhancing their own physical attractiveness. Although a libertine himself, Veblen never seemed to have recognized dress as a mode of sexual rivalry—one wonders what he would make of the plunging neckline or the miniskirt as a leisure-class symbol of physical incapacity! The difficulties in Veblen's analysis arise from his attempt to apply the characteristics of nineteenth-century fashion to the entire history of dress, placing the problems of the I. Magnin woman on the Cro-Magnon man.

Quentin Bell, a great admirer of Veblen, has pointed out the limitations of Veblen's analysis in *On Human Finery*. Bell questions Veblen's principle of "vicarious consumption." In history, Bell notes, when wives are actually reduced to the status of a "chattel," it is the husbands who display wealth upon themselves. "It is when women begin to acquire status on their own that they begin to dress for the world." One might add that in the history of fashion it is not so much the wife but the mistress who sets the styles of dress—a point made by Sombart in relating the rise of capitalism to the cultural acceptance of sensual love.[28] Bell also doubts that Veblen's analysis can explain why the mode of style sometimes turns toward simplicity and at other times toward "sumptuosity." Still, it was Veblen, Bell stresses, who first explored the relationship of the emulative process to class behavior, phenomena that go far toward rendering the history of fashion explicable. "I am convinced," Bell concluded, "that whatever modifications it may be necessary to make in history, it is Veblen who has shown us the true manner of approaching the problem. I do not see how any serious student of social history can afford to neglect his teachings."[29]

Unfortunately students and scholars have neglected Veblen's writings on fashion and the women question. This was also true of the feminists who were Veblen's contemporaries, writers and activists who found themselves inside the same "cage" of modern society and who wanted, like Ibsen's Nora Helmer, to slam the door to domesticity.

Veblen and Charlotte Perkins Gilman

What exactly was the status of women when Veblen wrote *Leisure Class* at the turn of the century? Contemporary social historians, having studied belles-lettres, marriage manuals, medical treatises, religious sermons, hygiene literature, and other guidance books, pamphlets, and articles on childhood, marriage, and the family, have reached no clear agreement about the position of women.[30] Nevertheless, two sketchy generalizations emerge from their research: first, American culture between the Gilded Age and shortly before World War One, roughly a period spanning the years 1875 to 1910, prescribed a fairly clear-cut picture of women's subordinate place in a male-dominated society based on well-defined gender roles; second, sex was a biological aspect of life that women should enjoy only after marriage, and then not too frequently or with too deep an expression of passion, lest a wife be regarded as unseemingly aggressive and perhaps neurotic. To a certain extent these and other similar attitudes about femininity became prevalent through children's reading materials, whose authors consciously imposed their own values in an attempt to socialize the young. Such a process involved "emulation" in the Veblenian sense, for many upper middle-class American authors, women as well as men, were anxious to internalize those features of life-style—dress, manners, and moral deportment—which appeared to signify and assure class status. Young women were brought up on the ideals of premarital chastity and postmarital domesticity, ideals which, if obeyed even at the sacrifice of impulsive romantic love, would mean a successful life of conjugal happiness. Feminists protested these and other "ideals" that implied the wife's subordination to the husband's career, the double standard of male morality, and the idea that youthful love should be rationally calculated, like a chessboard of strategic social moves, and that sex should be experienced calmly and passively, like the pleasures of a box of sweets.

However dubious may be such prescriptive sources as marriage manuals, the limitations imposed on women's personal autonomy, and the restrictions on her sexual freedom, have been interpreted by some scholars as evidence of cultural "repression" in general, a deliberate attempt to channel the libidinous energies of women and men away from pleasure and freedom and toward work and self-denial. This Freudian-Marxist interpretation sees sexual prescription as a means of meeting the needs of a developing capitalist economy. "The gospel of continence," writes one scholar who takes this position, "reveals its meaning when it is related to the dynamic quality inherent in the structure and functioning of the Respectable Economic System, the compulsion to accumulate and reinvest capital."[31] This interpretation may confuse moral aspirations for actual historical conditions, rhetoric for reality. Not only is it questionable, as some social historians have observed,[32] that Victorian standards hindered the biological imperatives of emotional growth, but *Leisure Class* demonstrated why the traditional Protestant ethic had already been transformed from a principle of work into a psychology of consumption. Perhaps the "purity crusades" of the late nineteenth-century were trying too late not to sustain capitalism but to hold back a revolution in morals that resulted from capitalism itself: the life of sensual gratification that accompanies the life of material acquisition.[33] It may be an exaggeration to relate the emergence of the erotic to the gross national product, particularly when we consider the plight of lower-class working women. Yet it is significant that several leading feminists maintained not that they were being denied their sexual freedom because they were forced to work, but rather that they were being forced to remain idle when they wanted to be active, to be producers instead of consumers. "She is forbidden to make, but encouraged to take," wrote Charlotte Perkins Gilman in *Women and Economics,* a book which has a striking resemblance to Veblen's analysis of the wife's place in modern industrial society.[34]

Gilman's *Women and Economics* was published in 1898, a year before *Leisure Class* appeared, and the same year that Veblen published his essay on "The Barbarian Status of Women." A chronological coincidence? Perhaps, for there is no evidence that either Gilman or Veblen was influenced by the other's writings. This seems all the more strange in light of the many similarities in their analysis. Both saw the women question as much wider than the historical stage of suffrage (Mill) or industrialization (Engels); instead each analyzed the problem in terms of the subtle social pressures in the culture of modern industrial society. Their mode of investigation was also spirited by a common Darwinian perspective, allowing Veblen and Gilman, who had been deeply influenced by the sociology of Lester Ward, to trace the social evolution of human relationships. In similar vein, each viewed the nature of men and women as endowed with a basic instinct to work and produce and to create as an artistic means of self-expression. "Socially organized human beings tend to produce, as a gland to secrete," wrote Gilman. "The creative impulse, the desire to make, to express the inner thought in outer form . . . this is the distinguishing character of humanity." Gilman and Veblen also discussed the implications of women's dress, attributed to women the qualities of cooperation and serviceability, and stressed, though Gilman more emphatically, the unrecognized economic value and social utility of women's household work and its isolation from the productive factors of the economy as a whole.[35]

Gilman, however, did not subscribe to Veblen's theory of the sexual division of labor, wherein the exclusion of women was due not to their incapacity for hard, physical work—the prevalent assumption in much of nineteenth-century Darwinist social thought[36]—but to their incapacity for the violence and aggression of primitive economic life. Gilman saw the division of labor originating differently and indeed actually contributing to progress. In the beginning of human life the female represented the forces of procreation and labor while the male, more impatient with the drudgery of work and more resourceful in adapting to environmental changes, was better able to invent ways to lighten the burden of labor. Woman also used her sex to humanize ("maternalize") man and to motivate him to become more than a hunter and destroyer. Women, then, were actually helpless, having only the steady instincts of preservation, while men devised the means through which life progressed rather than stagnated. In Gilman's account, which completely reverses Veblen's description, the female willingly allows the male to ascend to dominance because of his superior biological capacity in the "struggle for existence."[37] But that struggle, Gilman observed in the spirit of Lester Ward, is now over, and the "time has come when we are open to deeper and wider impulses than the sex-instinct; the social instincts are strong enough to come into full use at last." Veblen, of course, was far less optimistic about the disappearance of man's early barbarian instincts. Moreover, while Veblen wanted to see women participate in the move to take control of the productive processes of economic life, Gilman was interested in the wider network of human relationships and wanted to see changes within the home and family that would enable the woman to still be a loving mother as well as a productive worker. Gilman continued to believe that women needed to engage in useful, dignified work in the outside world in order better to enjoy the "delicate loveliness" and "simplicity" of life in the home, her real "place of rest."[38]

In light of Gilman's persuasive writings, and those of other feminists during the *fin de siècle,* why did Veblen feel it necessary to champion the cause of women's social emancipation? Unlike Mill, Veblen never expressed a commitment to sexual egalitarianism as an obligation of the liberal body politic. Unimpressed with Engels' analysis, he deliberately avoided the Marxist tendency of equating the women question with the class question. And in contrast to Gilman, he expressed little faith in moral progress. Indeed, what did Veblen actually experience with women as human beings, and why did he, like Henry Adams, look to women for the precious life-sense that would save the human race?

Veblen and the "New Woman"; H. L. Mencken and the Male Counter-Attack

Thorstein Veblen's relations with women are one of the most discussed and least documented affairs in American cultural history. Any person's love life is a challenge to serious scholarship; Veblen's is a frustrating cul-de-sac. Not only did he have his private correspondence destroyed but he was as reticent about his passions as he was about his convictions. Yet there is no question that Veblen was attracted to women, and throughout his professional life he was involved in one affair after another, once with a colleague's wife who later became the mistress of Anatole France.[39]

David Riesman suggests that both Veblen's theoretical defense of and physical and psychological attraction to women possibly derived from "a man who felt himself deficient in the usual manly virtues of self-reliance, aggressive comeback, social effectiveness, and so on. . . ."[40] One wonders whether such traits are peculiarly masculine and whether their absence actually describes what is purported to be explained. Veblen was a physically powerful figure who in his youth could be combative and as an adult capable of challenging authority and defying propriety; and his life in his austere shack in California, as well as his singular, pioneering explorations in early anthropological economics, indicates a "self-reliance" that is almost unique in the history of American scholarship.

If it is difficult to explain Veblen's interest in women, it is perhaps even more difficult to explain their interest in him, an unkempt, lethargic pedagogue who shunned the fraternal joys of companionship and conversation and seemed to have no need for intimacy. R. L.

Duffus, a journalist who had shared Veblen's cottage while a student at Stanford, suggests that Veblen was "more capable of affection than of passion." Veblen could inspire "an abiding devotion in a woman," Duffus found from talking to Veblen's first wife, the person to whom he had been unfaithful. Veblen was "a case," Duffus learned from another lady, "of a man who did not discover until well on in life that he *was* attractive to women."[41] Veblen did not go out of his way to pursue women, but neither did he resist their advances. Once he responded wearily with a question to a shocked friend: "What is one to do if the woman moves in on you?"[42] Ironically this unprepossessing man had that undefinable essence known as sex appeal. Whatever may have been Veblen's secret, he was clearly more seduced than seducing.

Veblen's first marriage, to Ellen Rolfe in 1888, turned out sadly: The niece of the president of Carleton College, Ellen was a woman of ideas and a warm, lively personality. In the early years there was a natural intellectual compatibility between the two. Veblen read Spencer to her and she read to him Henry George and Ruskin. She was a gifted story-teller and had a keen interest in ghost tales and mysteries. She also published children's nursery books. Veblen was enchanted with her, according to his biographer Joseph Dorfman. But one can only wonder whether there was much sensuality in their marriage. When Ellen died in 1926, an autopsy showed her sexual organs to have been retarded. Whether or not this misfortune itself explains Veblen's adulturous exploits,[43] the marriage grew more unstable with the passing of years. Ellen was to leave him periodically, sometimes prompted by his indiscretions, sometimes by his cold aloofness toward her. After a series of separations they were divorced in 1911. A marriage that began in glowing innocence ended in bitter acrimony. Ellen owned a number of houses and an Oregon lumber claim worth $4,000, but she felt insecure and rejected. In a letter to a friend she wrote: "Have never received a cent of help since divorce, though was awarded alimony. Such is men's gratitude."[44]

Veblen married his second wife, Anne Fessenden Bradley, in 1914. A divorcée whom Veblen had known in Chicago and California, the new Mrs. Veblen immediately set out to take complete care of her eccentric husband, doing his typing, washing his laundry, and keeping her own two children out of his way while finding time to make their clothes. Meanwhile, with no sense of contradiction, she brought up her own daughters on the teachings of Veblen as spelled out in *Leisure Class,* stressing feminine independence and economic autonomy. Anne was a radical, "impatient, explosive, and very doctrinaire," according to a neighbor, and she had been moved by the rebellious spirit of the prewar era. Perhaps she felt no violation to her feminist principles by waiting upon her husband because, as Riesman wryly noted, she regarded him as a valuable "national resource." During the war years she had a nervous breakdown, suffering delusions of persecution, and had to be institutionalized. No one seems to know how her sudden collapse affected Veblen inwardly (or her death in 1920), but he became more helpless than ever and his friends made arrangements to send the children to relatives and to have someone look after him. For a while he was taken care of by four ladies who called themselves "the Virolas." Curiously, women seemed to want to shelter him and serve his modest needs. Isador Lubin, an economist who worked with Veblen in Washington during this period, recalls his numerous visits to Veblen's house when he was living with Anne and her two daughters (ages 12 and 14):

> The thing that impressed me about all three of the women in the household was their protective attitude toward Veblen. They felt that they had to protect him against something. I could not understand what it was, but it was evident that they were going to see to it that nothing happened to him. Gradually all three of them developed a sort of motherly attitude toward me. By the time the year ended I had the feeling that this attitude toward me was partly due to the fact that they felt that I, too, wanted to protect Veblen. But again I'm not quite certain what he was being protected against.[45]

What, indeed? Riesman suggests that Veblen felt more comfortable with women because they made fewer demands upon his intellect, while D. R. Scott, a colleague of Veblen's at the University of Missouri, believes that Veblen found in women "a kind of psychological relief" from the loneliness of his self-banishment from the world of social relations.[46] It could also be that Veblen unconsciously experienced in women the very human emotions that he had so consciously purged from his social theory of scientific rigor and stolid workmanship: freedom, pleasure, beauty, and happiness. Whatever the source of his attachment to the opposite sex, Veblen was, together with Lester Ward, the first important social scientist to take a positive intellectual interest in the feminist cause around the turn of the century. In addition to his articles on the dress and status of women, he devoted a section of *Leisure Class* to studying the reasons behind the phenomena of the "New Woman" movement.

Veblen saw the feminist movement then as it is today, a predominantly white, upper middle-class expression of status unrest and resentment. The lower-class woman worker, Veblen observed, is still capable of putting up with mind-dulling activities, for her labor is immediate, tangible, and economically purposeful, and she also has "no time or thought to spare for a rebellious assertion of such propensity to self-direction as she has inherited." The educated, middle-class woman, however, is more prone to experience a "reversion to a more generic type of human character," which Veblen categorized, with masterful irony, as "proto-anthropoid" and "possibly sub-human." This woman is tired of seeing herself vicariously as an "expression of the man's life at second remove." Thus the watchwords of the movement are "Emancipation" and "Work," immediate liberation both from all current schemes of status and from all exclusion from useful employment.[47]

In the same section of *Leisure Class* Veblen took the trouble to answer the critics of the New Woman movement. He quoted one as saying of the female activist: "She is petted by her husband, the most devoted and hard-working of husbands in the world. . . . She is the superior of her husband in education, and in almost every respect. She is surrounded by the most numerous and delicate attentions. Yet she is not satisfied." Veblen had no difficulty using the critic's own words to show that man's habitual solution was precisely woman's problem; and he could show as well why feminism in America would always arise not from dire economic necessity but from the false promises of prosperity and luxury that had reduced the lives of women to the empty ceremony of consumption. But Veblen did not answer another critic who was both sympathetic to some women's causes and unsympathetic to what he regarded as all Veblenian cant: H. L. Mencken.

Mencken had been Veblen's nemesis for many years. Mencken not only resented the Veblen cult that sprang up during and shortly after the World War One years, he was even more upset by Veblen's abuse of the English language. But Mencken also itched to come to the defense of the much-maligned American male whom Veblen had been depicting as the finest flower of primitive barbarism. Mencken set out to accomplish this intellectual rescue first by reducing the entire 260 or so pages of the repetitious *Theory of the Leisure Class* to three simple propositions, and then by proceeding to try to demolish the entire edifice of Veblen's theory of status by exposing the fallacies in the principle of "exclusive possession":

> (1) The leisure class, which is the predatory class of feudal times, reserves all luxuries for itself, and disapproves their use by members of the lower classes, for this use takes away their charm by taking away their exclusive possession.
> (2) Women are chattels in the possession of the leisure class, and hence subject to the rules made for inferiors. 'The patriarchal tradition . . . says that the woman, being a chattel, should consume only what is necessary to her sustenance, except so far as her further consumption contributes to the comfort or the good repute of her master.'
> (3) The consumption of alcohol contributes nothing to the comfort or good repute of the woman's master, but 'detracts sensibly from the comfort or pleasure' of her master. Ergo, she is forbidden to drink.
>
> This, I believe, is a fair specimen of the Veblenian ratiocination. Observe it well, for it is typical. That is to say, it starts off with a gratuitous and highly dubious assumption, proceeds to an equally dubious deduction, and then ends with a platitude which begs the whole question. What sound reason is there for believing that exclusive possession is the hall-mark of luxury? There is none that I can see. It may be true of a few luxuries, but it is

> certainly not true of the most familiar ones. Do I enjoy a decent bath because I know that John Smith cannot afford one—or because I delight in being clean? Do I admire Beethoven's Fifth Symphony because it is incomprehensible to Congressmen and Methodists—or because I genuinely love music? Do I prefer terrapin a la Maryland to fried livei because plowhands must put up with liver—or because the terrapin is intrinsically a more charming dose? Do I prefer kissing a pretty girl to kissing a charwoman because even a janitor may kiss a charwoman—or because the pretty girl looks better, smells better and kisses better? Now and then, to be sure, the idea of exclusive possession enters into the concept of luxury. I may, if I am a bibliophile, esteem a book because it is a unique first edition. I may, if I am fond, esteem a woman because she smiles on no one else. But even here, save in a very small minority of cases, other attractions plainly enter into the matter. It pleases me to have a unique first edition, but I wouldn't care anything for a unique first edition of Robert W. Chambers or Elinor Glyn; the author must have my respect, the book must be intrinsically valuable, there must be much more to it than its mere uniqueness. And if, being fond, I glory in the exclusive smiles of a certain Miss —— or Mrs. ——, then surely my satisfaction depends chiefly upon the lady herself, and not upon my mere monopoly. Would I delight in the fidelity of the charwoman? Would it give me any joy to learn that, through a sense of duty to me, she had ceased to kiss the janitor?

Mencken maintained that Veblen's theory of conspicuous consumption and conspicuous waste proved to be, when applied to actual behavior, nothing more than a "wraith of balderdash." A husband may drink to excess but forbid his wife from doing so, not because her inebriation "detracts from his pleasure," but rather because her "dignity and happiness is precious to him." As for the presumption of the wife's dependency upon and subordination to the husband, Veblen simply could not comprehend what really motivated people and thus he failed to see who actually manipulates whom in a marriage partnership:

> No one denies, I take it, that in a clearly limited sense, women occupy a place in the world—or, more accurately, aspire to a place in the world—that is a good deal like that of a chattel. Marriage, the goal of their only honest and permanent hopes, invades their individuality. Thus the appearance she presents to the world is often the mirror of her husband's egotism. A rich man hangs his wife with expensive clothes and jewels for the same reason, among others, that he adorns his own head with a plug hat: to notify everybody that he can afford it—in brief, to excite the envy of the Socialists. But he also does it, let us hope, for another and far better and more powerful reason, to wit, that she intrigues him, that he delights in her, that he loves her—and so he wants to make her gaudy and happy. This reason may not appeal to Socialist sociologists. In Russia, according to an old scandal (officially endorsed by the British bureau for pulling Yankee noses) the Bolsheviki actually repudiated it as insane. Nevertheless, it continues to appeal very forcibly to the majority of normal husbands in the nations of the West, and I am convinced that it is a hundred times as potent as any other reason.

> The American husband, in particular, dresses his wife like a circus horse, not primarily because he wants to display his wealth upon her person, but because he is a soft and mooney fellow and ever ready to yield to her desires, however preposterous. If any conception of her as a chattel were actively in him, even unconsciously, he would be a good deal less her slave. As it is, her vicarious practice of conspicuous waste commonly reaches such a development that her master himself is forced into renunciations—which brings Prof. Dr. Veblen's theory to self-destruction.[48]

It would be facile to dismiss Mencken's observations as nothing more than male chauvinism, a charge that avoids the adversary instead of confronting him. Besides, the charge is not entirely accurate. If Veblen's Darwinian perspective led him to trace the causes of women's oppression to archaic man's barbarian strength, Mencken's Nietzschean standpoint led him to see the dilemma of modern women as lying in man's hopelessly weak and sentimental nature. It is the maudlin "slave morality" of Christendom that has placed women on the pedestal. Indeed, despite Mencken's attacks on Veblen, they shared many of the same attitudes toward women. Both praised women's superior intelligence and healthier emotional balance, and both admired women's disaffection from the world of business and politics, best exemplified in their aversion to war. Above all, the American woman could become what the American man could never be—a free spirit. "She is essentially an outlaw, a rebel, what H. G. Wells calls a nomad," wrote Mencken in *In Defense of Women*.[49]

Given these common sympathies, it is unfortunate that Veblen did not respond to Mencken. Had he done so he might have answered his adversary with the truths of anthropology. That a man, whether "mooney" or mighty, can either lavish wealth upon his wife or withdraw it indicates that she is the object of his will and power, and not necessarily the subject of her own desires. Veblen's understanding of the significance of potlatch enabled him to see that the "gift-ritual" is a way in which the giver asserts his authority over the receiver, a custom that, as we have seen, dramatizes through symbolic behavior the relationship of domination to subordination. Mencken, the crusty cynic, became the romantic idealist when he asked his readers to believe ("let us hope") that a husband adorns his wife because she delights and "intrigues" him and he "loves" her. Had he responded,[50] perhaps Veblen might have anticipated the four watchwords of the liberated wives of the 1970s: "Less Love, More Respect"—a manifesto that compels us to ponder again Ovid's troubling dictum: "Love and dignity cannot share the same abode."

Power Demystified

Feminists may find in Veblen's writings a number of useful ideas and insights. His explanation of the origins of property and the sexual division of labor offer a sociological dimension rooted in anthropological data that is lacking in Engels' economic interpretation of historical phenomena. His ideas about women's dress, status, and economic dependency seem, in light of recent trends, more valid than Mencken would care to acknowledge even if more emotionally complex than Veblen would like to admit. And his theory of the instincts of workmanship and the parental bent must surely strike a warm response in every women who has gagged on Freud's theory of the female's instinctual nature. What women may not find in Veblen, however, is a convincing practical solution to their situation in modern industrial society. Just as Marx and Engels believed that the "productive forces" would heighten the "contradictions" of capitalism, so too did Veblen look to the future to redeem the past. Although there always remained a brooding sense in Veblen that the forces of continuity would thwart the forces of change, his great hope was that the power of technology would loosen the psychological bonds that tied the barbaric past to the civilized present. Technology would be the housewife's ally as well as the engineer's, for machine work would liberate the mind and enable women as well as men to cast off the anthropomorphic ideas that are responsible for the current scheme of status. The mission of technology consists of freeing men and women from "animism," from a subservience to supernatural forces, "invisible" economic laws, sanctified institutions, and all the irrational forces that perpetuate the mystique of feminine subordination and male superiority as an unalterable fact preordained by God's mysterious will or nature's inscrutable ways.

The mystique has indeed been challenged, but it is difficult to see what role technology played in undermining it. To be sure, technology issued in the prosperity and the leisure time enabling greater numbers of women to obtain an education and thereby become conscious of their condition. But this path was not part of Veblen's forecast. The "discipline of the machine" was to nurture in women as well as men a mechanical, objective, scientific, "matter-of-fact" frame of mind, the only mentality, Veblen was convinced, that would be sufficiently purged of the sentiment of human emotions to challenge and overthrow a capitalist system sustained not by coercive power but by the hegemony of subjective ideas, the deep-rooted habits of property, class and status. It was indeed the machine, in fact a particularly innovative machine, that brought increasing numbers of women into the work force around the turn of the century, and that machine did succeed in "disciplining" women to think mechanically and submit themselves to the rhythms of industrial work and to the newer demands for scientifically precise clerical efficiency. That novel machine even gave rise to a whole new class of professional women and enhanced the "status" of the female as a reliable worker, and it did much to disseminate ideas and expand the horizons of culture. That machine did many things to bring about change; the one thing it could not do, except perhaps by its capacity to provoke revulsion, was to turn a typist into a feminist.

What then does Veblen have to say to the women liberators of our time? One should note, first of all, that if the machine failed Veblen so too did the "proletariate" disappoint Marx and the ballot John Stuart Mill. Neither science, class consciousness, nor democracy seems to have altered the status of modern women in ways radicals and liberals once hoped. Nevertheless, Veblen's interpretation of the cultural anthropology of sexual discrimination deserves attention. Unlike Marx and Engels, he was not content to explain the nature of social relationships without trying to explain their origins. He attempted to account not only for how things are but for how they came to be. His unique contribution to social theory bears repeating: in the simultaneous emergence of property and a leisure class he perceived the first formation of social role systems that would serve to legitimate not only class society and modern capitalism but male domination as well. Thus in contrast to Charlotte Perkins Gilman, Veblen did not see the evolution of the sexual division of labor as a natural necessity, nor did he look to man's "social instincts" as in any way redemptive until the culture of capitalism had been fully extirpated.

That culture itself had its deeper origins in the advent of masculine exploit and predation that developed when humankind passed from the stage of "peaceable savagery." Veblen's purpose was to point out that there was a "close connection" between the rise of three related developments: individual ownership, the paternal household, and the loss of women's status.[51] Whatever may be the underlying structure of these phenomena, Veblen made a distinct addition to feminist studies by describing the ways in which values function to sustain social relationships that had their birth at the dawn of human history. In doing so he challenged the conventional meaning of social and cultural "values." The modern "barbarian status of women" is the result not of "norms" and consciously accepted "ideals," as the consensus scholars would have it (nor is it necessarily the result of the "forces of production" and "relations of production," as Marxists insist). Rather the contemporary position of women is the outcome of power relations that originated in primitive acts of coercion, relations that become themselves reified into "natural" customs and thus take on the status of a scientific as well as a moral ideology. In tracing the brutish origins of masculine hegemony Veblen did much to reorient social consciousness by showing us why acts of power should never be dignified with the aura of authority. This is a perspective that liberals, radicals, and perhaps even conservatives, may fully share.

9 . . . The Tribes of Academe

Professor Veblen

Thorstein Veblen was a problem child of higher education. Tolerated as a colleague by an envious faculty, he was treated as a black sheep by a resentful administration. And with good reason. For Veblen's reputation followed him across the country from campus to campus, and seldom did he fail to live up to his image as an eccentric recluse and iconoclast. Even today his legend lives on in academic circles. Mention the name Veblen and one invariably draws a smile. What professor would not like to know more about a scholar who could be both a genius and a failure, to say nothing of an inscrutable misfit who made life so frustrating for administrators and so interesting for coeds?

Veblen was about as comfortable in an American university as a playboy in a European monastery. Much of his continuing troubles with academic officials stemmed from his notorious philandering. His association with the University of Chicago came to an end when he scandalized the authorities by traveling to Europe with a woman who was not his wife. During his brief stay at Stanford young coeds would visit his log cabin, and a few would linger on for more than tea and conversation. On one occasion a friend, trying to be discreet, referred to a young lady staying at his cabin as his niece. "That was not my niece," corrected Veblen. He made no attempt to conceal his life-style, and no doubt he delighted in shocking the sensibilities of Victorian America. When the chancellor at the University of Chicago, William Rainey Harper, expressed to Veblen his deep concern for the "moral health" of his colleagues' wives, Veblen more than obliged his superior. Legend has it that Veblen replied slowly in a low voice, slouching in front of the chancellor's desk. "I've tried them all," he whispered. "They are no good."[1]

If Veblen's erotic exploits were intolerable to authorities, his teaching methods were no less insulting. Veblen seemed to regard the three sacred rituals of academic life—grades, class attendance, and departmental meetings—as wasteful distractions from the pursuit of learning. He gave all his students the grade C, regardless of their work.

To a student who complained that his mark was the lowest he had received in college, Veblen explained: "My grades are like lightning. They are liable to strike anywhere." But when another student needed a higher score to qualify for a scholarship, Veblen cavalierly raised her evaluation from "medium" to "superior," and when that failed to do the trick, to "excellent," leaving the dean's office utterly bewildered. He seldom took attendance in class, and when ordered to do so by the authorities he would call the roll with a great display of precision, carefully placing to the side the cards of the students not present; then, once separated, he would seemingly by accident mix the decks of cards together again. Veblen had no use for faculty meetings, and he was heard to remark that committee work was useful only for "sifting sawdust."[2]

To undergraduates Veblen seemed as irresponsible a teacher as he was impenetrable a personality. His lectures were delivered in a low monotone, so mumbled and inarticulate that his humor and insights were often lost upon the audience. One student, sedulously taking notes, requested that a sentence be repeated, only to be told that it was not worth repeating. Veblen made no attempt to enliven his discussions, and he kept his classes small by asking prospective students if they could handle French and German. Once he told a sorority girl inquiring about his class: "I don't say that I will fail any member of a sorority or fraternity, but no member of such an organization has ever yet passed one of my courses." Sarcastic as well as intimidating, he once asked a devout student of religion to explain to him the value of her Church in terms of beer kegs. Reticent as well as whimsical, he replied, when asked his opinion of the work of a certain sociologist's writings in a journal edited by Veblen himself, "The average number of words on a page is 400. Professor ——'s average is 375." Veblen's classes dwindled as he continued to ramble and mumble; one ended up with only a single remaining student. His office hours changed accordingly. A door card which once read: "Thorstein Veblen, 10 to 11, Mondays, Wednesdays, and Fridays" was gradually revised to read: "Mondays: 10 to 10:05."[3]

Despite his reticence, or perhaps because of it, Veblen's reputation as a scholar quickly soared after the publication of *Leisure Class*. His erudition, until now buried in academic journals, began to be noticed. "There goes Dr. Veblen who speaks 26 languages," said a student. Some of his graduate students had already been awed by the sweep of his mind. "Interdisciplinary" before the word became a cant phrase, Veblen was adept in Norse literature, in Icelandic mythology, and in Cretan history, and his free-ranging mind enabled him, as Lewis Mumford observed, to break down "the conventional division between economics, ethnology, anthropology, psychology and the physical sciences." A number of his former students would later recall with affection as well as admiration what they had learned from Veblen. "To a well-brought-up scion of American culture," said Wesley Clark Mitchell, "taking one of Veblen's courses meant employing vivisection without an anaesthetic. Those who could stand the treatment, and not all could, came out with a much more critical attitude that included Veblen's own methods of arriving at conclusions." James Hayden Tufts, a noted social scientist, remembers coming upon Veblen while an oral examination was in session: "When I entered the room, the examination had begun and someone I did not know was asking questions. I thought his speech the slowest I had ever heard—it was difficult for me to keep the beginning of the question in mind until the end was reached. But after a while I began to see that here was a subtle mind penetrating to fundamental issues without disclosing its own views except the one determination to get to the bottom of things." Even Veblen's languid, discursive lectures could be appreciated by those few who sensed what he was about. Hence another former student: "In a low creaking tone, he began a recital of village economy among the early Germans. Presently he came upon some unjust legal fiction imposed by rising nobles and sanctioned by the clergy. A sardonic smile twisted his lips; blue devils leaped to his eyes. With mordant sarcasm, he dissected the tortuous assumption that the wish of the aristocrats is the will of God. He showed similar implications in modern institutions. He chuckled quietly. Then returning to history, he continued the exposition."[4]

It is almost painful to contemplate what ratings Veblen might have received had student evaluations been used in his era. His very erudition handicapped him as an instructor, college fanfare irritated him, administrative duties left him cold. On the other hand, many of his peers sensed his greatness and a number of his graduate students would later discover that he was more interested in their professional welfare than they had realized. If a teacher's contribution is measured more by his lasting impact than by his ephemeral popularity, Harold Laski explains why Veblen deserves to be so judged:

> I first met Professor Veblen shortly after the opening of the New School for Social Research. He was very shy, and, in the first weeks of our acquaintance, it was difficult to get on intimate terms with him. But, once the initial barriers had been overcome, he was an entrancing companion. He delivered himself, in a half-oracular, half-ironical way, of extraordinarily pungent judgments upon men and things. I remember particularly his admiration for Marx . . . his praise of F. J. Turner and Charles Beard. . . . He used to insist that we had entered upon an epoch of revolution and he doubted whether any American of his time would see again the kind of social peace characteristic of America in his youth. . . . He impressed me greatly both by his sudden flashes of insight—a streak of lightning which revealed unexpected vistas—and the amazing range both of his general knowledge and his memory for almost esoteric facts. It would have been easy to describe much of his talk as cynical; but one saw quite early that this was in fact merely a protec-

> tive colouring beneath which he concealed deep emotions he did not like to bring to the surface. I was moved by his patience, his willingness to consider difficulties, his tenacity in discussion, and his anxiety, in matters he regarded as important, to discover common ground. When I first knew him, he was beginning to get the recognition he deserved; and it was profoundly moving to watch his shy delight in realising that his long struggle was at last beginning to bear fruit. . . . I do not remember discussing anything with him without receiving illumination; and his kindness to a much younger teacher remains one of the abiding memories of my years in America.[5]

The estimate of Veblen's peers may have been more encouraging than the evaluation of his pupils. Yet there is a certain pathos in a mind so fine it is incapable of communicating its superior knowledge. Veblen himself, however, seemed untroubled by his limitations as a teacher. What did trouble him was the condition of the American university itself.

The Captains of Erudition

The Higher Learning in America: A Memorandum on the Conduct of Universities by Business Men appeared in 1918, a dozen years after the manuscript had been written. Veblen wanted to be free of the University of Chicago before he allowed this document to see the light of day. He may have also considered the old adage about satires—those who are clever enough to write them are foolish enough to publish them. At least he reconsidered and, at the suggestion of friends, dropped the original subtitle: "A Study in Total Depravity."

The Higher Learning opens with an anthropological generalization that by now had become characteristic of Veblen: in every known civilization there exists a body of esoteric knowledge whose bearers may be medicine men, savants, scholars, priests, shamans, clerks, or scientists. Whether such knowledge derives from science, philosophy, religion or mythology, it is revered as a "systematization of fundamental and eternal truth" that makes up the substantial core of civilization. Yet—and here is the crux—the custodians of culture are not free agents; their ideas are subjected to the institutionalized forces and habits that militate against the intellect. In the past the Church and the State intruded into the affairs of academe; today that role is being performed by business. The authority of the ecclesiastical and the political has given way to the hegemony of the commercial in society at large, and the university system is absorbing the pecuniary spirit as though it had found its cultural mission. "Plato's classic scheme of folly, which would have the philosophers take over the management of affairs, has been turned on its head; the men of affairs have taken over the direction of the pursuit of knowledge." Appointed to the strategic governing boards, businessmen at some universities had acquired discretionary control over huge endowment funds, a "penurious" management of finances that sacrificed the needs of the institution to the business ventures of the trustees. Engineers and inventors are seldom appointed to such positions, for success in the commercial world is the "conclusive evidence of wisdom" of managing affairs, even matters that have nothing to do with commerce. What then did the "honourable" businessman have to offer the university? The same qualities that the captains of finance brought to the economy: "a spirit of quietism, caution, compromise, collusion, and chicane," the "safe and sane" characteristics of "watchful waiting" best summed up in the "well-accepted" American colloquialism: "The silent hog eats the swill."[6]

Veblen's treatment of the hapless businessman remained as sardonic as ever in *The Higher Learning*. His more serious purpose, however, was to show how the principles of capitalism had permeated every aspect of the university: the meretricious "architecture of notoriety," new "bastard antique" edifices that served no useful academic purpose and only inculcated among students "a spirit of disingenuousness"; the expensive academic pageants, rituals, and other "genteel solemnities" that served to advertise the university and yield a return in gifts and donations, only at the cost of channeling more money to public relations and less to teaching and research; the rivalry among departments for funds and the "diplomatic contention" among chairmen bent on expanding their domains; the competitive hustling after students and the wasteful duplication of programs; and the amusing "side shows," such as athletics, Greek-letter fraternities, "student activities," and other frivolous devices of distraction and "politely blameless dissipation." Veblen wondered whether the faculty allowed itself to be the willing captives of the "ceremonial yoke" of academic life. The objections of professors are less felt than expressed, he observed, and they seem hardly to mind subjecting their wives to "this routine of resolute conviviality."[7]

The Higher Learning is more than a satire on the social manners of academe. In addition to exposing the pretensions of rank and status—Veblen himself removed the title "Dr." before his door card—the book offered a pioneering scholarly analysis of the bureaucratic operations of the modern university. The quantification of credits and the statistics of registration, the insidious jockeying for deanships and chairmanships, the pressures of conformity and sycophancy due to a seniority system of promotion and remuneration, a curriculum designed for mechanical accountancy and hierarchical control, evaluation of academic work in terms of livelihood or earning capacity—all such features of the modern university were easy targets for one who could not abide the domination of mind by the administration of things. The "captains of erudition" had done their job well in transforming learning itself into utilitarian calculus. "In all its bearings the work is hereby reduced to a mechanistic, statistical consistency, with numerical standards and units; which conduces to perfunctory and mediocre work throughout, and acts to deter both students and teachers from a free pursuit of knowledge, as contrasted with the pursuit of academic credits."[8]

To Veblen the university remained the last hope of the Enlightenment, the only institution in modern culture upon which the pure search for knowledge still devolves. Veblen acknowledged the preeminence of intellectual enterprise even in an American society dominated by leisure-class values. But he felt that the "higher learning" had to be protected, not only from the corroding forces of bureaucracy at work within but from society's tendency to impose its functions on the university. Veblen scarcely concealed his contempt for extension and correspondence courses ("and similar excursions into the field of public amusement"), for vocational training, the preparation of secondary-school teachers, and curricula offering "home economics," "domestic science," and even instruction in industrial skills (in *Leisure Class* he had expressed a preference for technological education over the humanities and fine arts). He protested vocationalism and utilitarianism in almost all branches of study. Schools of commerce were too imbued with the "business animus," and law schools too steeped in the study of the strategic use of knowledge to explore its theoretical foundations (Oliver Wendell Holmes, Jr., in contrast, found the study of law in America not steeped enough in worldly affairs). Veblen did make an exception for the training of physicians, surgeons, pharmacists, agriculturists, "engineers of all kinds," and "perhaps even of journalists," for their services were of use to the community at large. But whenever he heard the term "practical" in education, he sensed the misguided ambition of a young man on the make, the concern of the parents for their children's material success, or the request by businessmen for a "free supply of subordinates at reasonable wages."[9]

In anatomizing the spirit and structure of the American university, Veblen was not merely the mischievous critic to whom nothing is sacred. He did pose concrete suggestions. Perhaps the most controversial was his effort to distinguish a college from a university in order to separate better their respective functions. The attempt by administrators to integrate the two by offering undergraduate and graduate education within a single institution results less from pedagogical considerations than from bureaucratic calculations. The undergraduate college, Veblen observed, cannot be rated as an institution of higher learning since its aim is either to prepare students for the professions or, in more recent times, to provide the finishing cultural touches on those who are to enter a pecuniary life of "fashion or of affairs." While the university need offer no set curriculum, the college must continually adjust its offerings to meet the public's changing needs. One institution is dedicated to the pursuit of knowledge, the other to the service of society.

Veblen had gained a reputation in his economic writings as a cynic with nothing constructive to offer. In *The Higher Learning*, perhaps in answer to this charge, he offered a "positive" proposal "partly out of a reasonable deference to the current prejudice that any mere negative criticism and citation of grievances is nothing better than an unworthy experiment in irritation." The proposal had a Swiftian irony, modestly asking for the abolition of the president's office, the board of trustees, and the "organs" of other administrative functionaries. Veblen cautioned that at first thought his "heroic remedy" may seem "suicidal," since educators and laymen alike would fear the entire collapse of the university system. On reflection, however, those familiar with academic affairs will realize that members of the administration and governing boards serve only to publicize the university and to create new, superfluous functions to perpetuate their own bureaucratic sinecures. Once the "unreasoning faith in large and difficult combinations" (the same faith that sustains corporations) has been dispelled, the power of the university can be transferred to its rightful trustees, the teachers, and the "confirmed incompetence" and uselessness of the administration will be further confirmed. As the concluding paragraph of *The Higher Learning* suggests, it is difficult to say whether Veblen took his proposal seriously,* but one cannot fail to appreciate the syndicalist dream that inspired it:

> Now, all this speculation as to what might happen has, of course, little else than a speculative value. It is not intended, seriously and as a practical measure, to propose the abolition of the president's office, or of the governing board; nor is it intended to intimate that the captain of erudition can be dispensed with in fact. He is too dear to the commercialized popular imagination, and he fits too convincingly into the businessmen's preconceived scheme of things, to permit any such sanguine hope of surcease from skilled malpractice and malversation. All that is here intended to be said is nothing more than the *obiter dictum* that, as seen from the point of view of the higher

* This specific proposal may be tongue-in-cheek, but others made in the book need to be taken seriously. Veblen considered, for example, the possibility that foundations, institutes, and centers could take over the research function of the university; and hence some writers have maintained that he was an early advocate of what in our time came to be called "think tanks." Yet Veblen shrewdly noted that such institutions would cut off the creative "give and take between teacher and student" and thus leave the university more "routine" and "businesslike" than ever as it survives in the "sands of intellectual quietism." Far more important to Veblen was the creation of "academic houses of refuge," a proposal made in the "Introductory" chapter written after the outbreak of World War I. Veblen had the plight of the German intellectuals in mind, but he also saw such a proposal as a means of controlling the wasteful duplication among American universities. "A beginning may well be made by a joint enterprise among American scholars and universities for the installation of a freely endowed central establishment where teachers and students of all nationalities, including Americans with the rest, may pursue their chosen work as guests of the American academic community at large, or as guests of the American people in the character of a democracy of culture." A few years after Veblen's death in 1929, a "university-in-exile" was established at the New School for Social Research to support German scholars fleeing Hitler.

> learning, the academic executive and all his works are anathema, and should be discontinued by the simple expedient of wiping him off the slate; and that the governing board, in so far as it presumes to exercise any other than vacantly perfunctory duties, has the same value and should with advantage be lost in the same shuffle.[10]

Bureaucratic Realities

It is easy to dismiss Veblen's writings on education as a study in the perversity of brilliance, the work of wicked nonsense by an academic malcontent. It is even more tempting to trace the origins of his spleen to the frustrations of his academic career. His sense of the stultification of undergraduate education, for example, may have derived in part from his own student experience. At Carleton College even the conservative economist John Bates Clark felt a protective sympathy for the young Thorstein, "whose unconventional character," wrote Clark's son, "had not endeared him to authorities of an institution where smoking was grounds for expulsion and the professor of mathematics opened every class exercise with a prayer."[11] Setbacks in graduate school may have also influenced Veblen's animosity toward the university system. He failed to receive a scholarship to Johns Hopkins (as well as other fellowships for which he later applied as an established scholar), and even with a Ph.D. it took him, as we saw in an earlier chapter, nine years to find his first job. As a professor at Chicago, Stanford, and Missouri, he scorned academic entrepreneurship, refused to accommodate himself to administrative protocol, and mocked the university as the citadel of popular values. With the possible exception of Charles Sanders Peirce, under whom he briefly studied, and Henry Adams, another professor alienated from academic life, Veblen might be described as the most successful failure in the history of modern American education.

The Higher Learning is more than a peevish tract. The book's historical context justifies Veblen's apprehensions about the increasing influence of big business in education. Indeed the major universities at which he studied and taught had all been founded on the resources of personal or corporate wealth. Johns Hopkins, a merchant-banker, left in his will $3,500,000 to found a university in Baltimore; Leland Stanford, a railroad tycoon, gave $24,000,000 to a university named after his son and located on the family farm in California; and John D. Rockefeller, an oil magnate with a council of astute lawyers, contributed $34,000,000 to rescue the University of Chicago from obscurity.[12] Clearly capital had enriched the groves of academe, providing higher education its "primary accumulation," and no doubt businessmen assumed college directorates. But Veblen leaves the reader unclear as to whether the wealthy merely exercised influence or actually wielded power. He never bothers to discuss, for example, the sensitive issues of academic freedom. One need only compare *The Higher Learning* to Weber's *The Power of the State and the Dignity of the Academic Calling in Imperial Germany* to appreciate what is lacking in Veblen—a controlled moral anger at the violations of intellectual conscience. One would never guess from reading *The Higher Learning* that the parameters of professional behavior had been delineated by a series of academic freedom cases, notably the "heresy" trial of the University of Wisconsin's Richard T. Ely in 1894, and, in the following year, the dismissal of Ely's graduate student, Edward Bemis, from the University of Chicago for publicly stating opinions on the trusts, unions, and the Pullman strike that embarrassed the Rockefeller-supported university.[13] Veblen arrived at Chicago during the midst of the Bemis affair, and he later published *The Higher Learning* in 1918, when three Columbia University professors, including the eminent historian Charles Beard, resigned in protest against America's entry into World War One. Of these passionate human details Veblen seems to have been dispassionately untroubled.

Although Veblen felt the presence of power, he never fought power openly, never challenged authority directly, never joined the faculty in public protests. As David Riesman shrewdly noted, Veblen conducted himself "as an academic Wobbly, a slyly effective saboteur of Registrars, Deans of Students, and other officials."[14] Yet Veblen's indirection was as much artistic as political: a satirist as well as a syndicalist, he would lampoon the "imbecile institutions" instead of personally confronting them, accept his salary from a benefactor and then pun the gift-horse as a "philandropist." If satire is, among other things, a way of finding a certain psychological relief in expressing all that is ugly, incongruous, and excessive, Veblen's portrait of the university president served the author's purpose perfectly:

> A flabby habit of body, hypertrophy of the abdomen, varicose veins, particularly of the facial tissues, a bleary eye and a colouration suggestive of bile and apoplexy,—when this unwholesome bulk is duly wrapped in a conventionally decorous costume it is accepted rather as a mark of weight and responsibility, and so serves to distinguish the pillars of urbane society. Nor should it be imagined that these grave men of affairs and discretion are in any peculiar degree prone to excesses of the table or to nerve-shattering bouts of dissipation. The exigencies of publicity, however, are, by current use and want, such as to enjoin not indulgence in such excursions of sensual perversity, so much as a gentlemanly conformity to a large routine of conspicuous convivialities. 'Indulgence' in ostensibly gluttonous bouts of this kind—banquets, dinners, etc.—is not so much a matter of taste as of astute publicity, designed to keep the celebrants in repute among a laity whose simplest and most assured award of esteem proceeds on evidence of wasteful ability to pay. But the pathological consequences, physical and otherwise, are of much the same nature in either case.[15]

Veblen's aloof personality and his mordant style may explain the perspective and tone of *The Higher Learning*. They do not, however, explain Veblen's refusal to face power either personally as a moral confrontation or intellectually as a theoretical problem. For he was primarily concerned not with the sheer power of business but with the more subtle influence of capitalist values, and herein lies, I believe, the basic flaw of the book.

Veblen remained convinced that the clearest manifestation of capitalist culture could be seen not only in higher education's devotion to pecuniary goals but in the quantification of the learning process itself. "The underlying business-like presumption accordingly appears to be that learning is a merchantable commodity, to be produced on a piece-rate plan, rated, bought and sold by standard units, measured, counted and reduced to staple equivalence by impersonal, mechanical tests."[16] Yet in *The Higher Learning* we encounter not so much the creatures of capital as the agents of rationalization, the scientific coordination of all activities, the total bureaucratization of all procedures that is more a product of the engineer and efficiency expert than Veblen would care to acknowledge. We encounter, that is, the world of Weber, the spectre in Veblen's anarcho-technocratic daydreams. Veblen would have us believe that the administration was dedicated to the realities of capitalism and the faculty to the ideals of pure scholarship. Yet the faculty itself, in order to gain freedom from business influence and attain a measure of autonomy, could curb the power of the president only by promoting a network of committee structures that would depersonalize the university's operations. Veblen was too much the maverick to participate vigorously in faculty committees. Had he done so he may have realized what was behind all this seemingly wasted effort at "sifting sawdust"—maximum security through bureaucratic organization. Veblen, in short, could not fight bureaucratic power because he had no theory of power or bureaucracy. His own commitment to scientism left him in the paradoxical position of calling for the quantification of life in the social world and deploring it in the academic world.

Veblen's "faculty idyll," David Riesman has written, represents "a kind of Rousseauistic 'state of nature' thinking, of the very kind he so bitterly attacked, viewing scholars as a breed, so to speak, of 'scientific man,' single-mindedly pursuing the truth that lies at the margin of the already known, and not requiring any institutional support in that pursuit."[17] Veblen's proposal to abolish all administration may have been impractical, and clearly his innocence of the dynamics of power left him incapable of seeing that any movement in modern industrial society, even the movement for faculty autonomy, requires the power of bureaucratic organization for its realization. But would he be surprised at the condition of higher education today? Veblen wrote his book at a time when the faculty suffered from administrative interference and when many professors required independent means to supplement their nominal salaries.[18] Riesman, in turn, wrote his book on Veblen a quarter-century ago, when higher education was expanding responsibly, the university performing a most useful service in training students for professional work, offering educational opportunities to returning GI's, and providing Ph.D.'s when they were really needed. Today neither the context in which Veblen attacked the higher learning nor the situation in which Riesman thoughtfully defended it can make claims upon our judgment. Presently it is not the Rockefellers or the Stanfords who provide the personal funds for higher education; it is the great bulk of the middle class, upon whom taxes fall most heavily. Corporate capitalism may have supported the author of *The Theory of the Leisure Class;* now the public is being asked to support a massive body of academics who seem more and more in its eyes to represent "the leisure of the theory class." Veblen, a masterful ironist, would not be surprised by such developments. He was always quick to spot the incursion of business values into academe, and no doubt he would see how today's tenure system and other academic "privileges" can often be as abused a "property-right" as the oil depletion allowance.

Riesman has raised the most telling criticism of *The Higher Learning* by turning Veblen's own judgments back on himself. Not only did Veblen miss seeing that the university, instead of capitulating to business, actually provided alternative careers for young men of humanistic inclinations. Even more seriously, he became infected by the disease which he himself had so mercilessly anatomized in the body of capitalist culture. "Thus, in spite of his own hatred for snobbery, Veblen has ended by supporting, at least to some extent, certain current academic snobberies: the offensively superior attitudes to the business world; the extra meed of honor given those who don't teach at all, or who teach graduate-student males as against those who teach in secondary schools, or teach women, or teach extension classes."[19]

Can Veblen be accused of reverse snobbery? Was he an elitist parading as an egalitarian? Any judgment one makes of Veblen's educational ideas is bound to be ideological, based on our own views of the social or cultural (or even political) purposes of schooling. What then should be the mission of education? It must not, Veblen makes clear, perpetuate class or cultural distinctions, even the distinction between teaching and research which supposedly distinguishes undergraduate from graduate instruction. Veblen called upon all educators, in college as well as the university, "to take an investigator's interest in the subject in which he is called on to teach," for the "instruction offered can reach its best efficiency only in so far as it is incidental to an aggressive campaign of inquiry on the teacher's part." Veblen would make every teacher a scholar and have every scholar draw his students into his own life of research and reflection. The life of the mind, however, is frustrated by administrators who compel teachers to spread themselves thin by offering a variety of courses that can only become a routine of "amateurish pedantry."[20]

Rather than asserting the educator's "superior attitudes to the business world," Veblen described the immense prestige enjoyed by higher education, whose watchword commanded the respect of a moral imperative: "the increase and diffusion of knowledge among men." Why do the rich admire the learned? This behavior posed a problem for Veblen's simple dualistic scheme of prestige allocation. Perhaps, Veblen mused, "the pursuit of learning is a species of leisure," in which case the wealthy desire the honorific association which the scribes and shamans enjoyed in other cultures. Perhaps the rich admire knowledge because they worship power, and hence long to get their hands on "this highly sterilized, germ-proof system of knowledge, kept in a cool, dry place"—the archives and laboratories of the university. Whatever the case, Veblen recognized that the activity of learning commanded more respect than even "religious devotion, political prestige, fighting capacity, gentility, pecuniary distinction, profuse consumption of goods." Thus in *The Higher Learning* Veblen acknowledged what he had slighted in his previous works—the eminence of the academic calling even in a capitalist culture. Yet his awareness of history led him to sense how ephemeral this eminence could be and how learning could again become, as in the past, "only an instrumentality in the service of some dominant aim or impulse, such as vainglorious patriotism, or dynastic politics, or the breeding of a commercial aristocracy."[21] Although Veblen's proposal to abolish administration may seem a radical pipe dream, his ultimate aim was not so much to transform the university but to preserve it from both institutional deterioration and external political and social pressure. His elitism consisted in calling upon the "higher learning" to remain independent of power elites.

Veblen may have been *l'enfant terrible* of the modern university system, the iconoclastic scholar who posed embarrassing questions to the world of scholarship. Yet he was more than a disturber of the pedagogues. He was also a conscience, a moralist with elitist sensibilities and egalitarian sympathies who desired to save the "higher" learning from the "lower" realities of American life. He opposed the careerist tendencies of college life that would turn the university into a well-heeled agency for the production of well-adjusted young corporation men. Although an unsuccessful teacher himself, he criticized bureaucratic centralization for undermining "close or cordial personal relations" between student and teacher, and he questioned the "system of authoritative control, standardization, gradation, accountancy, classification, credits and penalties, [that] will necessarily be drawn on stricter lines the more the school takes on the character of a house of correction or a penal settlement."[22] He exposed the rituals of pomp and status and the inanities of many "extra-curricular" activities. Above all, he resisted the attempt of higher education to reach out and serve every need of society, only to discover that a consumer society will soon have little respect for its servants.

Idle Curiosity versus Pragmatism

The Higher Learning is, despite its cynicism, a hopeful statement. Veblen believed that the university could ultimately withstand the assaults upon its integrity by the commercial world. The true educator, naturally inquisitive and full of wonder and speculation, would always be at war with hierarchy, bureaucratic authority, sycophancy, and other forces detrimental to the pursuit of knowledge. Even under the corrosive influence of business principles the ideals of scholarship could survive, for the entire faculty could not be corrupted without suffering the sting of professional conscience. "Academic tradition gives a broad, though perhaps uncertain, sanction to the scientific spirit that moves this obscure element in the academic body. And then, their more happily gifted, more worldly-wise colleagues have also a degree of respect for such a single-minded pursuit of knowledge, even while they may view these naive children of impulse with something of amused compassion; for the general body of the academic staff is still made up largely of men who have started out with scholarly ideals, even though these ideals may have somewhat fallen away from them under the rub of expediency."[23] What remains to haunt the conscience of the academic with *mauvais foi* if he gives himself over to the culture of capitalism is the instinct of idle curiosity. Veblen's faith in the resiliency of this human endowment leads to perhaps the most optimistic utterance he ever committed to print:

> The permeation of academic policy by business principles is a matter of more or less, not of absolute, dominance. It appears to be a question of how wide a deviation from scholarly singleness of purpose the long-term common sense of the community will tolerate. The cult of idle curiosity sticks too deep in the instinctive endowment of the race, and it has in modern civilization been too thoroughly ground into the shape of a quest of matter-of-fact knowledge, to allow this pursuit to be definitively set aside or to fall into abeyance. It is by too much an integral constituent of the habits of thought induced by the discipline of workday life. The faith in and aspiration after matter-of-fact knowledge is too profoundly ingrained in the modern community, and too consonant with its workday habit of mind, to admit of its supersession by any objective end alien to it,—at least for the present and until some stronger force than the technological discipline of modern life shall take over the primacy among the factors of civilization, and so give us a culture of a different character from that which has brought on this modern science and placed it at the centre of things human.[24]

Veblen defined idle curiosity as " 'idle' in the sense that a knowledge of things is sought, apart from any ulterior use of the knowledge so gained." The aim of idle curiosity is a theoretical apprehension that allows the "disinterested proclivity to gain knowledge of things and to reduce this knowledge to a comprehensible system." Men have always possessed this propensity, for the nature of phenomena has always excited man's inquisitiveness and challenged his need to explain the curious behavior of things. Whether the pursuit of "unprofitable knowledge" is avowed as a legitimate end in itself is a matter of cultural circumstance.[25]

David Riesman has astutely observed how the notion of idle curiosity reflects Veblen's own personality: aloof, playful, uncommitted to the immediate "great issues" of the day, and defiantly independent of any vested interests.[26] The notion may also be seen as a central feature in Veblen's philosophy of education. Much as later psychologists like Jerome Bruner would argue that learning is not the acquisition of a body of knowledge but a "process" of thinking, so too did Veblen believe that one does not attain knowledge as a finished task but instead develops an ability to learn how to learn through the "work of inquiry." Veblen had always been concerned with the epistemological implications of the function of thought—what we do and why we do it when we think. He addressed himself to this issue in "The Place of Science in Modern Civilization" (1906), and it is here that the concept of idle curiosity was first introduced. It is also here, one may recall, that Veblen offers some unflattering comments on the philosophy of pragmatism. In this respect his essay on science, and not necessarily his book on the higher learning, may provide a key to Veblen's educational philosophy.

Veblen's attitude toward pragmatism is deeply ambiguous; one never knows what he means by the term, and while he refers to the philosophy itself with bemused skepticism, he is careful to express great respect for John Dewey and William James.[27] Nevertheless, it seems clear that Veblen wanted to show the limitations of pragmatism as a mode of knowing (or discovering) by introducing the notion of idle curiosity. Where Dewey and James believed that inquiry arises from a problematic situation, Veblen argued that idle curiosity derives from organic development in response to inhibited nervous complication. One reaction to this complication—a "naive pragmatism"—is a motor impulse directed to an expedient outcome for the stymied organism. The other reaction does not spend itself in a similar way and is not directed to practical use. Of the latter response Veblen says: "Pragmatically speaking, this outlying chain of response is unintended and irrelevant." What distinguishes idle curiosity, and renders it indifferent to expedient lines of thought, is that it takes its shape from an anthropomorphic or animistic interpretation of phenomena, an interpretation that incites primitive man's capacity for wonder because of its dramatic "consistency" and "cosmology." Veblen was convinced that throughout history idle curiosity had led to a more and more comprehensive system of knowledge, whereas in the pragmatic way of knowing, so steeped in the maxims of expediency, there is "scarcely a degree of advance from Confucius to Samuel Smiles." Moreover, while idle curiosity seems to have flourished in archaic, peaceable communities based upon blood relationships and clannish distinctions, pragmatic behavior develops when life is transformed from a culture of fecundity to an environment of predation involving mastery and servitude, gradations of privilege and honor, coercion and personal dependence. Now the pressures and uncertainties of everyday life cause men and women to behave pragmatically and expediently adjust themselves to a social system founded upon status distinctions and personal force. "A shrewd adaptation to this system of graded dignity and servitude becomes a matter of life and death." The habits of thought are now, Veblen observes while citing James's *Principles of Psychology,* shaped by discriminations enforced by daily life. Pragmatism is the counsel of conformity and survival; what is needed is the counsel of science—the interplay between idle curiosity and the discipline of technology, between the activity of mind and the reality of fact. Pragmatism renders inquiry cautious where it should be bold, submissive where it should be subversive.[28]

The pragmatic temperament, according to Veblen, was never completely absent after man left the stage of peaceful savagery. Even in the theologically drenched culture of the Middle Ages, the otherworldly "age of faith," one may discern an "accentuated pragmatism" in the way in which scholastic concepts are drawn in terms of experience, personal force, exploit, feudal hierarchy, and prescriptive authority. "The laws that are sought to be discovered in the natural universe are sought in terms of authoritative enactment. The relation in which the deity, or deities, are conceived to stand to facts is no longer the relation of progenitor, so much as that of suzerainty." Even the quest for God could not transcend the behavior of egoism and expediency. "The best of men in that world were not ashamed to avow that a boundless solicitude for their own salvation was their worthiest motive of conduct, and it is plain in all their speculations that they were unable to accept any other motive or sanction as final in any bearing." In social and economic behavior as well as in philosophical speculation all thought becomes a matter of practical sagacity and knowledge in general is turned to individual advantage. Whatever may have been the original communal and spiritual ideals of Christendom, its culture adapted to the altered requirements of life changes in the western world. The Christian ethic, Veblen suggests, was insufficiently strong to prevent the means of living to become confused with the ends of life. "The high era of barbarism in Europe, the Dark and Middle Ages, is marked off from what went before and from what has followed in the cultural sequence, by a hard and fast utilitarian animus." Veblen never made it clear whether culture determines conduct or reflects it, but he was certain that the higher learning of even classical humanism succumbed to the activist itch of daily life:

> The university of medieval and early modern times, that is to say the barbarian university, was necessarily given over to the pragmatic, utilitarian disciplines, since that is the nature of barbarism; and the barbarian university is but another, somewhat sublimated, expression of the same barbarian frame of mind. The barbarian culture is pragmatic, utilitarian, worldly wise, and its learning partakes of the same complexion. The barbarian, late or early, is typically an unmitigated pragmatist; that is the spiritual trait that most profoundly marks him off from the savage on the one hand and from the civilized man on the other. 'He turns a keen, untroubled face home to the instant need of things.'[29]

Veblen's generalizations may cause the intellectual historian to bristle. But there was a method to his cavalier treatment of the history of ideas. By attributing a utilitarian animus to classical culture Veblen made it clear that he was not, as some writers have maintained, calling for a return to the higher learning of a past age. Nor was he suggesting, as do some contemporary Marxists, that the philosophy of pragmatism emerged as the ideological equivalent of modern capitalism. The pragmatic temperament antedated industrial capitalism and had its roots in early man's mastery of the forces of nature. Pragmatism, insofar as it had nurtured an empirical approach to reality, should not be blamed for the cultural limitations of modern consciousness. But when pragmatism is applied to pedagogy and the question is asked, "What is the use of this learning?" here the trouble begins. The true scholar is under no obligation to answer this question. "If he were not himself infected with the pragmatism of the market-place, the scholar's answer would have to be: Get thee behind me!" To answer such a question is to concede the values of the person who posed it. "Ben Franklin—high-bred pragmatist that he was—once put away such a question with the rejoinder: What is the use of a baby?" Veblen made effective use of Franklin's shrewd remark, for it indicated how far modern "barbarian" man had deviated from the wholesomeness of his savage instincts. Yet Veblen also noted that "civilized" man could only admit with shame that he regarded children in pecuniary terms, and this suggests that humankind's two constructive instincts, idle curiosity and the parental bent, remain a potential force in modern life. "No doubt, what chiefly urges men to the pursuit of knowledge is their native bent of curiosity,—an impulsive proclivity to master the logic of facts; just as the chief incentive to the achievement of children has, no doubt, always been the parental bent." The urge to know and to understand, like the urge to procreate and to care, is itself an evaluative activity. The most basic instincts of men and women are self-justifying.[30]

Veblen's argument that learning exists for its own sake may not have resolved the ethical dilemmas in his philosophy of education; nor could it demonstrate how any process of inquiry divorced from the world of action could be translated into a philosophy of science. It would be interesting to know why Veblen felt it so necessary to distinguish idle curiosity from pragmatism. Did he foresee that Dewey's philosophy would leave the university theoretically defenseless whenever society demanded that knowledge be made useful in order to better meet the needs of society, even the conservative needs of the existing social order? Some writers have suggested that Veblen's *The Higher Learning* presages the student attacks on the "multiversity" in the 1960s.[31] But surely Veblen would have seen the hook within the bait: the student's demand for "relevance" amounted to a capitulation to the world-view of their bourgeois enemies, the urge to turn everything to practical account. The university, Veblen insisted, can serve no end but the "disinterested pursuit" of knowledge itself.

Veblen's early career in the academic world is testimony to the thesis he propounded in *The Higher Learning*. A fierce critic of society, he remained a castigator of any university that would surrender its cultural mission to society. After the outbreak of World War One, however, Veblen himself ceased being the "disinterested" inquirer and social theorist. When the ideals of Minerva confronted the forces of Mars, the ethic of "idle curiosity" became the first casualty of Veblen's higher learning.

10 . . . America and the World

World War One and Imperial Germany

Thorstein Veblen's response to World War I surprised nearly everyone who knew him. To be sure, he was not the only man on the left who supported America's entry into the conflict. Almost the entire intellectual left came around to advocating intervention between the outbreak of hostilities in August 1914 and President Wilson's war message to Congress in April 1917. Not only did liberals like Walter Lippmann, Herbert Croly, and Lincoln Steffens support the war, but even such militant socialists as Jack London, William English Walling, and Upton Sinclair broke with the Second International and rallied behind the Allied cause.[1] What makes Veblen's position so unique is that he alone among social theorists had relentlessly exposed modern war as a combination of barbarian fury and technological expediency. Veblen had always disdained warlike activity because he discerned in it the origins of private property and class stratification, and also the thwarting of his two highest values: productivity, the efficient output of useful goods, and serviceability, the concern for community welfare. Above all, the spirit of war undermined the objective pursuit of truth by nurturing a "conservative animus" based upon unquestioning cultural obedience and total political acquiescence. Veblen stressed the connection between war, capitalism, and barbarian predation in *The Theory of Business Enterprise*, published in 1906. Less than a decade later he would defend America's participation in the bloodiest war in modern history. Had the "bard of savagery" become the apologist for civilization?

Answers to such questions may be found in Veblen's fourth book, *Imperial Germany and the Industrial Revolution*. Veblen began the manuscript shortly before the war broke out in Europe, but the urgency of the international situation compelled him to finish it in a matter of months, an amazing feat for an author who had spent years working on his other books. One virtue of this haste is that Veblen no longer had the time to play the ironist and rhetorician. For once we know the aim of the book: to provide an historical account of Germany's exceptionally high degree of industrial progress and efficiency, an account based on "natural causes" that eschewed such pseudo-explanations as manifest destiny, national genius, and "Providential nepotism." Veblen was determined to expose as fallacious the racial explanation for Germany's supremacy in science and technological development. The German people were, like most people of other European nations, composed of a "hybrid race." By heredity, if not by habit, Germans had about the same characteristics at birth as other peoples who populate the European continent. *Das deutsche Volk* may be a cultural mystique, but it scarcely matches the native endowments of human biology. There was no scientific basis for believing that the German people, or for that matter any people, were a superior race.[2]

To explain the genius of Germany's superiority in industrial and military capacity, Veblen, the economist, anthropologist, and sociologist, turned historian. What now seemed crucial was not how institutions functioned or originated but how they changed during the course of development. Veblen approached the problem of Germany by contrasting her background with that of England to illustrate an obvious point with subtle and far-reaching implications: Germany was more technologically advanced while England remained more politically mature. Thus industrial England did not provide, as Marx suggested, the "classic ground" of the capitalist mode of production; that is to say, she did not provide the model of the more developed country that would show the less developed the image of its own future. Instead Germany overtook England by absorbing her technology, virtually adopting it afresh, without having also to assimilate her encumbering political institutions and ideological habits of mind. This did not mean that Germany would necessarily become more enlightened, for a "given technological system will have an economic value and a cultural incidence on a community which takes it over readymade, different from the effects it has already wrought in the community from which it is taken over and in which it has cumulatively grown to maturity. . . ." That modern technological advance was not made in Germany but borrowed by her from English science and industry suggested a quiet historical fact with many ramifications:

> Germany combines the results of English experience in the development of modern technology with a state of the other arts of life more nearly equivalent to what prevailed in England before the modern industrial regime came on; so that the German people have been enabled to take up the technological heritage of the English without having paid for it in the habits of thought, the use and wont, induced in the English community by the experience involved in achieving it. Modern technology has come to Germany ready-made, without the cultural consequences which its gradual development and continued use has entailed upon the people whose experience initiated it and determined the course of its development.[3]

In England, Veblen pointed out, the industrial arts endured long enough to affect the culture and customs of the people. The spirit of industrialism undermined institutions like the Crown and Church and engendered a constitutional order and commercial ethos, both of which were based upon a healthy skepticism, itself nurtured by technology, that could be directed against the power of the state. In Germany, on the other hand, technology arrived almost as an alien import and thus had little or no effect on the political culture. Here machine technology was merely harnessed to an existing political order that had its roots deep in Germany's medieval past. The institutional system, the habits and values of the German people, still dominated technology and science; and those habits and values were still influenced by a dynastic state and semi-feudalistic class system that had as their aim the internal centralization of power and the external expansion and domination of people. The Germans imposed their new technology on their older dynastic state, and out of this synthesis came an "unstable cultural compound" that was susceptible to accelerated change and to aggression and world conquest as well.

In Veblen's eyes Germany presented a threefold danger: its peculiar history of nation building, its peculiar pattern of economic development, and its peculiar philosophy of authority. In contrast to England, whose insulated geography enabled it to avoid the foreign wars and rivalries that rocked the Continent, Germany forged its unity and nationhood out of centuries of offensive and defensive warfare and protracted internal struggles of "ruthless exploitation, terror, disturbances, reprisals, servitude and gradual habituation to settled allegiance, irresponsible personal rule, and peaceable repression." In contrast to England's economic history, which nurtured individualism and enterprise in opposition to the state, that of Germany was guided by the Prussians who, beginning with the *Zollverein*, identified commercial development with the power of the state and its fighting capacity, a policy presently manifested in Germany's transportation system, a unified rail network strategically laid out on the basis of military need. And in contrast to England's political philosophy, whose libertarian natural-rights doctrine amounted to the principle of "live and let live," that of Germany inculcated the idea of duty and obedience. The German concept of authority, Veblen noted, placed sovereignty neither in the people nor in the ruler but in a mystical, super-organic moral community called "the State." The English notion of loyalty was tempered with self-interests, just as British empiricism was itself preoccupied with "material realities." German philosophy, on the other hand, in both its metaphysical and romantic tendencies, had turned away from the actualities of sense perception to seek the "idealistic, spiritual, transcendental." This "nobler" and "profounder" philosophy resulted in an acquiescence to dynastic politics and bureaucratic rule insofar as the German concept of the state made the nation's power and glory the highest aim of its citizens. In the German idea of liberty the truer and higher freedom inhered not in resistance to power and authority but in the ability to obey orders and carry out commands.[4]

In *Imperial Germany* Veblen betrayed a fondness for English liberty that was completely absent from his earlier works. Not only had he suggested that democracy nourished the scientific spirit and represented a more perfect adjustment to modern industry than did the dynastic state; he also treated the British liberal tradition as a valuable intellectual resource worth fighting for. Only a year earlier, in *The Instinct of Workmanship*, Veblen had relegated English natural rights to the museum of historical relics, a philosophy of competitive individualism no longer relevant in an age of corporate capitalism. Now he took another look at English history and, by turning defects into virtues, found much to be admired as well as disparaged.

In England, according to Veblen, machine technology and business enterprise arrived earlier and matured more slowly than in Germany. As commercialism and science developed over the centuries, the old order was undermined and English social philosophy became imbued with the utilitarian canon of self-interest. "The British subject's loyalty to the reigning monarch or to the crown is conditioned on the serviceability of such allegiance to his own material interests. A loyalty which raises the question What for? comes far short of the feudalistic ideal and of that spirit of enthusiastic abnegation that has always been the foundation of a prosperous dynastic state."[5] The emergence of liberal skepticism out of capitalist materialism proved, however, to be a mixed blessing. While the philosophy of self-interest transferred sovereignty to the individual self, it also transferred power to the captains of industry. Earlier, in the sixteenth and seventeenth centuries, the rising capitalist class in England played its role well in borrowing technological methodologies from the more advanced continental nations and in integrating the agricultural, industrial, and financial activities of the country. By the nineteenth century, however, the institutionalized values of capitalism—ownership, competition, and the profit system—served to hinder the full development of industrialism in England. Instead of keeping abreast of the newest technological innovations, British capitalists engaged in the strategy of "depreciation by obsolescence" as they allowed their railways, factories, and harbors to fall into disrepair. Corporate profits, not technological efficiency, inspired the English businessmen who no longer had a vested interest in change and innovation. In Veblen's account of the logic of modernization, the capitalist emerged as less the villain than the victim:

> All this does not mean that the British have sinned against the canons of technology. It is only that they are paying the penalty for having been

thrown into the lead and so having shown the way. At the same time it is not to be imagined that this lead has brought nothing but pains and penalties. The shortcomings of this British industrial situation are visible chiefly by contrast with what the British might be doing if it were not for the restraining dead hand of their past achievement, and by further contrast, latterly, with what the new-come German people are doing by use of the English technological lore.[6]

Germany's combination of philosophical idealism and technological efficiency greatly disturbed Veblen. This unexpected synthesis seemed to offer evidence that science may not, as Veblen once hoped, liberate society from cultural lag, from the "dead hand" of old values and habits of mind. Idealism led to political subordination, efficiency to national power. Germany was poised as the leading "disturber of the peace" precisely because her industry and commerce were developed to strengthen a nation whose cultural outlook remained almost medieval while her economy was thoroughly modern. From these observations Veblen concluded that a constitutional state like Britain will fight mainly when provoked, whereas dynastic states like Germany use war as a means to expand power and domination. Yet Veblen remained convinced that Germany's combination of idealism and efficiency was unnatural and therefore unstable. Although somewhat chastened by the spectacle of Prussian might, he continued to believe that industrialism would eventually sweep away all cultural impediments. Thus he foresaw two possible alternatives for Germany. First, her old dynastic pattern might be gradually transformed into a constitutional state composed of a capitalist economy and liberal political institutions; second, the German people "may yet be able to retreat into that more archaic phase of Western civilization out of which they have latterly been escaping," a retreat that would mean "so drastic a reaction in their civil and political institutions as will offset, presently neutralise, and eventually dispel the effects wrought by habituation to the ways and means of modern industry and the exact sciences."[7]

The second alternative has led some scholars to believe that Veblen foresaw the rise of fascism, not only in Germany but also in Japan, another rapidly modernizing country on whose future he also speculated in 1915. We shall return to these "prophetic" claims at the conclusion of the chapter. Here it is important to note that Veblen did not offer a "devil theory of war" and saddle Germany with sole responsibility for the outbreak of hostilities. In Veblen's estimate, the war was the result of a number of factors affecting all belligerent western nations: technological developments that broke down the defensive buffers of geography, the scramble for colonies that whetted imperialistic appetites, the quickened pace of transportation and communication that increased fear of aggression, and, above all, the volatile spirit of patriotism that made military success the test of national manhood. The burden of Germany's dynastic history made it inevitable that she would be placed in the "seat of the disturbance, whether on the offensive or defensive," but other western nations also contributed to the diplomatic situation even if Germany suffered "the distinction of taking the lead and forcing the pace." All nations protested their peaceful intent, Veblen wryly noted; yet "it was not necessary formally to desire the war in order to bring it to a head, if only care was taken to make the preparations so complete as to make war unavoidable."[8]

If no country wanted war and yet each and every national leader took actions that led inexorably to war, what measures could be adopted to prevent future international conflicts? If World War One was inevitable, was perpetual peace impossible? This question Veblen took up in his next book.

Peace Without Honor

Imperial Germany and the Industrial Revolution perplexed those few Americans who bothered to read the book. Veblen's description of British capitalism as wasteful and inefficient offended American anglophiles, and his dismissal of German *Kultur* as metaphysical hogwash seemed too much for American intellectuals who had once studied at the universities of Berlin and Heidelberg. So ambiguous a reception did the book receive that even government officials could not make up their minds whether Veblen should be praised or imprisoned. After America entered the war, President Wilson's propaganda expert, George Creel, tried to exploit the book's anti-German arguments; but the Post Office, perhaps uneasy about Veblen's harsh treatment of the British and his depiction of the Prussian business imagination as superior to the American, barred the book from the mails as pro-German.

The war years were perhaps the only period in which Veblen took politics and diplomacy with utter seriousness. For the first time the aloof cynic became the involved citizen. In the fall of 1917, Wilson authorized setting up the U.S. Inquiry into the Terms of Peace, a study group to prepare the groundwork for a possible peace conference. The group was officially headed by Colonel Edward House but it was actually directed by the secretary, Walter Lippmann. Veblen corresponded with Lippmann over the possibility of working with the Inquiry, pointing out that the aim of the committee coincided exactly with the aims of a book he had just completed, *The Nature of Peace*. Lippmann responded, prompted in part by a suggestion from a subordinate, by asking Veblen to prepare a memorandum dealing with "the economic penetration of underdeveloped countries by foreign interests," a study aimed at "protecting backward or semi-backward peoples from unjust exploitation" and "reducing to a minimum the economic and political advantage of concession holders as against nationals of other allegiance." Veblen undertook the investigation for the Inquiry, and he also took on a number of other studies that would aid the war effort. Among them were a schedule on price regulation prepared for the Food Administration; a proposal to the Department of Agriculture that federal prosecution of the I.W.W. be "immediately squashed" so that Wobblies could be used to harvest grain during the manpower shortage; a similar proposal to release "menial servants" from the household chores of the rich in order to employ them in war industries; a study of the foreign and domestic policies of Japan; and even a memorandum, "Wire Barrage," suggesting to military officials a practical method for fighting submarines.

Many of Veblen's reports were lost in the labyrinth of government agencies (and were only later retrieved through the diligent research of Joseph Dorfman).[9] But one study, "Suggestions Touching The Working Program Of An Inquiry Into The Prospective Terms Of Peace," was received by the Inquiry "about the time we were preparing the memorandum for the fourteen points," Lippmann later recalled.[10] Whether Veblen exercised any influence on Wilson's policies is difficult to say. Yet his studies on the terms of peace and postwar reconstruction, as well as his book-length analysis, *An Inquiry Into The Nature Of Peace And The Terms Of Its Perpetuation* (1917), deserves close attention. For now Veblen was thinking as a political and diplomatic strategist, and not only as a social theorist. His studies on war and peace provide the link between his cultural criticism and his political thought.

In the preface to *The Nature of Peace* Veblen discussed Kant's *Zum ewigen Frieden*, pointing out that the German philosopher regarded the quest for an enduring peace as an intrinsic human duty rather than as a promising enterprise. Although Kant exhorted man to endeavor to make peace real, he remained convinced that in the end peace would be installed not as a deliberate achievement of human wisdom so much as "a work of Nature and the Designer of things—*Natura daedala rerum*." The question of peace today, Veblen noted, has changed considerably since Kant's time. The answer cannot be found in what man ought dutifully to do or in what nature will do in her own mysterious ways. Rather, the answer must be sought in "terms of those known factors of human behavior that can be shown by analysis of experience to control the conduct of nations in conjunctures of this kind."[11] For Veblen these "known factors" constituted the whole psychological substructure of values and mentalities that determine a country's political culture. And World War One provided, ironically enough, the opportunity to scrutinize those values and habits of mind and perhaps even sweep away their institutional foundations. In one sense Veblenism added a corollary to Wilsonianism: World War One would be the war to end all wars, a war to make the world safe for technocracy.

The Nature of Peace contained several provocative arguments. First of all, Veblen noted with anarchistic relish, peace cannot be established by negotiations among the warring states. Such maneuvering and bargaining could only result in an armistice, "in effect terminable at will and in short notice." At best, the state, or the government, served as an instrument for making peace, not for perpetuating it. And the state meant to Veblen not so much the "executive arm" of the capitalist class, as it did to Marx, but a modified lineal descendent of feudal establishments (Veblen noted the exceptions of the governments of Switzerland and the Scandinavian countries as well as the ancient republic of Iceland and its insubordinate citizenry). Veblen conceded that there were important differences between the dynastic and the democratic states, but despite the variations both types were vested with certain attributes of "sovereignty." Whether in Germany or in England the citizen was in some measure a "subject" of the state in that he owed his allegiance to inherited or constituted authorities. As the recent preoccupation with treason and sedition indicated, modern governments possessed many of the same discretionary, coercive rights that belonged to the feudal chieftain, and they possessed such power not necessarily because they were oppressive as much as they were venerated. The psychological glue that bound the citizen to the state was patriotism.

Veblen had long regarded patriotism with the same disdain he held for capitalism—the animistic curse that plagued the collective mentality of modern man. In *The Nature of Peace* he devoted a lengthy chapter to the subject, a revealing discourse that indicates that Veblen saw patriotism as something more than the ideology of the capitalist class. As a phenomenon that generates "a sense of partisan solidarity in respect of prestige," patriotism was not simply a manufactured false consciousness but rather a propensity that had evolved out of earlier archaic habits.

> The patriotic spirit is a spirit of emulation, evidently, at the same time that it is emulation shot through with a sense of solidarity. It belongs under the general caption of sportsmanship, rather than workmanship. Now, any enterprise in sportsmanship is bent on an invidious success, which must involve as its major purpose the defeat and humiliation of some competitor, whatever else may be comprised in its aim. Its aim is a differential gain, as against a rival; and the emulative spirit that comes under the head of patriotism commonly, if not invariably, seeks this differential advantage by injury of the rival rather than by an increase of home-bred well-being.[12]

Although patriotism may be seen as tribalism writ large, Veblen was careful to point out that it was not universal. Certain communities, like the Eskimos and the people of the ancient Icelandic republic, had no knowledge of such sentiments; and even the Chinese, who had outlived and civilized their barbarian conquerors, appeared to be "incorrigibly peaceable" and lacking a "solidarity of prowess" to such an extent that they were presently entering international politics not as a "power but as a bone of contention." The promptings of patriotism thus derived from an acquired bias, not from a basic trait of human nature; they were a matter of habit, not of heredity.

The patriotic loyalty commanded by the state was in many respects the political expression of the cultural deference commanded by the captains of industry. The patriotic spirit, like the emulative propensity, also had its origins in humankind's vague beginnings, when hunting and fighting in solidarity with one's clan were requisite for survival and material well-being in primitive times. Even after this requisite was no longer necessary because of the advent of technology, the habits of tribal solidarity persist in the form of modern nationalism, in which citizens take pride in the physical magnitude of their countries, in the size of their monuments and buildings, their aggregate wealth, natural resources, and military prowess. Veblen was convinced that the common citizens, the "underlying populations," had no stake in patriotism. After the rights of ownership begin to take effect, so that property and profit now govern men's relations, the collective material concerns of life cease to run on lines of group solidarity. As the state of the industrial arts developed, property rights displaced the community of usufruct and invidious distinctions between persons emerged. "The material interests of the population . . . come to be divided between the group of those who own and those who command, on the one hand, and those who work and who obey, on the other." With this division of labor, and of privilege and prescription, joint effort became beneficial to only one class and patriotism was exploited to forge a solidarity of emotions to replace the loss of a community of interests. Thus the modern protective tariff and commercial subvention, for example, were accepted by the common man because they supposedly promised an increase of national power and prestige, and thus were part of his "psychic income," whereas in reality such conspiracies in restraint of free trade worked against the interests of the commonweal. The interests of the privileged classes in the common welfare, observed Veblen, "is of the same kind as the interest which a parasite has in the well-being of his host."[13]

In his skillful anatomy of patriotism, Veblen made a contribution to modern social thought that has been given little recognition. Both classical liberal pluralists (i.e., Madison) and to a certain extent even conflict theorists (i.e., Marx) assumed that classes in a given social strata knew—or, in Marx's case, would inevitably come to know—their own class interests, and that therefore moral ideals and ethical motives were all but irrelevant to the study of history. Veblen, in contrast, may have been, together with Georges Sorel, one of the first modern social thinkers to insist that the working class is psychologically incapable of being moved by material interests alone. Hence such diplomatic shibboleths as the "Open Door," "Freedom of the Seas," or, more quaintly, "A Place in the Sun," could stir mass emotions not because the common man had a clear grasp of the realities of foreign policy but rather because his sense of equity and fair play, however misguided, could be aroused. Thus patriotism, far more than radical class conflict or even liberal interest politics, commanded the greatest allegiance because it had the sanction of moral necessity.

> Any promise of gain, whether in the nation's material or immaterial assets, will not of itself carry full conviction to the commonplace modern citizen; or even to such modern citizens as are best endowed with a national spirit. By and large, and overlooking that appreciable contingent of morally defective citizens that is to be counted in any hybrid population, it will hold true that no contemplated enterprise or line of policy will fully commend itself to the popular sense of merit and expediency until it is given a moral turn, so as to bring it to square with the dictates of right and honest dealing . . . To give the fullest practical effect to the patriotic fervor that animates any modern nation, and so turn it to use in the most effective way, it is necessary to show that the demands of equity are involved in the case. Any cursory survey of modern historical events bearing on this point, among the civilised peoples, will bring out the fact that no concerted and sustained movement of the national spirit can be had without enlisting the community's moral convictions. The common man must be persuaded that right is on his side. 'Thrice is he armed who knows his quarrel just.'[14]

Veblen had his work cut out for him. Faced with the delusions of the common man on the one side and the deceptions of the capitalist classes on the other, how could peace possibly be obtained? Like Max Weber, Veblen was critical of the endeavors of the pacifists to bring forth a peace based on "good will." He was also critical of the "old fashion" nineteenth-century plan of competitive defensive alliances, the Bismarckian balance-of-power school of thought that collapsed like a house of cards in August 1914. Thus according to Veblen only two options remained for the Allies: unconditional surrender and submission to the dynastic hegemony of Germany and Japan,* or elimination of the war-prone states, together with all resources suitable to the formation of subsequent formidable coalitions.

Terming submission "peace without honor," Veblen called for an international organization to eradicate every vestige of German militarism and imperialism, to grant her government only administrative status until a democratic regime could be established, and to con-

* Japan was then, of course, on the side of the Allies, but Veblen regarded her as equally menacing to peace as Germany. For Veblen's observations on Japan, see below, pp. 313–314.

fiscate the estates of the Junkers and to use the proceeds to indemnify civilians of invaded countries. The organization that was to carry out this second alternative Veblen called a "League of Neutrals"—countries capable of the "neutralization of all outstanding national pretensions." The principal members would be the North Atlantic countries, including not only the United States and the English-speaking dominions and France, but Scandinavia and the Netherlands as well. Veblen regarded such countries as less warlike and mature enough to have "abjured dynastic ambition and dominion." Other countries of eastern Europe would, once freed from dynastic rule, be incorporated into the league, as would eventually the less developed colonies overseas. Although the degrees of influence would vary, the relations among the three groups would no longer be imperial and exploitative. The league would be somewhat patterned after the evolution of America's federal system, in which states, territories, and outlying possessions exercised varying degrees of sovereignty and autonomy. In that part of the world governed by the league there would be no economic discriminations or privileges, all peoples would have equal access to natural resources, trade would be free, diplomacy "open and public," and a system of collective security would serve as a "League to Enforce Peace."[15]

Although Veblen shared Wilson's conviction that America's entry into the League of Nations was imperative, he was too skeptical that American business would support any enterprise that might curb nationalism and economic liberty in the interests of the common good—the book's final chapter is entitled "Peace and the Price System." Veblen went far beyond Wilsonian internationalism and demanded much more than the defeat of Germany and the establishment of world government. His "peace without honor" referred to the policy of nonresistant submission to imperial domination, but he implied that Wilson's policy of national self-determination was no less defeatist, leaving, as it did, the power of the capitalist classes intact. Veblen never lost sight of the fact that war encourages the forces of nationalism and reaction, yet he also believed that World War One offered a great opportunity. To the extent that the conflict is prolonged, Veblen observed, the public may come to see the waste and greed of business enterprise as well as the stupidity of the ruling classes, whose "gallant gentlemen officers" have piled up such a high death rate on the battlefields that one wonders about their fitness for survival. The war could unhinge the psychological bond that ties the lower class to the older order. The "common man," wrote Veblen in a moment of optimism, "who gathers nothing but privation and anxiety from the owner's discretionary sabotage, may conceivably stand to lose his perception that the vested interests of ownership are the cornerstones of his life, liberty, and pursuit of happiness."[16] Veblen was never a man of much hope, but for a brief historical moment in 1919 he did believe that war would be able to break the spell of capitalist hegemony. What encouraged his belief that World War One might be the seedtime of liberation was the most volcanic historical event of the early twentieth century—the Russian Revolution.

A Soviet of Technicians

Veblen's interest in the Bolshevik Revolution was aroused in 1917, peaked in 1919, and lapsed after 1921. With Lenin's dramatic seizure of power, Veblen faithfully read the newspapers to learn about the successes of the Bolshevik Party and the Red Army, anxiously following the course of the civil war. He also conversed with Lenin's engineering representative in America, and he began to study Russian. Then in February 1919, he wrote a long essay in *Dial*, "Bolshevism Is a Menace—To Whom?"

An appropriate question, no doubt; yet Veblen's essay must be judged an exercise in self-deceit. With his anarcho-syndicalist convictions as a touchstone, Veblen insisted that the Bolsheviks aimed to translate political democracy and majority rule into economics by carrying both principles into the domain of industry. The liberal Kadets and the Kerensky Mensheviks were only prepared to disallow the rights of privilege, while the Bolsheviks were willing to push the revolution to the left and challenge the rights of ownership itself. The idea of Bolshevism spreads by communication, and the conservative forces in the west would no doubt resist this "contagion." But the measures taken by the elder statesmen, such as the blockade, can scarcely do more than enervate the remnants of the old order in Russia. After a brief period of disorganization, the Bolsheviks have restored the transportation and food-supply systems. Meanwhile the workers are being won over to the Bolsheviks, whose "scheme of ideas comes easy to the common man because it does not require him to learn much that is new, but mainly to unlearn much that is old." The training afforded by "the mechanical industries and strengthened by the experience of daily life in a mechanically organised community lends no support to prescriptive rights, or ownership, class perquisites, and free income." Bolshevism, in short, fulfilled the function of the "machine process," emancipating man from "older preconceptions, older habitual convictions." In this respect Bolshevism is a "menace to the vested interests, and to nothing and no one else." The true Bolshevik, concluded Veblen, "is the common man who has faced this question: What do I stand to lose? and he has come away with the answer: Nothing."[17]

In a subsequent essay on Bolshevism, published in 1921, Veblen displayed no loss of enthusiasm for violent revolution. Dismissing the democratic socialists as "dead horses," he described the Russian soviet as "very closely analogous to the town meeting as we know it in New England history." The mystique of a "soviet" occupied

Veblen's thoughts in these critical years, and in *The Engineers and the Price System,* also published in 1921, Veblen proposed a "Soviet of Technicians" as the only alternative to the rule of absentee owners. His faith in a mass uprising by the common man now shaken, Veblen looked desperately to the engineers as the only group indispensable to the running of modern industrial society, hoping that they would join with mechanics and other workers and collectively withdraw their skills from business and prepare to take over its operations. It is doubtful that Veblen really believed in such a possibility. Writing on "The Technicians and the Revolution" in 1921, he observed that "there is nothing in the situation that should reasonably flutter the sensibilities of the Guardians or of that massive body of well-to-do citizens who make up the rank-and-file of absentee owners, just yet." The "just yet" only indicates Veblen remained an ironist of rhetoric and never really became a theorist of revolution. "Veblen could not point out the weak spots in the [social and economic structure] with a more dry and masterly accuracy, if he were consulting engineer to His Satanic Majesty who contrived it," wrote Max Eastman, the Leninist editor of the *Liberator*. But "Veblen's 'Soviet of Technicians' may be set down as a soviet of abstractions—interesting as an intellectual experience, but irrelevant to the problem of defining and organizing a dynamic force sufficient to alter the essential course of history."[18]

The course of history was actually beginning to turn to the right after 1920, and no one knew this better than Veblen himself. The Red Scare of 1919 already served as an omen and its meaning was not lost upon Veblen, who wrote on the subject in anonymous *Dial* editorials and later summed up the whole significance of postwar reaction in a foreboding essay in *The Freeman,* "Dementia Praecox." All the old hopes and new fears of the revolutionary left in America are reflected in this document: the failure of the great steel strike, the suppression of the Wobblies, the suspension of civil liberties, and the rise of the Klan, the American Legion, and the "secret service," which "kept faithfully on the job of making two suspicions grow where one grew before." Had not America intervened in Europe, Veblen speculated with cold melancholy, the old order would have been liquidated due to the sheer exhaustion of resources and an inevitable fiscal crisis. But American interference ended the war before such developments could run their course, and as a result the vested interests remain in power while the common man now suffers unemployment, privation, disorder, and an inconclusive peace that can only result in future hostilities. At home America has become "something of a psychiatric clinic" as a "certain fearsome and feverish credulity" leads citizens to "resort to unadvised atrocities as a defense against imaginary evils," while the capitalists do business as usual and the government does their bidding with protective tariffs and overseas concessions to oil companies. "Unreflecting patriotic flurry has become a civic virtue," lamented Veblen, who no longer had the humor left to satirize a nation deranged by "persecutory credulity."[19]

In the twenties Veblen was tired and deeply disillusioned. His hopes for revolution, always tinged with doubt, were now too painful to recollect. His final book, *Absentee Ownership*, may be read as a premonition of the changing structure and culture of the American economy in the "prosperous" but unstable twenties: the rise of advertising, credit buying, financial speculation, and towering corporations. In his remaining years Veblen lost interest in politics entirely. Save for an essay on economic theory, his last two scholarly endeavors involved translating the Icelandic epic *The Laxdaela Saga* and writing an article on eugenics. Veblen's mind remained as probing as ever, but the passionate intelligence and wit that marked his earlier works could no longer be sustained. During the throes of war and revolution he had watched eagerly for signs of the coming of a new order, and he allowed himself to believe that the Bolsheviks might show the way. But it was the hope of a lapsed skeptic, a desperate belief in the occurrence of the impossible. Thus "when the thing failed to come off," recalled Horace Kallen, a colleague at the New School, Veblen "gave signs of a certain relaxation of will and interest, of a kind of turning toward death. . . ."[20]

Social Theory and World Realities

Veblen's wartime writings are generally regarded as a response to the disruptive world events of the teens and early twenties, a body of work that is more than a *pièce d'occasion* but something less than a *chef d'oeuvre*. Whereas his earlier books, *Leisure Class, Business Enterprise,* and *Instinct of Workmanship*, are something of "classics" in the sense that a timeless quality inheres in the original ways in which Veblen explored the perennial issues in social theory, his writings on world events seem at first glance to be limited to a particular historical context. There is some validity in this assessment of the time-bound nature of his studies of war, peace, and revolution. No one today would read Veblen for an accurate account of the outcome of the Bolshevik Revolution. Nevertheless, many of Veblen's writings during this period can still be read for their enduring insights. Perhaps the greatest compliment on this body of work came from Albert Einstein, who wrote to a friend:

> An excellent and exhaustive analysis of these characteristics of the [German and Japanese] ruling classes was also presented by an American economist Thorstein Veblen, in my opinion one of the most remarkable political writers not only in America but in the entire world. You will find this analysis particularly in Veblen's books *The Nature of Peace* and *Imperial Germany and the Industrial Revolution*. It seems a great pity that this great man is not sufficiently appreciated in his own country.[21]

Einstein's lament, written in 1942, proved a bit premature, for Veblen would be rediscovered by future generations as he had been by different generations of scholars in the past.

The most significant contribution of Veblen's wartime writings, the one theory that scholars in various disciplines have rediscovered in the post–World War Two period, is his account of the process of modernization. Veblen's analysis of Germany and England offers both a pioneering study in what would later be called "comparative history" and a novel technological theory of history and social change. His theory of the "merits of borrowing" and of the "penalty for taking the lead" has been effectively applied by scholars interested in explaining why England, where the Industrial Revolution began, has fallen behind in the twentieth century, while America, Germany, Japan, and Russia have become leading industrial powers because their "take-off" began at a later and therefore higher technological level.

In Germany in particular scholars like Ralf Dahrendorf have not only employed Veblen's analysis to explain Germany's "breathtaking" advance to industrial maturity at the hands of the Prussian state in the late nineteenth century; they have also drawn on Veblen to stress the dangerously incomplete process of modernization that took place. Dahrendorf shifts Veblen's chemical metaphor, "unstable compound," to a geological one when he describes Germany as a "faulted society," just as Barrington Moore shifts to an architectural metaphor when he describes late nineteenth-century Germany as a "victorian palace" with "electricity"—a nation comprised of a highly rationalized economic system and an atavistic social stratum of traditional elites devoted to a patriarchal conception of authority. Students of German history may be critical of Veblen for underestimating the real benefits gained by the German working class under the imperial regime, but they acknowledge his pioneering efforts at explaining Germany's history in terms of objective forces rather than the variables of personality, national character, or *Realpolitik*. Indeed Veblen was the first scholar, in Europe as well as America, to play down the role of Otto von Bismarck and to approach modern German history from what today would be called a "structuralist" point of view, stressing not the dramatic actions of statesmen but the inexorable processes of industrialization.[22]

Historians and economists have also drawn upon Veblen to account for the benefits of backwardness that redound to latecomers in developing countries, while sociologists cite Veblen's analysis as a pioneering study of the differences between traditional and modern societies due to technological determinants.[23] Veblen's thesis has not only come into the common parlance of contemporary economic thought, it has also been used by one anthropologist to develop the "Law of Evolutionary Potential": "The more specialized and adapted a form in a given evolutionary stage, the smaller is its potential for passing to the next stage."[24] Veblen's dialectic between technological development and historical decline, between specialization and eventual obsolescence, is a kind of moral allegory that has also been pondered by Arnold Toynbee. Describing "host" cultures and their "parasites," Toynbee quotes the biologist J. B. S. Haldane: "A step in evolution in any animal group is followed by an evolutionary advance on the part of the parasites."[25]

Ultimately the value of Veblen's analysis goes much further than the study of the formation and transformation of traditional and modern societies. It is not only as a theorist of modernization that one should reflect on Veblen's war writings; he may also be read as a moralist. Today, when every nation seems to want to "catch-up" with, to "emulate," as Veblen would put it, every other more advanced nation, and when those more developed nations continue to exploit their limited resources for fear of falling behind, Veblen's analysis of historical evolution may serve as a cautionary tale to human egotism and national pride. For Veblen was, with the possible exception of Mark Twain and Henry Adams, America's greatest ironist of progress, and his message is as perverse as it is profound: the leaders will eventually be the losers, and in the end the future will belong, not to the innovators, but to the predators.

The recurrence of predatory behavior in modern society raises another issue implicit in Veblen's war writings—the prophecy of fascism. Social scientists like Max Lerner, Douglass Dowd, and David Riesman believe that one may find in Veblen's works premonitions of the rise of Hitler and the Third Reich, or at least some aspects of that grotesque phenomenon. "Anyone reading *Imperial Germany* today," wrote Lerner shortly after World War Two, "will be startled at how clearly he foresaw the mixture of racism, industrial efficiency, military caste, and imperial adventure that were to form Nazism, and how close to the totalitarian state the German dynastic state described by Veblen comes."[26] Riesman is less certain that Veblen foresaw the terror and fanaticism of Hitler's Germany than he did its use of mass psychology and propaganda, while Dowd does not specify exactly what Veblen predicted other than to quote Veblen's description of a "drastic reaction in civil and political institutions."[27] Clearly the most emphatic argument for Veblen's prophesying fascism was made in the *Political Science Quarterly* in 1940 by the then Secretary of Agriculture Henry Wallace. Reviewing the new edition of *Imperial Germany*, brought out in December 1939 after Hitler had marched on Poland, Wallace praised Veblen's study as "the most acute analysis of modern Germany which has ever been written." Wallace noted how difficult it is for Americans to see Germany correctly, the nation which has given America so many immigrants of plain decency and civility, the Germany of Goethe, Kant, Beethoven, and Heine. "But," he added, "if Veblen were living today he would almost certainly look on Hitler merely as the current expression and extension of the pre-war Prussian imperial spirit."[28]

With the outbreak of World War Two it was understandable that Veblen would be reappraised in a positive light; indeed one of his disciples, Walton H. Hamilton, informed readers of the *New Republic* that Veblen anticipated the Munich pact.[29] Looking back, it does seem that Veblen had described many of the factors that would lead to another war: the weakness of a league that enforced a peace settlement leaving untouched the German social order; the danger of a Germany suffering from national humiliation and nursing patriotic grievances; the pretentious commitment of the West to preserving democracy and hence the decadence of British diplomacy in the thirties.

What makes Veblen's case even more compelling is not only his glum expectations for Germany but his uncanny warnings about the future course of Japanese history. When he wrote "The Opportunity of Japan" in 1915 there was no Axis; Japan was fighting on the side of the Allies against Germany. Yet Veblen showed that Japan was not different from Germany in its pattern of historical development. "It is in this unique combination of a high-wrought spirit of feudalistic fealty and chivalric honor with the material efficiency given by the modern technology that the strength of the Japanese nation lies." Adopting western industrial methods while retaining the archaic institutions and customs of the pre-Meiji era, Japan stood in a "transitional" period, a country that would become increasingly torn between the commercial and industrial values of the new world and the militaristic and nationalistic values of the "Spirit of Old Japan." The chivalric and honorific ethos could be matched with the technological culture only for a limited time, before it becomes clear that the "new industrial era carries the faults of its own qualities"—the "spiritual deterioration" of ancient institutions and the creation of new outlets that will deflect the energies of the people. Thus if Japan is to avoid the mistake of England, if she is to harness her new technological power to her older imperialistic ambitions, she must make her move before the full impact of modernization transforms her from a well-poised industrial machine into a complacent and decrepit bourgeois society.

> If this new-found efficiency is to serve the turn for dynastic aggrandisement of Japan, it must be turned to account before the cumulatively accelerating rate of institutional deterioration overtakes and neutralises the cumulatively declining rate of gain in material efficiency; which should, humanly speaking, mean that Japan must strike, if at all, within the effective lifetime of the generation that is now coming to maturity. For, facile as the Japanese people have shown themselves to be, there is no reason to doubt that the commercialisation of Japan should be passably complete within that period. It is, therefore, also contained in the premises that, in order to [forge] an (imperialistically) successful issue, the imperial government must throw all its available force, without reservation, into one head-long rush; since in the nature of the case no second opportunity of the kind is to be looked for.[30]

Statements such as the above have led some Veblen admirers to laud his "prophetic qualities." One must resist the temptation of claiming that he anticipated Munich and Pearl Harbor. If Japan's need for an inevitable "one head-long rush" may help explain her move into Manchuria in the thirties, it can hardly explain the development of postwar Japan. Here an emperor reigned and a patriarchal and paternalistic culture remained almost intact while a democratic parliament thrived and a demilitarized capitalist economy flourished, all of which contradicts Veblen's thesis that modernity and traditionalism make an "unstable compound." There are similar problems with Veblen's analysis of Germany. Ironically it was the Nazi regime itself which finally destroyed the hegemony of the old aristocracy and Junker class. Hitler's veritable "social revolution" brought to power new elite groups which had little or no connection with the dynastic state of historic Germany.[31] And Hitler's foreign policy, instead of representing a continuation of either Bismarckian *Realpolitik* or Wilheimian imperialism, whose aims were contiguous and limited, expressed a dynamic *Weltanschauung* that made war an end in itself. It is even questionable whether big business in Germany gave substantial support to the Third Reich.[32]

That Hitler's Germany was characterized more by change than by continuity is not what ultimately casts doubt on Veblen's predictions. If scholars claim that Veblen's wartime writings "foreshadowed" fascism, why did he so signally fail to comment on the rise of fascism in Italy, Hungary, Poland, and other parts of Europe in the twenties? Many of Veblen's contemporaries did so (e.g. Charles Beard, Lincoln Steffens, Walter Lippmann, Herbert Croly, Oswald Villard, Horace Kallen), some as fellow travelers (e.g. George Santayana and Ezra Pound), others as discerning critics (e.g. Max Eastman and Albert J. Nock, who published Veblen's essays in their respective journals, *The Liberator* and *The Freeman*).[33] Because of Veblen's total silence on the subject, the historian is left reconstructing his implied prognostications from guesses and hints, mistaking some scattered or incidental remarks as omniscient prophecies. Indeed, one can only wonder what Veblen would have made out of the conspicuously bombastic regime of Benito Mussolini. Il Duce knew the value of patriotism, laid claim to the entire heritage of Italian history while paradoxically worshiping the power and precision of the machine and at the same time destroying with utter contempt the traditional Italian state. He was the first leader to exploit both the radical doctrines of class conflict and the conservative work ethic while fabricating a national solidarity of heroic example and leading a personal life of debauchery that reads like a chapter from *The Theory of the Leisure Class*. Here was a political hero who believed in both the mystique of technology and in the romance of national greatness, who attacked both liberalism and Marxism, who accepted irrationality yet aspired to efficiency. True, after 1933 he suffered the "penalty for taking the lead."

One can only speculate on how Veblen would have interpreted the revolutions from the right that arose in Italy and Germany (some Americans, after all, saw in the corporate state the realization of syndicalism and guild socialism, full political representation for the producing groups).[34] Veblen's writings on left-wing revolutions are another matter. If his scheme of historical analysis may have been awkward for grasping the meaning of fascism, it proved totally inadequate as a basis for understanding what was going on in the Soviet Union.

The amazing thing about Veblen's interpretation of Bolshevism is not that he saw the soviets functioning as a New England town meeting; almost the entire American left suffered delusions of wish-fulfillment in 1917. The amazing thing is that he did not apply the same mode of analysis to Russia as he did to Germany, even though the burden of Russia's feudalistic past was greater than that of Germany. In almost all his writings Veblen displayed a keen sensitivity to the slow pace of historical change and to the persistance of archaic values and customs. In his essays on Bolshevism, however, Veblen assumed that the machine psychology would so permeate Russian life that the "older preconceptions" and "habitual convictions" would be immediately swept away. Why the same mechanization of life would not produce the same effect in Germany is not clear. The upshot is that Veblen's assumption proved more utopian than the premises of the Bolsheviks themselves, especially Lenin, who appreciated the accumulated forces in Russian history that worked against a rapid transition to "communism": the primitive state of agriculture, the autocratic and repressive political legacy, the illiterate population mired in the doctrines of the orthodox Church, the vast peasantry incapable of responding to socialist incentives, and the powerful farm owners (later termed "Kulaks") capable of only *embourgeoisement*. Lenin had his own answers to these problems, and his solutions had more to do with the imperatives of political organization than with the transformative power of technology.

Six months before his death in 1929, Veblen remarked to a neighbor: "Naturally there will be other developments right along, but just now communism offers the best course that I can see."[35] This remark was made at the time the anti-Stalinist opposition was being crushed and Stalin himself was embarking upon the brutal program of rural collectivization. The Bolshevik Revolution had eliminated the two institutions of modern life that Veblen had regarded as the curse of barbarism—property and patriotism. With the elimination of these institutions Veblen could feel, at least in the euphoric years of 1919–1920, that all other cultural and political impediments would be extirpated as well. They were not, of course, and within a few years after Veblen's death Stalin would introduce wage differentials, dismiss the idea of equality as "bourgeois rubbish," revive traditional Russian nationalism, and exploit the cult of personality with the acumen of an American captain of industry. Viewed from the perspective of Slavic history, Veblen, had he lived another decade, might have dismissed Stalin's despotic rule as the vengeance of ancient Russian barbarism upon Soviet communism. But for a theory of liberation Veblen would have to go beyond Russian history to find the roots of freedom elsewhere, either in primitive communal life or in the political institutions of the West, neither of which could help explain the dilemmas of a socialist experiment that defiantly skipped the bourgeois stages of historical development. Indeed Veblen astutely described in *The Instinct of Workmanship* the process by which the Anglo-American tradition of freedom emerged with the rise of private property and a liberal economy. How freedom could develop in a country where political liberty never sank roots, and where the traditional communal units, such as the ancient *mir*, were being drastically transformed by industrialization, remains the central burden of Veblen's interpretation of Bolshevism. It may even be said that Veblen ignored his own Darwinian sensibility when he allowed himself to believe that communism did not have to evolve from preexisting historical conditions but instead could be imposed upon the course of history by an act of will. In this sense Marx, with his conviction that each stage of history must reach its fullest development before passing over into another stage, may be judged a better evolutionist than Veblen, who believed what even Lenin regarded as an infantile fantasy: that the flower of democracy can burst forth in full bloom from the bowels of despotism.

Veblen never really developed a theory of politics or power. He approached the phenomenon of the modern state and authority relations by analyzing the economic power and cultural influence of the capitalist classes. Confronted by an episode like soviet communism, where the influence of property interests had been eliminated, Veblen had no theoretical framework for analyzing the political and bureaucratic dynamics of a revolutionary regime. In the end his writings offer not so much a political theory of power as a psychological theory of submission. As Max Lerner observed, Veblen was quick to explain "the readiness of the victim for the slaughter. He stressed the willingness of the capturable mind to be captured even more than the strategic position the captor holds."[36]

In the Soviet Union, however, it was the strategic position of the party, and certainly not the acquiescent tendencies of the Russian masses, that accounts for the success of Bolshevism. Veblen's theory of "emulation" may explain why even citizens in a democratic society surrender their sovereignty to capitalist elites; it may also explain why peoples living under fascist regimes are prone to identify with power by submitting to authority. In the early years of the Soviet Union, however, what is remarkable is the popular resistance to the centralization of power and authority in the hands of the communist party.

This resistance came from all elements outside the relatively small group of Bolsheviks: the peasants, the Mensheviks, the Kadets, the Kulaks, the anarchists, the non-Russian ethnic groups, even many of the intellectuals. Veblen's great hope was, of course, that the engineers would rise to the top and guide the party apparatus. This hope followed from his analysis of modern technology, which supposedly delivers power and responsibility into the hands of the technicians, who by virtue of their empirical activities become increasingly skeptical of conventional truth. The grim irony is that the Russian engineers did begin to move to important positions at the end of the twenties, only to become one of the first professional groups to fall victim to the earliest purge, the industrial party trials of 1930–1931.[37] More than anything else, this purge signified the incompatibility of Veblenism and Bolshevism. The engineers, who had now superseded the capitalists in assuming control over the means of production, posed a threat to the party and constituted a "new class" whose leaders had to be liquidated.

Veblen was fortunate in passing away before he saw how his ideas (and Marx's) would be appropriated by the Russian communist party for its own ends. As Herbert Marcuse has noted, *The Instinct of Workmanship* illustrates how the mechanization and rationalization of labor generates attitudes of standardized conformity and exacting submission to the machine process, which in turn require adjustment and response rather than autonomy and spontaneity.[38] Insofar as industrialism corrodes old attitudes only to nurture new forms of regimentation, science itself cannot be a counterforce to a totalitarian regime. In essence, Marx's and Veblen's insistence upon science as the highest reach of human comprehension, and upon productivity as the highest principles of social relations, offers no ethical or political ground from which to criticize the Soviet state. Indifferent to the qualitative aspects of life, to the dimensions of human freedom and even to the values of leisure and the pursuit of happiness, technology, by emphasizing only efficiency and productivity, becomes an instrument of control rather than liberation.

Although Veblen's presuppositions led him to misread the nature and direction of Russian communism, his wartime writings may tell us something about the condition of third-world countries today. That borrowing countries do not necessarily take over every aspect of industrialization from advanced societies, that the state plays a crucial role in promoting or retarding development, that economic growth involves the impact of technological change on both the culture and on the institutional framework in which the economy functions, that "capital equipment" is a public resource embodying the community's joint stock of technological knowledge, than an economy of production rather than distribution and consumption maximizes its full capacity for serviceability—such ideas are urgently relevant to countries presently struggling to overcome backwardness. Having said this, however, one is obliged to note that Veblen himself failed to anticipate the rise of the third world. Although he wrote an important document for the Wilson administration on using an international league to prevent the economic exploitation of backward countries by western powers—thereby protecting primitive cultures he respected from the technology he admired—he appears to have had no inkling that much of the underdeveloped world would achieve colonial independence and political autonomy. One reason Veblen could not anticipate such a development is that he had dismissed as archaic nonsense the single motivating factor that did so much to stir the political consciousness of the third world—patriotism.

With the subject of patriotism we come to the final irony in Veblen's life and thought. It was Veblen's estrangement from American society which enabled him to scrutinize everyday normalities with the surgical tools of a pathologist and the inspired madness of a literary artist. It was that very same estrangement, however, that led Veblen to misinterpret the historical significance of patriotism. Veblen regarded the patriotic sentiment as a heritable propensity with roots deep in man's primitive legacy. This fact in itself, however, could not be sufficient grounds for Veblen's rejecting the promptings of patriotism. Veblen's own sense of what constitutes ethical behavior, such as workmanship, parental obligation, and idle curiosity, indicates that genuine ideals could have a natural basis. But while the instincts and ideals that Veblen espoused were somehow distorted through the processes of historical change, patriotism seemed to him a kind of curse from the very beginning of human history. Of the concatenation of propensities that make up the "patriotic animus," Veblen noted that there is a "sentimental attachment to habit and custom that is called love of home, or in its accentuated expression, home-sickness." In addition there is an "invidious self-complacency, coupled with a gregarious bent which gives the invidious comparison a group content; and further, commonly, if not invariably, a bent of abnegation, self-abasement, subservience, or whatever it may be called, that inclines the bearer unreasonably and unquestioningly to accept and serve a prescriptive ideal given by custom or customary authority." Although patriotism inculcated "abnegation," Veblen did not believe it could lead to a devotion to higher communal ideals and thus to a renunciation of individual egotism. As an "edifice for national prestige," patriotism can only really be vitalized when the dogs of war are unleashed, when group solidarity is realized only because human sympathy is relinquished:

> It is, at least a safe generalization that the patriotic sentiment never has been known to rise to the consummate pitch of enthusiastic abandon except when bent on some work of concentrated malevolence. Patriotism is of a conten-

tious complexion, and finds its full expression in no other outlet than warlike enterprise; its highest and final appeal is for the death, damage, discomfort and destruction of the party of the second part.[39]

Veblen's hostility to patriotism is understandable in its historical context. Many of the best literary minds of that age—Dos Passos, Hemingway, Cummings, Eliot, Pound—came out of World War One convinced that patriotism is the lie of old men; and Max Eastman and Randolph Bourne, two of Veblen's contemporaries, wrote blistering essays on the deadly poison of nationalism in times of war. Thus one might dismiss Veblen's attitude only if he had not been so bold as to offer a solution to the problem of patriotism: the elimination of national frontiers. Veblen remained convinced, even in the face of the nationalistic aspirations of east European peoples, that modern culture and technology had become so complex and integrated as to render the nation obsolete as an "industrial unit." The forces of change would only benefit the common man to the extent that patriotism and its blood brother, the price system, could somehow be undermined. Thus Veblen looked forward to the "submergence of national divisions and national integrity."[40] In so doing, Veblen challenged the liberal assumption that national self-determination made democracy possible. As a cultural evolutionist, Veblen could not identify nationhood with freedom. There could be nationalities tied together by linguistic and religious bonds, such as the Scots, Welsh, and Irish, but the nation as a state functions only as an "organization for collective offense and defence."

To the historian there is much in Veblen's argument worth pondering. While many other contemporary social scientists—especially those who, like the historians John Burgess and William Dunning, did their graduate work in German universities—looked to the state as a source of political and spiritual strength, Veblen was one of the first American scholars to point out that the nation-state came into existence as an instrument of security and aggression and that nationalism functioned as an ideology of cohesion and organization. Nationalism triumphed only when the forces of liberalism and modernization had undermined the older bonds of church and religious faith, the solid network of family relations, and the intimate sense of locality and place.

Although Veblen was perceptive in seeing the relation of nationalism to the pride and "emulation" engendered by international rivalry, his fundamental error was to equate nationalism with patriotism. In historical perspective nationalism may have superseded patriotism as the industrial state came into being, but the two are not synonymous and thus it does not follow that patriotism and nationalism alike will disappear with the transnational integration brought about by technology. It is not only that such technological unification as exists has been forged, as we see today, by multinational corporations. The problem is that patriotism is a natural sentiment that lies deep in man's archaic past, while nationalism is a modern historical development that represents no more than an episode in the story of western civilization. Indeed it may be that nationalism will increase with the advance of technology since the nation-state is based on instrumental rationality, a process of technical organization that has as its aim the conversion of the world into resources for economic and political power. Nationalism and technology share a common premise, the doctrine of progress; and thus, as John Schaar has observed, exponents of nationalism can use ideology to translate baser ambitions into universal principles, whether it be W. W. Rostow's mystique of modernization or G. W. F. Hegel's idealization of the Prussian state.[41]

Veblen was correct in two respects. The nation-state has historically signified the division of the earth into bellicose factions; its very existence is the symbol of lost innocence, suggesting the impossibility of perpetual peace. Moreover, it is pure fiction—and here Veblen was most prophetic—that blood or race is the biological foundation of nationality and the primal bond among human groups. Yet Veblen's equation of nationalism and patriotism led him to dismiss almost contemptuously one of humankind's healthiest sentiments. Even if the nation and the nation-state were to disappear with the blurring of national boundaries due to cultural and technological integration, as Veblen hoped, patriotism would still remain viable. Unlike nationalism, patriotism is essentially an emotional bond fired by a sense of community. The patriotic impulse signifies love of one's habitat and homeplace, a feeling for that which is familiar, an identity with rooted values and customs. As a source of devotion to old ways and intimate things, patriotism is a concrete sentiment that one returns to, while nationalism is an ideological abstraction, a bastardized form of patriotism that one attempts to expand as a universal export, by military force if necessary.

Caught up in the wonderful promises of technology, and disdainful of all archaic traits, Veblen could not distinguish between nationalism and patriotism and thereby discern a radical potential in a conservative sentiment. As a reverence for a world we have forsaken, patriotism may be the only perspective from which to criticize contemporary society. In such an exercise in social criticism non-Marxist theorists need all the help they can get. Veblen exposed leisure and consumption as wasteful, an insult to man's full productive powers; a century earlier John Adams reproached luxury and idleness as a danger to the republic. Both rejected the gods of bourgeois comfort, both explored the implications of "emulation," both denied the pretense of America's uniqueness, and both remained ambivalent about modernity. Had Veblen turned back to American intellectual traditions, instead of mischievously calling for a "soviet of technicians," he may have been able to accomplish the most difficult task that is called for in time of war—to take patriotism away from the patriots.

11 . . . Disciples and Dissenters: Veblen's Legacy in American Thought and Social Action

Truth and Technocracy

The Theory of the Leisure Class and *The Theory of Business Enterprise* aimed to undermine, both by satire and by scholarly analysis, the two fundamental assumptions upon which the entire ethos of modern capitalism rested. Veblen's first book exposed as false the orthodox conceit that wealth and virtue walk hand in hand and that the life of physical labor had always been and therefore must always be the burden of the lower classes. His second book denied that the capitalist played an essential role in the march of industrial progress and that the profit motive necessarily was the handmaiden of productivity. Such generalizations were shocking to the Victorian mind of the turn of the century, and no doubt they can still jar conventional sensibilities. Were they true?

Actually there was almost as much factual history as there was comic hyperbole in Veblen's studies. His second book especially drew upon contemporary economic investigations, census data, and the various testimony submitted to a congressional inquiry into business practices, published as a 19-volume *Report of the Industrial Commission.* Veblen could gather from these sources, as he could have from Charles and Henry Adams' *Chapters on Erie*, ample evidence to confirm his charge that the capitalist was not only a "robber-baron," the epithet of liberal intellectuals, but a "saboteur" who conspired against the interests of production. The creation of the U.S. Steel Corporation in 1901, for example, illustrated how enormous profits could be made without any substantial reduction of prices or increased efficiency in output. J. P. Morgan and Company made $12,500,000 by selling watered stock worth twice the value of the real assets of the plant, an exercise in the new phenomenon of "intangible property" that Veblen would also expose, in his essays on economic theory, as a means of "getting something for nothing."

Veblen's distinction between the engineer and the businessman could also be documented in the building of the great transcontinental railroads. Resourceful engineers like General Grenville Dodge and Theodore Judah did the constructive work of planning safe and efficient roads for the Union Pacific and Central Pacific. But their careful maps and blueprints were often deliberately set aside by financiers scrambling to obtain the lion's share of federal bounties and land grants. When the famous golden spike was hammered in 1869, connecting the transcontinental Northern Pacific line, thousands cheered and economists lauded the organizing genius of the financiers who coordinated the men and materials for this great entrepreneurial venture. But they would have had little to cheer about had they seen a letter written by an eastern railroad man, James J. Hill. "The lines are located in good country," wrote Hill after observing the Northern Pacific empire, "some of it rich and producing large tonnage; but the capitalization is far ahead of what it should be for what there is to show and the selection of routes and grades is abominable. Practically it would have to be built over." Rather than build over dilapidated lines, many railroad promoters went on to bigger and better pursuits. The "Big Four" who organized the Central Pacific—Collis P. Huntington, Mark Hopkins, Leland Stanford, Jr., and Charles Crocker—competed for land grants with the Union Pacific in its race to lay tracks westward across the Sierra mountains and Nevada desert. Their capital and equipment were subsidized generously by the federal government, while the heroic task itself rested gruelingly on the backs of Irish immigrants and Chinese coolies. The "Big Four" lost the race, but they made enough to go on to buy the state government of California.[1]

Veblen's analysis might also have been documented by Populists who believed that depressions are inherent in the credit and monetary system, not the economy. Farmers who saw the market value of their wheat controlled by the Chicago exchange while they paid 12 percent to an eastern mortgage company could likewise understand Veblen's distinction between those who make products and those who manipulate prices. And industrial laborers who worked the mine fields and steel mills to eke out a subsistence wage while corporate profits soared knew from experience that the Protestant work ethic was neither admirable nor workable. Indeed there were some production-minded capitalists who could agree with Veblen—James J. Hill and Andrew Carnegie, and later Henry Ford and Henry Kaiser, were honest spokesmen for hard work and industrial efficiency. But the Goulds, Fisks, Drews, Morgans, Rockefellers, and Stanfords of the late nineteenth century were more interested in the exciting maneuver of huge piles of intangible wealth than in the tedium of turning out useful goods.

Veblen's satiric attacks on business inefficiency represented the negative side of his more positive desire to promote a scientific understanding of the modern industrial system. His devotion to productivity attracted a small following among a handful of theorists and moralists who began to preach the gospel of efficiency in the late nineteenth century. The most prominent was Frederick W. Taylor, an industrial sociologist convinced that the solution to all social conflicts lay in "scientific management."[2] Taylor's chief concern was the physiological problem of fatigue and the technical problem of maximum output. He developed time-motion studies as a means of rationalizing work and justifying its rewards to strike-prone wage earners. Once labor processes were scientifically planned, Taylor believed, there could be no dispute about how much effort one must expend or how much pay one should receive. Veblen thought all such theories regarding work and pay irrelevant; but both Veblen and Taylor shared a common disgust with the waste and confusion of the industrial system and a common faith that increased productivity guided by the canons of science rather than profit would mean social progress for the masses.

Around 1910, when the idea of "scientific management" was beginning to catch on, hundreds of persons started calling themselves "efficiency experts." One of the Taylorites, Henry L. Gantt, founded an organization named the New Machine, which attacked the incompetency of "financiers," claimed the business system was about to collapse, and called upon the "engineer" to prepare to take his place. But the few technicians who rallied to Gantt were drawn into government work with the outbreak of war in Europe. Another Taylorite was Morris L. Cooke, vice-president of the American Society of Mechanical Engineers. Cooke was instrumental in formulating a new code of ethics that obligated the engineer's loyalty to the standards of his profession, not to the needs of his employer. Veblen had been made acquainted with the writings of Cooke by a Stanford professor of machine design, Guido Marx. Years later, when Veblen was teaching at the New School, he asked Marx to come to New York and give a course on the state of industrial conditions from the point of view of the engineer. Marx came only to find that, in his own words, "no mature members of the A.S.M.E. appeared in the picture." The imminent revolutionary consciousness of the engineers, which Veblen had in mind when he referred vaguely to a "soviet of technicians" emerging from the example of the Russian Revolution, remained as distant a dream as an American "proletariat."

But one man who followed the Veblen-Cooke plan was Howard Scott, a controversial figure who organized the Technical Alliance in the twenties. The organization lay almost dormant until the depression, when Scott's name suddenly flashed into front-page news as the leader of what was now called "Technocracy." Scott had listed as founders of his movement such eminent figures as the late Veblen and the famous electrical engineer Charles Steinmetz. Scott's claim is dubious, but the program of Technocracy, calling for the elimination of the price system and the inauguration of government by engineering expertise, attracted some important writers like Stuart Chase and Harold Loeb. As an alternative to the chaos of capitalism and the coercion of communism, Technocracy was widely discussed in the conservative *Business Week* as well as the liberal *Nation*. Veblen now became the center of conversation, and *The Engineers and the Price System* was readvertised by its publisher and for a short time became a best-seller. "An old man named Thorstein Veblen who died in 1929," stated one magazine, "and whose works were read previously only by the intelligentsia, would be astonished if he were to learn that his name is on everyone's lips today."[3]

Veblen's followers included more than the Technocrats. Long before the depression another group of reformers who admired the eccentric theorist were the Institutional Economists at Johns Hopkins and Wisconsin. Such scholars as Richard T. Ely and John R. Commons assimilated Veblen's mode of economic analysis, especially his rejection of apriorism, the myth of beneficent competition, and the mystique of "economic man." But Ely and Commons departed from Veblen when they looked to the traditional state as a positive agency of social reform. The writings of the Institutional Economists had a considerable impact in the academic and intellectual world, and in the thirties their work influenced such New Deal officials as Rexford Guy Tugwell, Thurman Arnold, Jerome Frank, Henry Wallace, and Mordecai Ezekiel. To several Roosevelt liberals the Veblenian idea of production-for-use served as a kind of moral equivalent to the Keynesian idea of deficit spending.[4]

Perspectives on Veblen from Three Decades

As a social critic as well as an economist Veblen also achieved recognition. But his stature waxed and waned with the mood of each generation of American writers. Perhaps his uncertain position in American intellectual history can best be understood if we trace three decades of appreciation and criticism: the teens, an era of cultural ferment and political rebellion; the thirties, a decade of radical hopes and Marxian analysis; and the fifties, a period of political silence and historical reflection.

After the turn of the century *The Theory of the Leisure Class* became a familiar document even though its author remained strange and unfamiliar. The book's vocabulary entered the idiom of social criticism, and its ideas echoed through the Chicago-based novels of Robert Herrick and Ben Hecht, whose characters abided the sufferance of capitalist society while quoting Veblen and Nietzsche. (Although William Dean Howells announced in his two-part review of *Leisure Class*, "An Opportunity for American Fiction," that the material for the "great American novel" may be found in Veblen's treatment of the "aristocraticisation" of a democratic society by old world values like luxury and idleness, no American novelist, neither Henry James nor John Dos Passos, followed up this specific advice.) Not until the immediate prewar years did Veblen become a genuine cultural hero. To the Greenwich Village left he was a valuable resource for national self-scrutiny, an ally in the revolt of the young against "tribal customs" and the respectability of the starched-collar class. The radicals of *The Masses* and the literary intellectuals of the *Dial* turned to Veblen as a veritable sage who illuminated the morphology of business operations and leisure manners. A few writers were especially stirred by Veblen's notion of the "instinct of workmanship" as one of the primary drives of human nature. Lewis Mumford, a young philosopher who worked with Veblen on the *Dial*, would make use of the latter's ideas when he wrote his seminal study of the history of the machine and its effects on the natural and human environments, *Technics and Civilization.*

During the World War One period, when he was writing on current political issues, Veblen's fame reached its peak in America. "He was," H. L. Mencken complained of his *bête noir*, "all over the *Nation*, the *Dial*, the *New Republic* and the rest of them, and his books and pamphlets began to pour from the presses, and the newspapers reported his every wink and whisper, and everybody who was anybody began gabbling about him." For the entire year of 1918, Veblen actually "dominated the American scene," groaned Mencken. "All the reviews were full of his ideas. A hundred lesser sages reflected them. Everyone of intellectual pretensions read his books. Veblenism was shining in full brilliance. There were Veblenists, Veblen clubs, Veblen remedies for the sorrows of the world. There were even, in Chicago, Veblen girls—perhaps Gibson girls grown middle-aged and despairing."[5]

In the twenties Mencken had no further need to complain. The "New Era" economics of Calvin Coolidge promised prosperity for everyone, and the leisure class set the tastes for the flappers and the financiers. In an era of seemingly burgeoning affluence Veblen's discourses were no match for Gatsby's dreams. But the following decade Veblen emerged as a Cassandra who presumably had foretold the economic crash of 1929. The generation of the thirties rediscovered Veblen and immediately used his principle of "business sabotage" as an explanation for Wall Street's collapse. The once-eclipsed Veblen "now . . . shines like a star of the first magnitude," wrote John Chamberlain in *Farewell To Reform*. To writers like Chamberlain, Mumford, Max Lerner, and Alfred Kazin, Veblen was the surgical anatomist of "plunder economics," the keen satirist of the vested interests, and even the modern tragedian who saw the desperate need for social change yet himself doubted its historical possibility. It was this fatalistic view that disturbed the liberal intelligentsia of the thirties. Veblen offered no program of political action, no prospective means by which the technical creators could be expected to oust the creatures of the price and profit system. After 1929 it was no longer necessary to have merely a critique of capitalism but instead a realistic alternative to business enterprise. Yet Veblen, who seemed to be able to analyze and explain everything, could affirm nothing. He was constitutionally unable, wrote John Dos Passos, "to get his mouth round the essential yes."[6]

The novelist Dos Passos learned much from Veblen, particularly the thesis that industry and business operate at cross purposes. He etched a masterful portrait of him in *The Big Money*, published in 1936, and that same year he told his friend Edmund Wilson that Veblen's "work is a sort of anthropological footnote to Marx."[7] To the Marxist left of the thirties Veblen was indeed a valuable reference, but he was also an intellectual frustration. Writers in the *Marxist Quarterly* and the *New International* could admire his sympathetic essays in 1919 and 1921 on the Russian Revolution and Bolshevism. They could also respect his criticisms of liberalism and piecemeal reforms, his dissection of the premises of classical economic theory, and his comprehensive analysis not only of the foundations of capitalism but its ideology and "superstructure." But old left intellectuals also shared the doubts that had troubled writers in the *International Socialist Review* at the turn of the century. Both generations of Marxists looked askance at Veblen's aloofness from radical causes. Equally disturbing were his rejections of the idea of class struggle and the labor theory of value, his psychological theories of "habits" which made the human mind the primary motive force, and, above all, his repudiation of the idea of progress and perfectibility for the Darwinian idea of cumulative change without consummation. Communists wanted to use Veblen but, like everyone else, they frankly could not figure out what to make of him. An uncommitted comrade in life, Veblen remained an uncertain legend in death. The most sympathetic radical sociologist, Lewis Corey, could only hope that "all that is vital in Thorstein Veblen may fulfill itself in Marxism and socialism."[8]

Between 1934 and 1936 four literary events occurred that enhanced Veblen's reputation among writers of the depression generation. Leon Ardzrooni and Wesley C. Mitchell, two former students of Veblen, edited, respectively, his uncollected papers in *Essays In Our Changing Order* (1934) and *What Veblen Taught* (1936); Joseph Dorfman, a young Columbia University history professor, published *Thorstein Veblen and His America* (1934); and Dos Passos published the final volume of the Veblen-inspired trilogy *USA, The Big Money* (1936). Veblen's posthumous anthologies drew favorable reviews by radicals and liberals alike, Dos Passos' novel brought wide recognition to Veblen's defiant career and penetrating mind, and Dorfman's book, still the definitive biography, compiled a mountain of factual information about the man's life and a chronicle of contemporary impressions of his work, a monumental study that caused even the jaded Mencken to have second thoughts about Veblen. Perhaps the greatest tribute to

Veblen occurred in an anthology put together by Malcolm Cowley, *Books That Changed Our Mind* (1938). Cowley and the editors of the *New Republic* asked a number of leading American intellectuals to cite the non-fiction authors and books that had had the greatest "jolt" on their own thought and writings. Veblen came in way ahead with 16 mentions, followed by Charles Beard (11), John Dewey (ten), Sigmund Freud (nine), Oswald Spengler and Alfred North Whitehead (seven each), and V. I. Lenin and I. A. Richards (six each). Rexford Tugwell wrote the essay on Veblen for the anthology.

After World War Two Veblen's reputation would never achieve the stature it enjoyed in the teens and again in the thirties. Much of the reason for the demise of interest in Veblen is connected to the rise of consensus attitudes in the late forties and fifties. We shall return to this momentarily, but here it is helpful to observe three trends that developed in the study of Veblen in America. First, he became the subject of dissertations by graduate students in various departments at Columbia, Harvard, and the New School for Social Research. Second, his body of work was no longer of interest only to economists of the Institutional school; it was now explored by sociologists, analytical philosophers, Freudian psychologists, cultural anthropologists, and intellectual historians. Third, there developed what we have referred to as "The Veblen Problem" in American scholarship, the difficulties of explaining the odd peculiarities of his mind, of assessing the enduring validity of his thought, and of relating his life and work to the main currents of the American intellectual tradition.

If anything even resembling a mild Veblenian revival occurred after the Second World War, it was due in large part to Max Lerner's perceptive and valuable "Introduction" to *The Portable Veblen*, published in 1948. To Lerner the "core meaning" of Veblen lay in the fact that the most advanced and "tenacious" "business civilization" had sprouted its most consummate and trenchant critic. A sociologist with a deep concern for the fate of America as a civilization, Lerner described Veblen as "the most creative mind American social thought has produced." Veblen's insights are now more than ever relevant to a world that has gone through years of "economic and cultural disintegration and dynastic war," advised Lerner. Although critical of the primacy Veblen accorded to economic activity, Lerner was impressed by Veblen's attack on orthodox economic theory, and he appreciated the "dualistic" sensibility which enabled Veblen to see the clash of opposing forces without committing the Marxist error of forecasting the triumph of one over the other. Above all, Lerner respected Veblen's "Rousseauistic belief" that man is born peaceful yet everywhere is in conflict, that his instincts of curiosity and productivity are at war with the institutions of waste and futility that he himself has created. No one could any longer look to Veblen for economic solutions, as had the Technocrats and to a lesser extent the Institutional Economists, but

Lerner's "Introduction" suggests why Veblen's ironic mode and melancholy wisdom could still appeal to the postwar generation.[9]

Did Veblen, the immigrant descendant who rarely cited an American author, really fit into the American intellectual tradition? Three scholars tried to answer this question in the late forties and early fifties. In *The American Mind* (1950) Henry Steele Commager maintained that Veblen was too sardonic and aloof to be identified with the Populists, Progressives, or socialists. "His rebellion went so deep that it confounded even dissenters; his heresies were so profane that they baffled orthodoxy and heterodoxy alike."[10] Commager could state clearly what Veblen was against; it was more difficult for him, as it has been for all intellectual historians, to state precisely what Veblen was for. Veblen's indifference to programs and ethical issues also troubled the philosopher Morton White, who titled his chapter "The Amoral Moralist" in *Social Thought in America* (1949). White believed that Veblen was the "patron saint" of the progressive intellectuals who were in " revolt against formalism." John Dewey, Charles Beard, Oliver Wendell Holmes, and James Harvey Robinson all opposed abstractionism and deductionism, and they could follow Veblen in casting off the metaphysical chains of their early education and turn to the real, everyday processes of life. But White confessed that "we are mildly confused" when trying to find out Veblen's moral position, and our "confusion is complete" when we find Veblen telling us that he intends "to discuss the place and *value* of the leisure class as an economic factor in modern life."[11] The confusion may only mean that Veblen's ironic rhetoric is more apt to catch the eye of the literary historian, and indeed the style encountered the right scholar in Daniel Aaron's *Men of Good Hope* (1951). Aaron was unimpressed by the cult of strangeness that had grown up around Veblen's reputation, and he shrewdly observed that Veblen is best understood as a literary artist who, in the tradition of Swift, conceals his ethical stance with claims of objective detachment while anatomizing society as a "moralist, satirist, and rhetorician."[12]

While Aaron was the first to focus on Veblen's style to place him squarely within the mainstream of progressive thought—though at the cost of slighting the almost total European and anthropological orientation of Veblen's sources—other intellectual historians have stressed how uniquely American was the quality of Veblen's ideas. Perry Miller believed that Veblen possessed such independence of mind that he could revise concepts and conceive ideas "which could have been uttered in no land but America."[13] One such idea has been elaborated by David Noble: Veblen's conviction that the industrial machine will redeem man from the evils of industrial society and deliver him to a preindustrial utopia. Noble maintained that such an assumption was characteristic of the "paradox of progressivism" in general.[14] Noble's characterization misses the mark. Saint-Simon, Marx, Sorel, and other

European socialists celebrated technology as the agency that would liberate man from the pains and confusions of modernity. Perhaps it would be more accurate to say that the hope of using science and industry to restore a community of pre-scientific moral precepts is the central dilemma of all modern social theory resting on empirical foundations.

If postwar intellectual historians tried to render Veblen comprehensible, other scholars tried to make him usable. The radical economist Douglas Dowd believed that Veblen is "useful for the process of *unlearning*"; but in an attempt to make Veblen into a socialist, Dowd drew parallels between Marx's "ruling class" and Veblen's "vested interests," and between the former's idea of the "proletariat" and the latter's reference to the "underlying population," only to conclude that such analogies must be taught in order to better be unlearned. In the end Dowd wisely concluded that "Veblen had no panacea for our sickness, but he enabled us to perceive its causes."[15] To the economist Robert Heilbroner Veblen's world was not so much sick as it was "savage." In *The Worldly Philosophers* (1953), Heilbroner brilliantly recreated the brutal milieu of industrial warfare which Veblen gazed upon with the "eyes of a stranger." Veblen's chilling portrait of the businessman as predator need not concern us, Heilbroner advised; that "climate" of economics belongs to the past. What remains to be pondered is Veblen's theory of "competitive emulation," his dichotomy of "technical genius" on the one hand and "financial recklessness" on the other, and the "somber social and economic conclusions" he drew from his own observations.[16] The radical sociologist C. Wright Mills could agree that Veblen's conclusions were pessimistic, but he was less certain than Heilbroner that Veblen's descriptions of the business world were no longer true. In his "Introduction" to a 1953 edition of *The Theory of the Leisure Class,* Mills described the "crackpot realism" of capitalists who posed as practical men of affairs but in reality are "utopians" who live in their own "delusional world" of profits, war, and destruction. Mills found Veblen most useful as a thorn in the side of the complacency of the fifties, and, as an academic outcast himself, he readily identified with "the only comic writer among modern social scientists." But Mills also believed that Veblen was "not quite serious enough about prestige because he did not see its full and intricate relation to power."[17] Here Mills seems to have been so fascinated by the *idée fixe* of a "power elite" in America that he mistook an effect for a cause, equating power as the source rather than the result of prestige. Power requires the ability to compel, prestige the ability to persuade. Veblen realized that in a democratic society prestige is as important, if not more important, than raw power itself. Indeed, if we define power in the classical sense as used by the founding fathers, that is, as the ability to command influence by virtue of deference, Veblen's theory of scientific knowledge and status emulation goes to the heart of the problem of power in modern American society.

This problem has preoccupied the economist John Kenneth Galbraith. In the fifties and sixties the liberal Galbraith drew upon some aspects of Veblenism to support the economic platforms of the "vital center." As in Mills' case, Galbraith found himself attracted to Veblen, but for different reasons. Like Veblen, Galbraith was raised by hardworking immigrants (Scotch Canadians) who derided, not with envy but with "amiable contempt," the upper class's disdain for soiling their hands in manual labor. Hence both grew up to be men "of animus and not of revolution." And like Veblen, Galbraith felt that the "dismal science" of economics is a matter of literary persuasion and wit as much as facts and figures. Thus both were sensitive to the deceptions of rhetoric: Veblen spoke of the "ceremonial adequacy" of orthodox thought, Galbraith of the "conventional wisdom" of traditional ideas. In substance the parallels between Veblen and Galbraith are also striking. Both denied the free-market premise of "consumer sovereignty," especially in the face of modern corporate techniques of advertising, which emphasizes the production of "vendible" rather than "serviceable" goods. Both concerned themselves with the effect of wealth on behavior, with the cultivated wastefulness of affluence, and with the priority of production and economic growth over price stability and income distribution. Both, finally, believed that the complex nature of modern industrial processes necessitates the separation of ownership from actual operation, and that the power of specialized knowledge will give rise to a managerial class—Veblen's "new order," Galbraith's "technostructure." Thus in the 1960s Galbraith could use Veblen to show the deficiencies of an economy which allows the vested interests to impose a created demand upon a gullible public living in a culture that welcomes technological advance while resisting social innovation. He could also call for a "New Industrial State" run by specialists interested in maximized output and technical virtuosity. It is here, in his prescriptive role, that Galbraith encounters the dilemma confronting all the Technocrats. Insofar as he recognizes competition as an antiquated principle, Galbraith's hope for social reconstruction along Veblenian lines still leaves unresolved the question of power that Veblen refused to face—the autonomy of the producing organizations. Nevertheless Veblen remains for Galbraith "a genius, the most penetrating, original, and uninhibited—indeed the greatest—source of social thought of [his] time."[18]

In the writings of a number of postwar scholars—Heilbroner and Galbraith in economics, Lerner and Mills in sociology, Aaron and Commager in history—Veblen became both a valuable intellectual resource and an important vehicle for social criticism. A number of other American scholars, however, believed that Veblen remained too outside the American value system to be himself of any enduring significance. Conversely, a number of European exile scholars believed Veblen remained too inside that value system to be of any enduring importance. A study of this convergence represents one of strangest syntheses in modern intellectual history.

Consensus Scholars and Critical Theorists

After World War Two many of the politically estranged radicals returned home like prodigal sons. It may be unfair to say that they all engaged in what C. Wright Mills called "the great American celebration," but an influential number discovered or rediscovered the basic health of American society and the forgotten beauties of American history. Many also supported the rise of "consensus" scholarship, a school of thought which stresses the stability and continuity of American institutions and values. As far as the demise of Veblen is concerned, the cult of consensus can be traced to three historical developments that presumably rendered his work irrelevant.

First, the spectacular performance of American industry during the war seemed to put an end to the Veblenian complaint about the waste and inefficiency of the economic system, whether competitive or corporate. Although Veblen himself might not have been surprised by the feats of war capitalism, a few former radical critics could hardly believe their eyes when the wonderfully "collectivized" Third Reich fell before the onslaught of General Motors assembly lines.[19] Second, the Cold War, with its Marshall Plan and Truman Doctrine, not only called upon American enterprise to shoulder the economic burden of defending the democratic West; it did much to restore the viability of the natural-rights tradition of liberty which Veblen had so cavalierly dismissed. After Stalinism who could read Veblen's ludicrous essays on Bolshevism? Third, the postwar era witnessed the "economic miracle" in western Europe and the advent of abundance in America, dramatized in suburban housing tracts and supermarkets, tail-finned Chevrolets and Cadillacs, television sets and kitchen appliances. When former luxuries became necessities available to the great majority of citizens, with the claptrap of gadgets and accessories arising out of the very credit system that Veblen had once regarded as the frail crutch of capitalism, consumers could scarcely resist the temptations of the "installment plan." Even though historians now began to look to economic abundance as the central key to the "American Character," the thesis of David Potter's influential *People of Plenty* (1953), Veblen would have been no more surprised by the democratization of affluence after the war than by the rationalization of industry during the war. When the charge account became almost universal along with the five-day work week, the Protestant ethic of thrift and endeavor lost all meaning in American culture, and hence Veblen was more relevant than ever as a mocking conscience in an acquisitive society that advertises the false promises of leisure. But consensus scholars would have no part of Veblen.

Neglect of Veblen actually began in the thirties, particularly in the work of Talcott Parsons, the Harvard sociologist who became one of the most influential academic intellectuals in the postwar era. Parsons is a rare specimen in modern American intellectual history. Writing in a period when most American consensus scholars were convinced that European ideas had no relevance for America, he set out to bring to native shores the theories of Durkheim, Pareto, and Weber. Parsons' indifference to Veblen is unfortunate. The school of "structural functionalism" that he originated—a theory which holds that all human societies, no matter how complex or simple, share some of the same basic organizing principles and that all social phenomena have a necessary function in holding society together—is not that alien to the status functions of consumption in Veblen's analysis. Indeed the absence of Veblen in recent sociological scholarship is a curious omission on the part of consensus theorists who made so much of status roles and social strain in America's political culture during the McCarthy era.[20] Although Parsons' students addressed themselves to Veblen,[21] Parsons himself remained convinced that what Veblen had to say had been more adequately presented in Weber's writings. That Veblen and Weber had entirely different views on the meaning of capitalism, work, and bourgeois morality hardly mattered. Instead of confronting Veblen, Parsons chose to dismiss him—a case of a sociologist treating American intellectual history with what might charitably be called "benign neglect."

Daniel Bell also approached Veblen as though he were no more than an irritable footnote to the great classical social theorists of the nineteenth century. In 1960, Bell announced the "exhaustion" of all radical theories of social conflict in *The End of Ideology*, and he, like many consensus scholars, was certain that the tradition of liberal pluralism which Veblen attacked had become solidified and could now in fact be appreciated as the central political reality of American life. As a political testament of the postwar mood, Bell's thesis was as prescient as it was profound.* Yet however accurate it remained as a

* The attempt on the part of New Left scholars to uncover the forgotten layers of poverty and to bring to public awareness the plight of dispossessed ethnic groups, both in the historical past and the present, by no means refuted the conclusions of consensus scholars like Bell, Daniel Boorstin, or Louis Hartz. The very "conflicts" which historians discovered—slavery, Indian wars, the labor movement—had little or nothing to do with class conflict in the Marxist sense of the term. The central question is whether such struggles were directed against the doctrine of property or against its distribution. The search for a radical tradition in the American past requires evidence that a certain social stratum posed a potential "negation" of the existing social order and not only a demand that its wealth be redistributed, a demand of familiar interest politics that is, in principle, incorporated into the very structure of Madison's constitutional system. It was easy for the New Left to assume that a radical past existed. The question is where to find it.

description of the American social condition, it resulted in a double standard of political morality. The ideologies of the nineteenth century, Bell claimed with implicit reference to the Marxist heritage to which he once swore allegiance, were based on the "universalistic" and "humanistic" goals of social equality and freedom, while the neo-ideologies of the twentieth century are "parochial" and "instrumental" and spring from the "impulsions" of economic development and national power.[22] Thus formulated, it was inevitable that Bell would identify Veblen with the latter tradition and claim that his aim, like that of all technoauthoritarians from Saint-Simon to James Burnham, was to find a "new class" capable of overthrowing the existing order. Veblen "must be ranked on the side of the elitists," Bell wrote in his "Introduction" to *The Engineers and the Price System* in 1963. Bell based much of his case on Veblen's writings on Bolshevism, and his explanations of Veblen's "elitist" motives tends to read like a parody of pop psychohistory. "A woman spurned in love turns to reform as a second choice; a man scorned by power often turns to revolution. Veblen had always been subversive in his verbal irony; now, in the next two years, from 1919 to 1921, he began to entertain hopes, always somewhat masked, of becoming an active political force."[23] It is one thing to claim that Veblen's infatuation with engineers carried elitist implications; it is quite another thing to argue that Veblen himself sought power for the simple reason that power had eluded him. Such an interpretation ignores Veblen's own skepticism of the engineers as politically ineffectual, his sympathies with the powerless and nomadic Wobblies, and his maverick personality which rendered him incompatible with the demands of any organized movement. Veblen had no more interest in becoming an American Lenin than he had in becoming president of the American Economic Association. Perhaps this says something for his sense of power!

Veblen frustrates the ex-Marxist who is searching for an alternative vision of social change;[24] he also intrigues the ex-Marxist who, even as a liberal or conservative, is nostalgic enough to try to salvage something from the radical tradition in America. In 1953, the sociologist Lewis S. Feuer explicated Veblen for the readers of the *American Quarterly*, the national journal of American studies. Feuer, an Old Left veteran, displayed much admiration for Veblen, "the first American scientific thinker . . . to set forth a socialist critique of American society and thought." When comparing Veblen's epistemology to that of William James, however, Feuer found that the former's "materialism" failed to plumb the full depths of human experience. Not only was Veblen's philosophy shallow, his theory of the "instinct of idle curiosity" may have arisen from the psychic needs of an "interned immigrant." "There is the sense," Feuer argued, "in which 'idle curiosity' is a similar defensive myth for Veblen himself, a portrayal of himself, shaped into a detached observer, in the visage of an instinct of mankind. But was his own 'idleness,' his bitter silence, his inability to speak and act, the expression of a free, natural impulse? Or by a strange irony, had Veblen confused the neurosis which society had inflicted upon him with the natural, instinctive constitution of man? In that case, Veblen himself had been touched with 'contamination' in the heart of his thinking. The repressed wrath against the leisure class had turned into self-hatred and an anxiety of brooding silence."[25] Feuer touched upon a delicate matter that consensus scholars were bound to raise—the state of Veblen's mental health.

"If Veblen were around now," wrote David Riesman in 1953, "his friends would almost certainly, with the best will in the world, urge him to consult a psychoanalyst." Riesman's *Thorstein Veblen: A Critical Interpretation* is a discerning analysis that "emphasizes above all the ambiguity, even internal contradictions, of his thought." It remained a "problem" for Riesman that Veblen could simultaneously praise primitive communal life and workmanship and at the same time welcome industrial technology, and that he could condemn war as a recurring trait of "barbarism" and yet support wholeheartedly America's entry into the First World War. Riesman successfully unraveled some of these riddles, but as a Freudian analysis of Veblen's ideas, his book is a speculative essay that begins in conjecture and ends in inference. Riesman tells us that Veblen "appears never to have exorcised his own father," whose power and authority he saw symbolized in the engineer. We also learn that Veblen's lack of "masculine prowess" led him to sympathize with the cause of feminism, that his "peasant roots" explain ("perhaps") his revulsion toward luxury and extravagance, and that his "masochistic tendencies" and "fear of success" may account for his ineffectual teaching and inability to rise in the academic world, and this in turn partly resulted in his perverse *The Higher Learning in America*. Not only does Riesman subject Veblen to Freudian treatment, he subjects the readers of Veblen as well. "What is the source of Veblen's power over us?" It could very well be our life of well-fed affluence in a society that has still to solve the problems of poverty and unemployment; hence, our "guilt" and "our willingness to let Veblen punish us for our sins."[26]

There is truth in Riesman's psychoanalytical approach, but it is far from the whole truth. If his richly suggestive book helps us understand Veblen, it also helps us understand why consensus scholars of the fifties were puzzled by Veblen's hostility to capitalism, and why they were inclined to trace the origins of his "alienation" to individual pathology rather than to social reality. However that perspective may be, it is still difficult to see how one can dismiss Veblen's observations as psychologically rooted unless one is prepared to claim that American society as it existed constituted a rational norm to which the intellectual community itself gave assent. The danger lies in attributing a causal role to a unique personal background for social problems that concerned a whole generation of writers. Moreover, it is one thing to judge Veblen's thoughts irrational because of "internal contradictions"; it is another thing to so judge his thoughts because they violate our norms, as Riesman was prone to do in his discussion of education. Veblen was an idiosyncratic personality, to be sure, perhaps the most "inner-directed" character ever to appear in the history of American social science. But an account of his ideas which stresses childhood determinants slights the enormous influence of many writers (Kant, Hume, Darwin, Mill, Clark, Bellamy, Peirce, Marx, and Sombart) who contributed to his intellectual growth, as well as the historical experiences (the Populist movement, socialism and industrial conflict, Coxey's protest march, etc.) to which he responded. Finally, even if we grant that the process by which Veblen arrived at his ideas derived from personal eccentricities, it does not follow that his ideas about modern society have no merit and cannot be critically examined and rationally assessed. In intellectual history, as opposed to psychohistory, it is the man's work, and not his life, that poses questions for social theory that must be examined on the basis of observations, assumptions, and evidence. Veblen may have had his share of "neurosis," but not all neurotics shared his insights.[27]

The above survey of Veblen historiography illustrates that one's reaction to Veblen may depend upon one's judgment of America. Yet we cannot simply conclude that only those who celebrated the health of American society remained unsympathetic to Veblen. Actually his most telling critics were men with no country to defend, intellectual wanderers like himself.

These were the German exile scholars who had been associated with the Frankfurt Institut für Sozialforschung (Institute for Social Research) and had fled Hitler's regime in the early thirties. Theodor Adorno, Max Horkheimer, and Herbert Marcuse, the chief spokesmen for Frankfurt social theory in America, had been nurtured in their early years on the reassuring "dialectical imagination" of Hegelian-Marxist tradition. But they were also philosophers-turned-sociologists who had grown melancholy over the failure of the proletariat—the "heirs of classical philosophy" (Engels)—to fulfill its historical mission and liberate man from the snares and false comforts of bourgeois society. What interested the German exiles in Veblen was the same historical development that would interest Riesman, the phenomenon of mass society. In the forties Riesman had been exploring the conformist pressures in American culture, while the German exiles had earlier discovered in America what had remained less clear in Europe: the "integration" of the working class. Thus they both looked to Veblen as a possible key to the future nature of advanced industrial society, and the Germans, especially Horkheimer, believed that Veblen, "America's greatest sociological critic of culture, would help us better to understand the catastrophic change in human nature" dramatized in the barbarism of the Second World War.[28]

The work of Veblen was only a point of departure, however, and understandably the American and German scholars interpreted him differently. Where sociologists like Riesman and Feuer saw Veblen as a queer introvert alienated from American society, German exiles saw him as a typical American thinker assimilated into the dominant values of that society. Where some American scholars criticized Veblen from the standpoint of consensus, German writers consensualized him from the point of view of "critical theory." The idea of critical theory suggests a style of thought which proceeds from negation to negation and which presumably enables the mind to question all social phenomena and to see all reality as transitory because, in Hegelian terms, the "becoming" is everything. Thus in the minds of the German scholars Veblen failed to question sufficiently the values of American culture because he offered as a solution what in reality should be seen as part of the problem itself: the "positivist" values of practicality and efficiency. Even more serious was Veblen's inability to appreciate the contributions of Marx, an inability rooted in Veblen's rejection of Hegel. Without the dialectical understanding afforded by Hegel, Veblen could only think along the scientific lines of mechanical causation that precludes the dualistic tension between the "is" and the "ought." In Veblen's mode of analysis, charged Adorno and Marcuse, thinking and reality were one and the same, and the ideal and the real merged into an acceptance of the "given" as the norm. Veblen also lacked a conception of "totality," and thus his epistemology represented not so much an effort at radical vision as mere "adaptation." All Veblen's limitations stem from the fact that he could not appreciate the Hegelian-Marxist principle of "negation," the denial of the existent world and the affirmation of ultimate ideals that transcend present reality.[29]

No contemporary scholar of Veblen can ignore this learned critique. Adorno brilliantly demonstrated that "Veblen's critical motive and his reverence for the historically given are irreconcilable." But Adorno and Marcuse tried to prove much more, and herein lays the problem. On this crucial point listen to Adorno:

> In Veblen's view, Marx had made a brave beginning in cultural analysis, though handicapped by a superficial psychology derived from Bentham and by a romantic metaphysics derived from Hegel. Bentham's influence led Marx to develop a commonplace theory of class interests that overlooked the way in which certain habits of thought are drilled into business men by their pecuniary occupations and quite different habits of thought are drilled into wage earners by the machine process in which they are caught. Hegel's influence made the Marxian theory of social evolution essentially an intellectual sequence that tends to a goal, 'the classless economic structure of the

socialistic final term,' whereas the Darwinian scheme of thought envisages a 'blindly cumulative causation, in which there is no trend, no final term, no consummation.' Hence Marx strayed from the narrow trail of scientific analysis appropriate to a mechanistic age and attained an optimistic vision of the future which fulfilled his wish for a socialist revolution. The Darwinian viewpoint, which supplies the needed working programme, will spread among social scientists, not because it is less metaphysical than its predecessors or nearer the truth (whatever that may mean), but because it 'harmonizes better with the thoughts begotten by daily work in the twentieth century.' The thesis that the 'Darwinian viewpoint' is not 'nearer the truth' than Marx but merely more adequate to working conditions in present day society implies the decisive shortcomings of Veblen's theory. The 'harmony' of thinking and reality for which his doctrine of adaptation stands may finally be a harmony with the selfsame oppression which he elsewhere condemns. It is a harmony that is certainly not superior to the discordant views of Marx. The latter did not have a 'superficial psychology.' He had no psychology at all, and for good theoretical reasons. The world Marx scrutinized is ruled by the law of value, not by men's souls.[30]

To assert that Marx's world is "ruled by the law of value" may be as misleading as declaring that it is ruled by the value of law. On the question of value theory it was not Veblen who was submerged in the ideas and assumptions of capitalist culture but Karl Marx himself, and Veblen was the first social scientist to point out the ways in which the labor theory of value rests awkwardly on Ricardian foundations and Hegelian fantasies. Adorno's otherwise discerning treatment suggests why Veblen will always remain an intellectual embarrassment to Marxists and to critical theorists who can be critical of everything save their own premises. Veblen could neither believe in Marxism as a philosophical proposition nor accept capitalism as a human condition. It is this tension between belief and doubt which made Veblen such an estranged outsider and turned his mind on the satirical and the absurd, the only escape for an intelligence which took critical theory critically. Mordant, detached, a skeptic with a cynical appreciation of the ridiculous nature of social reality, he raised the inanities of society to the dignity of social theory.

12 . . . Conclusion: Whither Capitalism?

Bourgeois society has enjoyed few friends among the intelligentsia, and capitalism, its lifeblood, has usually been analyzed by means of gloomy metaphors having to do with pathology, decay, and inevitable demise. Though they flourish best precisely in capitalist society, intellectuals may be justly charged with having harbored a death wish for capitalism. So frequently have they proclaimed its impending collapse that its perverse ability to survive disaster, and to thrive anew, must seem to them little less than miraculous, like the spontaneous remission of symptoms by a terminally ill patient.

The latest in a long line of grim prognoses is that of Daniel Bell, who is too sophisticated to succumb to the one-dimensional analysis—Marxist or otherwise—but whose recent study of the "modalities" of capitalism, its expressive and symbolic forms, is nearly as doom-laden as that of the Marxists who focus on the mode of production. Bell is convinced that contemporary industrial society is in the grip of grave "cultural contradictions" chiefly because the bourgeois ethos which fueled its rise has given way to the "sensate" culture of modernism.

> The bourgeois world-view—rationalistic, matter-of-fact, pragmatic; neither magical, mystical, nor romantic; emphasizing work and function; concerned with restraint and order in morals and conduct—had by mid-nineteenth-century come to dominate, not only the social structure (the organization of the economy), but also the culture, especially the religious motivation in the child. It reigned triumphant everywhere, opposed only in the realm of culture by those who disdained its un-heroic and anti-tragic mood, as well as its orderly attitude toward time.[1]

Bell laments the passing of this world we have lost. This triumphant outlook succumbed in the twentieth century to a culture of freedom and pleasure, a life-style that made the mystique of self-realization tantamount to an inalienable right, and a mass consumption economy of unlimited gratification. The value system of capitalism, Bell concludes, is at last experiencing a fundamental crisis of legitimacy.

Significantly, both Marxist writers and anti-Marxists (in some cases ex-Marxists themselves) are willing to grant capitalism its ascetic, rationalistic world-view that was first formulated by Max Weber. Yet such a world-view cannot explain how modern capitalist society is possible. If early capitalism has its genesis in the ethic of self-restraint, mature capitalism has come to be, as Weber himself acknowledged, the rational systematization of irrational needs, an enslavement to the sovereignty of desire. Seen from this perspective, we may better understand why capitalist culture retains its legitimacy and hegemony and seemingly absorbs all challenges, turning crises and conflicts into further evidence of an all-pervasive consensus.

The problem of hegemony, man's subjugation to ideas and not only to force alone, could very well be the future reality of bourgeois society. If so, it is necessary to add another dimension to the anguished speculations of Daniel Bell. The present "cultural contradictions" of capitalism may derive not only from the disjunction between its work ethic and its pleasure principle. On the contrary, ever since the philosophy of property received its classical liberal formulation in the writings of Locke one may discern a central paradox: labor is considered to have value as a source of wealth, but the laborer himself is regarded as cursed with the burden of work; the more the principle of labor is praised economically, the more the activity is denigrated socially.[2] It would be facile to dismiss such attitudes as an aspect of "alienation" or a species of "false consciousness." Indeed Veblen's analysis suggests that the distinction between the fruits of labor and the acts of workmanship, between the esteem for the product and the disesteem for the producer, is reified thinking experienced as anthropomorphism, and that therefore alienation itself may have its roots in the sphere of consumption rather than in production. In our age, when fewer and fewer people are engaged in industrial labor, and when technology and affluence have enabled more people to engage in the "pursuit of happiness" in leisure activities, it would seem that we need to turn our attention from the "productive forces" to the commodity culture, perhaps the crucial formative element in the development of modern popular consciousness. Veblen's writings may serve as a starting point for a study of the anthropological ties which bind the "civilized" present to the "barbaric" past.

Veblen's writings may also illuminate a new dimension in the contemporary debate between the consensus scholars and the conflict or coercion theorists of modern society. Representatives of both schools are interested primarily in the Hobbesian question: How does social order exist? In the consensus model, first articulated by Alexis de Tocqueville, and in our time by Seymour Martin Lipset and Talcott Parsons, a society exists because the mass of citizens share common norms, ideas and beliefs, a value system and structure of organizing principles that function to hold together the social order. In the conflict school, first put forward systematically by Marx, and in contemporary thought revised by non-Marxists like Ralf Dahrendorf and Lewis Coser, social phenomena are explained by either the interaction of class interests or the reality of authority relations, and hence the social system is perpetuated not by norms but by power.

Veblen's position bears similarities to both schools of thought yet is distinct from each. The America that he described at the turn of the century appears as a class society in which the workers suffered not so much from economic misery as from status deprivation, a phenomenon that indicated the pervasiveness of the capitalist norms of pecuniary achievement. But it is also a society in which the values of the dominant industrial class prevail because of its prior success in the struggle for power. The captain of industry is admired for much the same reason that primitive man stood in awe of the warrior: he is "gifted with ferocity." The persistence of such deferential attitudes toward personal force is the result both of biological evolution and ideological coercion. "This effect," wrote Veblen in reference to leisure-class hegemony,

> is wrought partly by a coercive, educational adaptation of the habits of all individuals, partly by a selective elimination of the unfit individuals and lines of descent. Such human material as does not lend itself to the methods of life imposed by the accepted scheme suffers more or less elimination as well as repression. The principles of pecuniary emulation and of industrial exemption have in this way been erected into canons of life, and have become coercive factors of some importance in the situation to which men have to adapt themselves.[3]

To Veblen the structure of power is the basis from which social attitudes evolve. The ideas and culture of the victorious class take on a life of their own and give modern capitalist ideology the same reified status that previous ruling-class ideologies enjoyed in the past. In one respect Veblen offers a synthesis of the consensus-conflict debate: the history of society is the history of power struggles that issue in a culture of status fetish, a cult of masculine triumph around which a consensus is formed and through which society itself is sustained. It is no coincidence that Veblen discerned in capitalist ideology what other philosophers like George Santayana and William James saw as the curse of American culture itself: the worship of "the bitch-goddess of success."

Had Veblen merely demonstrated nothing more than the authority which the strong acquire over the weak, he would have asserted nothing more than a variation of nineteenth-century Social Darwinism. Yet by grounding his analysis in the anthropomorphic nature of cultural phenomena, Veblen's approach to attitude formation not only absorbed the distinction between norms and power that divide the consensus and conflict theorists, it also called into question an assumption shared by liberals and Marxists as well as Social Darwinists—the assumption of historical progress. Where the theorists of progress saw change, he saw only continuity; where they saw man's increasing rationality and mastery of the environment, he observed man acting out in symbolic forms of animistic behavior the residues of his barbaric nature; and where they looked either to "intelligence" or to "class consciousness" in order to undermine the old order and produce a new society and perhaps even a "new man" (Trotsky's phrase), he looked to the "discipline of the machine" to liberate man from his archaic traits by restoring almost intact his productive, wholesome nature that had supposedly flourished in the early stage of "primitive savagery."

Veblen's ultimate hope has always seemed "paradoxical" to intellectual historians;[4] and one must say that the idea that the machine, a product of modern man, could revitalize the healthy primal instincts of human nature does seem a dubious proposition. Yet viewed in historical perspective the liberating power of science and technology cannot be denied. What, after all, is more threatening to false social distinctions than a "machine process" that makes no cultural distinctions? What is more revolutionary than an impersonal mode of cognition which has a logic and independent reality apart from the user? What is more democratic than an empirical enterprise that has no higher obligation than to the practical and useful? The problem, as Lewis Mumford astutely observed, is that in western culture the machine emerged purely as an "external instrument" for the conquest of the environment rather than as an extension of man's intellectual powers; and thus as modern life became more mechanized, and work dull and alienating, civilization assimilated the objects that technology brought forth rather than the "spirit" that had produced them. Mumford deserves to be quoted at length since he has expressed the Veblenian promise of the machine "aesthetic" more lucidly than Veblen himself:

> The possibility that technics had become a creative force, carried on by its own momentum, that it was rapidly ordering a new kind of environment and was producing a third estate midway between nature and the human arts, that it was not merely a quicker way of achieving old ends but an effective way of expressing new ends—the possibility in short that the machine furthered a new mode of *living* was far from the minds of those who actively promoted it. The industrialists and engineers themselves did not believe in the qualitative and cultural aspects of the machine. In their indifference to these aspects, they were just as far from appreciating the nature of the machine as were the Romantics: only what the Romantics, judging the machine from the standpoint of life, regarded as a defect the utilitarian boasted of as a virtue: for the latter the absence of art was an assurance of practicality.
>
> If the machine had really lacked cultural values, the Romantics would have been right, and their desire to seek these values, if need be, in a dead past would have been justified by the very desperateness of the case. But the interests in the factual and the practical, which the industrialists made the sole key to intelligence, were only two in a whole series of new values that had been called into existence by the development of the new technics.

> Matters of fact and practice had usually in previous civilizations been treated with snobbish contempt by the leisured classes: as if the logical ordering of propositions were any nobler a technical feat than the articulation of machines. The interest in the practical was symptomatic of that wider and more intelligible world in which people had begun to live, a world in which the taboos of class and caste could no longer be considered as definitive in dealing with events and experiences. Capitalism and technics had both acted as a solvent of those clots of prejudice and intellectual confusion; and they were thus at first important liberators of life.[5]

One suspects that Marx would immediately have agreed with Mumford's assessment of the liberating role of capitalism and science. But what went wrong? How did the acquisitive culture of capitalism gain ascendancy over its rationalized system of production? Against the objectivity of the machine, why does the subjectivity of man continue to prevail? How did ideology come to triumph over technology? In Veblen's writings, where capitalism is not so much a definitive break with the past as a continuation, in modified form, of feudal status relations and barbarian survivals of prowess and esteem, where the market economy did not so much "tame the passions" of glory and power as rechannel them, we may find a compelling answer to this problem in contemporary social theory.

This extended analysis of Veblen's ideas and theories cannot conclude without some final reflection on the man himself. In some deep personal sense his life remains as interesting as his ideas. Yet any attempt to assess Veblen in relation to his writings leads only to a plethora of baffling paradoxes which reveal the man as: an empiricist who derided the value of literature and art but who spent his last years translating Icelandic poetry; a social philosopher who denounced leisure as wasteful and who yet wrote an essay to prove that idleness was the highest state of knowing; a radical who attacked property and absentee ownership but who fought fiercely for possession of his own land and cabin; a feminist who championed the liberation of women but who allowed his own wives and mistresses to wait upon him hand and foot; an inveterate seducer who developed a theory of human nature that was coldly indifferent to the sex instinct so crucial to Freud; a technocrat who called upon the engineers to take power while declining the presidency of the American Economic Association; and a social scientist who looked forward to modern technology and backward to primitive harmony. One may well wonder whether such contradictions ever bothered Veblen. Perhaps he merely agreed with Emerson that a probing mind cannot permit itself to be vexed by the bugaboo of consistency.

No less enigmatic were Veblen's last days in California. Who can surmise what thoughts must have occupied him as he sat in his cabin in the hills outside of Palo Alto, staring into space as a stray wood rat or skunk brushed up against his baggy trousers? Did he succumb, in his final mood of elegiac resignation, to some secret suspicion that capitalist society had eluded the powerful net of his analysis? One thing is certain: the dynamics of Veblen's personality still elude the intellectual historian, even as they baffle the psychohistorian. Perhaps this is as it should be. He gave us the ideas and insights with which we now know better the subtle cultural forces, social pressures, and power realities of modern industrial society. He made the invisible world of values, habits, and customs seem real and tangible, and even a little silly. Indeed, he not only succeeded in adding comic relief to the "dismal science" of economics but endured the absurdities of social existence while keeping his own individuality stubbornly intact. What more can one ask of life? Should we trouble ourselves over the enduring "mystery" of his personality? Apparently it did not trouble him. Must we analyze the sources of his "discontent," or should we accept his alienation as the necessary condition of consciousness in the act of perception? "The world owes its onward impulses," advised Nathaniel Hawthorne, "to men ill at ease."

Notes

Introduction: Social Theory and Anthropological Imperative

[1] Perry Miller, "Introduction," *American Thought: Civil War to World War One* (New York, 1954), p. xlix.

[2] On Veblen's "substantive revolution" in this field see *Economic Anthropology: Readings in Theory and Analysis,* ed. Edward E. LeClair, Jr. and Harold K. Schneider (New York, 1968); for a more discerning appraisal of Veblen as a "pioneer," see Norman O. Brown, *Life Against Death: The Psychoanalytical Meaning of History* (New York, 1959), pp. 254–57.

[3] George Santayana, *Character and Opinion in the United States* (Garden City, N.Y., 1956), pp. 102–03.

1 . . . Veblen's America

[1] Edward Chase Kirkland, *Dream and Thought in the Business Community, 1860–1900* (Chicago, 1964), pp. 29–49.

[2] George Santayana, *Winds of Doctrine and Platonism and the Spiritual Life* (New York, 1957), pp. 1–24, 186–215.

[3] Theodore Roosevelt, *An Autobiography* (New York, 1913), pp. 462–63.

[4] Woodrow Wilson, *The New Freedom: A Call for the Emancipation of the Generous Spirit of a People,* ed. William Leuchtenberg (Englewood Cliffs, N.J., 1961), p. 6.

[5] Henry Steele Commager, ed., *Lester Frank Ward and the Welfare State* (Indianapolis, 1967), p. xxxvi.

[6] Cotton Mather, *A Christian At His Calling* (Boston, 1791), pp. 36–48.

[7] On the "vogue of Spencer" in America, see Richard Hofstadter, *Social Darwinism in American Thought* (Boston: Beacon edn., 1955), pp. 31–50.

[8] William Graham Sumner, "Sociology" and "The Absurd Effort To Make The World Over" in *American Thought,* pp. 72–104.

[9] Quoted in Henry Steele Commager, *The American Mind* (New Haven, 1950), p. 230.

[10] Robert Bannister, "'The Survival of the Fittest Is Our Doctrine': History or Histrionics?" *Journal of the History of Ideas* 31 (1970) 377–98; for a valuable discussion of Darwinism and economic theory, see also Paul F. Boller, *American Thought in Transition: The Impact of Evolutionary Naturalism, 1865–1900* (New York, 1969), pp. 70–93.

[11] Quoted in Hofstadter, 45.

2 . . . Enter Veblen: "Disturber of the Intellectual Peace"

[1] Veblen, *LC*, p. 28.
[2] *Ibid.*, p. 30.
[3] *Ibid.*, p. 103.
[4] *Ibid.*, pp. 173–74.
[5] *Ibid.*, pp. 181–82.
[6] Veblen, *BE*, p. 49.
[7] *Ibid.*, p. 310.
[8] Veblen, *AO*, p. 110.
[9] *Ibid.*, p. 116.
[10] Veblen, *ECO*, pp. 175–93.
[11] Veblen, *POS*, p. 96.
[12] *Ibid.*, pp. 32–55.
[13] *Ibid.*, pp. 1–31.
[14] Miller, pp. xlviii–xlix.

3 . . . The Social Scientist as "Stranger"

[1] Madge Jenison, *Sunwise Turn: A Human Comedy of Bookselling* (New York, 1923), pp. 125–26. I am indebted to Professor Joseph Dorfman for this reference.

[2] Quoted in Dorfman, I, p. 504.

[3] Quoted in *Ibid.*, p. 497.

[4] *Ibid.*, p. 456.

[5] *Ibid.*, p. 498.

[6] Quoted in *Ibid.*, pp. 12–13, 56.

[7] Quoted in *Ibid.*, p. 504.

[8] Quoted in *Ibid.*, p. 250.

[9] Georg Simmel, "The Stranger" in *The Sociology of Georg Simmel*, ed. Kurt Wolf (New York, 1950), pp. 402–09.

[10] Veblen, *ECO*, pp. 219–31.

4 . . . Economics and the Dilemma of Value Theory

[1] David Ricardo, *Principles of Political Economy and Taxation* (Homewood, Ill., 1963), pp. 5–28.

[2] Maurice Dobb, *Theories of Value and Distribution Since Adam Smith* (Cambridge, 1973).

[3] R. L. Meek, *Studies in the Labor Theory of Value* (London, 1973); Murray Wolfeson, *A Reappraisal of Marxian Economics* (Baltimore: Penguin edn., 1968); Joan Robinson, *An Essay on Marxian Economics* (New York, 1966); Geoffrey Pilling, "The Law of Value in Ricardo and Marx," Economy and Society 1 (1972), 281–307.

[4] Veblen, *POS*, p. 422.

[5] *Ibid.*, p. 443.

[6] *Ibid.*, pp. 415–18.

[7] *Ibid.*, p. 97.

[8] Arthur K. Davis, "Sociological Elements in Veblen's Economic Theory," *Journal of Political Economy* 53 (1945) 132–49.

[9] On Veblen's method of reasoning in economic analysis, see Morton White, *Social Thought in America: The Revolt Against Formalism* (Boston, 1957), pp. 24–26.

[10] Veblen, *POS*, p. 70.

[11] *Ibid.*, p. 193.

[12] *Ibid.*, pp. 73–74.

[13] *Ibid.*, pp. 204–05.

[14] *Ibid.*, pp. 155–56.

[15] *Ibid.*, p. 74.

[16] Adam Smith, *Theory of Moral Sentiments* (London, 1759), pp. 144–45.

[17] Veblen, *POS*, pp. 156–58.

[18] Veblen, *BE*, p. 63.

[19] Bell, "Introduction," *EPS*, p. 30.

[20] Kenneth Arrow, "Thorstein Veblen as an Economic Theorist," *American Economist* 19 (Spring 1975) 5–9; see also Donald A. Walker, "Thorstein Veblen's Economic System," *Economic Inquiry* (forthcoming).

[21] Michael Harrington, *Socialism* (New York, 1972).

[22] Veblen, *POS*, p. 144.

[23] David Riesman, *Thorstein Veblen* (New York, 1953. Reissued in paper by The Seabury Press, 1975), p. 163.

[24] A discussion of Veblen and Keynes may be found in Riesman, pp. 164–66; and John S. Gambs, *Beyond Supply and Demand: A Reappraisal of Institutional Economics* (New York, 1946), pp. 6–8; David Dowd, *Thorstein Veblen* (New York, 1964), pp. 644–48.

[25] Veblen, *BE*, p. 211.

5 . . . Marx, Veblen, and the "Riddle" of Alienation

[1] Whereas Veblen had access to the work of Boas, Fraser, Malinowski, and other late nineteenth-century anthropologists, Marx drew upon the earlier studies of Morgan, Maine, and Lubbock. See *The Ethnological Notebooks of Karl Marx*, transl. Lawrence Krader (Assen, Netherlands, 1972).

[2] Karl Marx, "Economic and Philosophical Manuscripts" in *Writings of the Young Marx on Philosophy and Society*, eds. Loyd D. Easton and Kurt Guddat (New York, 1967), pp. 265–301.

[3] Karl Marx and Friedrich Engels, *A Contribution to the Critique of Political Economy* (Chicago, 1907), p. 13.

[4] E. J. Hobsbawm, ed., *Karl Marx: Pre-Capitalist Economic Formations*, transl. Jack Cohen (New York, 1964), p. 26.

[5] Friedrich Engels, *The Origins of the*

Family, Private Property, and the State (Chicago, 1902), pp. 194–95.

[6] István Mészáros, *Marx's Theory of Alienation* (London, 1970), p. 155.

[7] Bertell Ollmann, *Alienation: Marx's Conception of Man in Capitalist Society* (Cambridge, 1971), pp. 163–64.

[8] Marx, *Pre-Capitalist Economic Formations*, pp. 67–139; see also Karl Marx and Friedrich Engels, *The German Ideology* (London, 1965).

[9] Karl Marx, *Grundrisse*, transl. Martin Nocolaus (London, 1973), p. 492.

[10] Veblen, *IOW*, p. 147.

[11] Marx also considered this possibility but then tries to explain away war by tracing it to the mode of production. He noted as an objection to his theory of property and the division of labor that "the fact of conquest appears to contradict this whole conception of history," and then proceeded to demonstrate that "for the conquering barbarian people, war itself is a regular form of intercourse, which is exploited all the more energetically the more the growth of population together with the traditional . . . primitive mode of production arouses the demand for new means of production." Marx, *The German Ideology*, pp. 12–13.

[12] Veblen, *ECO*, pp. 36–39.

[13] *Ibid.*, pp. 32–49.

[14] *Ibid.*, pp. 42–47.

[15] M. I. Finley, ed., *Slavery in Classical Antiquity* (Cambridge, 1960), pp. 1–14, 53–72, *passim*, but see especially Henri Lévy Bruhl, "Esquisse d'une théorie sociologique de l'esclavage a Rome," pp. 151–69; M. I. Finley, "Slavery," *Oxford Classical Dictionary* (Oxford, 1970), pp. 994–96.

[16] Rodolfo Mondolfo, "The Greek Attitude to Manual Labor," *Past & Present* 6 (November 1954) 1–5.

[17] "This theory today has been refuted: since nomadism occurs later than the first civilizations, the emergence of the state must have had indigenous causes." Jurgen Habermas, "Toward a Reconstruction of Historical Materialism," *Theory & Society* 2 (1975), 287–300.

[18] Veblen, *IOW*, pp. 1–37.

[19] See Bernard Rosenberg's defense of Veblen against these criticism in *The Values of Veblen: A Critical Appraisal* (Washington, D.C., 1956), pp. 44–46; for a full discussion of the problem, see Louis Schneider, *The Freudian Psychology and Veblen's Social Theory* (New York, 1948).

[20] Veblen, *IOW*, p. 2.

[21] Quoted in Dorfman, II, p. 100.

[22] Talcott Parsons, *The Structure of Social Action* (New York, 1968), II, p. 529.

[23] Lewis Mumford, *Technics and Human Development* (New York, 1966).

[24] Veblen, *IOW*, pp. 24–25.

[25] *Ibid.*, pp. 9–11; see also Stanley Matthew Daugert, *The Philosophy of Thorstein Veblen* (New York, 1950), p. 89.

[26] Veblen, *IOW*, pp. 1–37, *passim*.

[27] Veblen, *LC*, pp. 31–32; *IOW*, p. 100.

[28] *IOW*, pp. 36–37.

[29] *Ibid.*, p. 149. In his essay on "The Beginnings of Ownership" (1898), Veblen offered one possible explanation for the emergence of the psychology of human possession. In *The Instinct of Workmanship* (1914), however, he discusses several other interpretations that could account for the transition from the savage stage of "free workmanship" to the barbarian stage of pecuniary control of property. These hypotheses are discussed in a future chapter (see pp. 128–33).

[30] Marx, "Economic and Philosophical Manuscripts," p. 266.

[31] Veblen, *IOW*, pp. 53–54.

[32] *Ibid.*, pp. 58–59.

[33] Marx, "Economic and Philosophical Manuscripts," p. 304.

[34] Among the "animistic" phenomena that even a modern matter-of-fact attitude has been unable to extirpate, Veblen mentions the concept of causality, particularly the search for unseen causes in observed effects, natural law, and God. Even the skeptical modern scientist can only replace old deities by substituting himself as a new wonder-worker. "It is as the creative workman, the Great Artificer, that he has taken his last stand against the powers of spiritual twilight." Veblen, *IOW*, pp. 59–60.

[35] *Ibid.*, pp. 34–35.

[36] Veblen, *POS*, p. 392.

[37] A. R. Radcliffe-Brown, *The Andaman Islanders* (Cambridge, 1933), p. 50; Raymond Firth, *Primitive Economics of the New Zealand Maori* (London, 1929), pp. 164–67; Bronislaw Malinowski, *Coral Gardens and their Magic* (London, 1965).

[38] Jean-Jacques Rousseau, *The Social*

Contract and Discourse on the Origin of Equality (New York, 1967), pp. 212–19.

[39] Veblen, *LC*, p. 29.

[40] *Ibid.*, p. 40.

[41] Veblen, *BE*, p. 310.

[42] See John P. Diggins, "Thoreau, Marx, and the 'Riddle' of Alienation," *Social Research* 39 (1972) 571–98.

[43] Ortega y Gasset, "Man the Technician" in *History as a System and Other Essays Toward the Philosophy of History* (New York, 1962), pp. 87–161. I am much indebted to this essay.

[44] Marx, "Economic and Philosophical Manuscripts," p. 310.

[45] Alvin Johnson, a colleague of Veblen's at the New School, came close to making a similar point in another context. "Teleology is Veblen's specialty. Let another scientist produce a generalization, however abstract, Veblen will extract a teleological element, an ulterior motive from it. He is like a skilled pathologist, competent to prove that all the world is suffering from his pet disease. . . . Such pathologist usually ends by taking the disease himself, if it is communicable; and even if it is not, he is likely to reproduce the symptoms. So it has befallen Veblen." (Johnson, review of *The Instinct of Workmanship* in the *Political Science Quarterly* 31 [1916] 631.)

[46] Theodor Adorno, "Veblen's Attack on Culture," *Studies in Philosophy and Social Science* 9 (1941) 389–413.

[47] Robert Heilbroner, *The Worldly Philosophers* (New York, 1961), p. 212.

[48] Veblen, *BE*, p. 313.

[49] Veblen, *IOW*, pp. 318–34.

[50] Quoted in Dorfman, II, p. 113.

[51] Veblen, *POS*, p. 19.

[52] Veblen, *IOW*, pp. 88–89.

6 . . . Reification, Animism, Emulation: The Cultural Hegemony of Capitalism

[1] Veblen, *POS*, pp. 436–37.

[2] The phase which Marx and Engels call "modern industry" does not arise until the end of the eighteenth century. The technical evolution of machinery, dramatized on a large scale by the factory system, is a response to the growing demands of an ever-expanding market which hand labor can no longer supply. Marx, *Capital*, I, pp. 368–69, 430, 502; see also Marx, *The Poverty of Philosophy* (New York, 1973), pp. 150, 152.

[3] Marx, *Capital*, I, pp. 676–77.

[4] Lawrence Stone, *The Crisis of the Aristocracy, 1558–1641* (New York: Galaxy edn., 1967), p. 8.

[5] Veblen, *IOW*, p. 184.

[6] *Ibid.*, pp. 159–60.

[7] Mumford, p. 238.

[8] The element of animism remains in modern science, however, especially in the concept of causality. "Causation," wrote Veblen, "is conceived as manual work—to use a French term, it is a *remaniement* of raw materials at hand. Physiological or chemical explanations must finally be recast in terms of physics, to satisfy the modern scientist's sense of finality, and physics must be made to run in terms of impact, pressure, displacement in space, regrouping of material particles, coordinated movements and a shifting of equilibrium." It is here, in this early effort to apply the concept of physical science to an understanding of economics, that one first discerns the difficulties that develop over value theory, according to Veblen. "Through all this runs the concomitant requirement of quantivalence, statable in statistical form. The scientist's results are not finally merchantable, on the scientific exchange, until they have been reduced to such terms of accountancy as would be comprehensible to the man trained in the merchandising traffic of petty trade, for whose conviction things must be punctiliously rated in exchange value. But . . . it is only as an expedient of scientific accountancy that the facts under inquiry are kept account of in an itemised bill of values. This meticulous statistical accountancy is necessary to safeguard the accuracy of the work done and its conformity with the facts in hand; but the work so done handles these facts as active factors which go efficiently to the production of the results observed. The cause is conceived to produce the effect, somewhat after the fashion in which a skilled workman produces a finished article of trade. But when the scientist has set forth the operations and working conditions that

have brought forth the effects which he is engaged in explaining, he must also, in order to the conviction of his fellow craftsmen, show a statistically itemised statement of receipts and expenditures covering the facts engaged,—in quantitative values he must show that the costs are balanced by the values that emerge in the finished product of that workmanlike process of causation whose recondite nature and course he has so laid bare to the light of understanding." Veblen, *IOW*, pp. 264–65.

[9] Veblen, *IOW*, p. 200.

[10] Mumford, p. 25.

[11] John Locke, *The Second Treatise of Government* (Indianapolis: Liberal Arts Press edn., 1952), p. 28.

[12] Georg Lukacs, *History and Class Consciousness: Studies in Marxist Dialectics*, transl. Rodney Livingston (Cambridge, 1971), pp. 83–222.

[13] Marx's critique of capitalist value theory, observes Foucault, could hardly refute capitalism since it was based on the same metaphysical foundations, the same order of knowledge based on a world of things and objects. "At the deepest level of Western knowledge, Marxism introduced no real discontinuity; it found its place without difficulty, as a full, quiet, comfortable and, goodness knows, satisfying form for a time (its own), within an epistemological arrangement that welcomed it gladly (since it was this arrangement that was in fact making room for it) and that it, in return, had no intention of disturbing and, above all, no power to modify, even one jot, since it rested entirely upon it. Marxism exists in nineteenth-century thought like a fish in water; that is, it is unable to breathe anywhere else. Though it is in opposition to the 'bourgeois' theories of economics, and though this opposition leads it to use the project of a radical reversal of History as a weapon against them, that conflict and that project nevertheless have as their condition of possibility, not the reworking of all History, but an event that any archaeology can situate with precision, and that prescribed simultaneously, and according to the same mode, both nineteenth-century bourgeois economics and nineteenth-century revolutionary economics. Their controversies may have stirred up a few waves and caused a few surface ripples; but they are no more than storms in a children's paddling pool." Foucault, *The Order of Things: An Archaeology of the Human Sciences* (New York: Vintage edn., 1973), pp. 261–62.

[14] Marx, *Capital*, I, p. 91.

[15] Veblen, *POS*, p. 56.

[16] Veblen, *LC*, p. 65.

[17] Marcel Mauss, *The Gift*, transl. Ian Cunnison (London, 1954).

[18] Johan Huizinga, *Homo Ludens: A Study of the Play Element in Culture* (Boston, 1955), pp. 60–63; Maurice Godelier, *Rationalité et irrationalité en economie* (Paris, 1966); Marshall Sahlins, *Stone Age Economics* (London, 1974), p. 169.

[19] C. Tullio-Altan, "La Teoria del valore-lavoro di K. Marx nel quadro dei problemi attuali i dell' antropologia economica," *La Critica Sociologica* 23 (1972) 5–23; Walter Goldschmidt, "The Economics of Brideprice Among the Sebei and in East Africa," *Ethnology* 13 (1974), 311–331; Melville J. Herskovits, *Economic Anthropology* (New York, 1940).

[20] See, for example, Eugene E. Ruyle, "Slavery, Surplus, and Stratification on the Northwest Coast: The Ethnoenergetics of an Incipient Stratification System," *Current Anthropology* 14 (1973) 603–17; and the "Comments," 618–31, and *ibid.*, 15 (1974) 200–01.

[21] Jean Baudrillard, *The Mirror of Production*, transl. Mark Poster (St. Louis, Mo., 1973); Jurgen Habermas, *Knowledge and Human Interests* (Boston, 1971), pp. 1–63.

[22] Marx, "Economic and Philosophical Manuscripts," pp. 265–69; *Grundrisse*, pp. 138–66.

[23] Baudrillard, *Mirror;* Roland Barthes, *Système de la mode* (Paris, 1967).

[24] George Herbert Mead, *Mind, Self, and Society: From the Standpoint of a Social Behaviorist*, ed. Charles W. Morris (Chicago, 1934) p. 292.

[25] Veblen, *IOW*, p. 200.

[26] "If it be declared that the social characters assumed by objects, or the material forms assumed by the social qualities of labour under the regime of a definite mode of production, are mere symbols, it is in the same breath also declared that

these characteristics are arbitrary fictions sanctioned by the so-called universal consent of mankind." (Marx, *Capital*, I, p. 94.) On money and language, see *Grundrisse*, pp. 162–63.

[27] "A commodity is, in the first place, an object outside of us, a thing that by its properties satisfies human wants of some sort or another. The nature of such wants, whether, for instance, they spring from the stomach or from fancy, makes no difference. Neither are we here concerned to know how the objects satisfied these wants, whether directly as a means of subsistance, or indirectly as a means of production." (Marx, *Capital*, I, p. 43).

[28] Veblen, *ECO*, pp. 32–43.

[29] It is highly likely that Veblen's comprehension of the implications of semiology derived from Peirce, under whom he studied as a graduate student. Peirce, like Veblen in his later writings, regarded "habit" and "custom" as the starting point of knowledge. Beliefs are the individual's biased meaning of events mediated by the active mind responding to the "sign-character" of reality. The key to thinking is the efficacy of objects to transmit to the knowing subject a meaning; and the mind, a product of living habits, is the final interpretant of the series of purely representational or verbal meanings. Unfortunately, Veblen was reticent about the thinkers and ideas influencing him, not only on this subject but on knowledge in general. For a discussion of Peirce and Veblen, see Allen G. Gruchy, *Modern Economic Thought* (New York, 1947), pp. 16–17; for an analysis of Peirce's philosophy as a sort of supplement to Marx's epistemology, see Habermas, pp. 99–112.

[30] Gaetano Mosca has described in specific terms the process that Veblen only alludes to. Discussing how in India, Russia, Poland, and medieval Europe militarism ushers in a plutocracy, Mosca writes: "Poland offers a characteristic example of the general metamorphosis of a warrior class into an absolutely dominant class. Originally the Poles had the same organization by rural villages as prevailed among all the Slavic peoples. There was no distinction between fighters and farmers—in other words, between nobles and peasants. But after the Poles came to settle on the broad plains that are watered by the Vistula and Niemen, agriculture began to develop among them. However, the necessity of fighting with warlike neighbors continued, so that the tribal chiefs, or voivodes, gathered about themselves a certain number of picked men whose special occupation was the bearing of arms. These warriors were distributed among the various rural communities. They were exempt from agricultural duties, yet received their share of the produce of the soil, along with the other members of the community. In early days their position was not considered very desirable, and country dwellers sometimes waived exemption from agricultural labor in order to avoid going to war. But gradually as this order of things grew stabilized, as one class became habituated to the practice of arms and military organization while the other hardened to the use of the plow and the spade, the warriors became nobles and masters, and the peasants, once companions and brothers, became villeins and serfs. Little by little the warrior lords increased their demands to the point where the share they took as members of the community came to include the community's whole produce minus what was absolutely necessary for subsistance on the part of the cultivators; and when the latter tried to escape such abuses they were constrained by force to stay bound to the soil, their situation taking on all the characteristics of serfdom pure and simple." (Mosca, *The Ruling Class* [New York, 1939], pp. 54–55.)

[31] Veblen, *LC*, pp. 30–31.

[32] Veblen, *ECO*, pp. 35–36; *POS*, pp. 101–03.

[33] Veblen, *IOW*, pp. 54–55.

[34] Veblen, *LC*, p. 35.

[35] Veblen, *POS*, pp. 82–179.

[36] Jean-Jacques Rousseau, *The Social Contract and Discourse on the Origin of Inequality*, ed. Lester Crocker (New York, 1967), pp. 153–358; Denis Diderot, *Rameau's Nephew*, trans. L. W. Tancock (Baltimore, 1966).

[37] Adam Smith, *The Theory of Moral Sentiments* (London, 1790), p. 173; Bernard de Mandeville, *A Fable of the Bees* (London, 1725); Thomas Hobbes, *Leviathan*, ed. Michael Oakshott (Oxford, 1946), pp. 101–02; see also Arthur O. Lovejoy, *Reflections on Human Nature*

(Baltimore, 1961) for a penetrating study of the role of "pride" and "emulation" in Enlightenment thought.

[38] Veblen, *LC*, pp. 45–46.

[39] Peter Berger and Stanley Pullberg, "Reification and the Sociological Critique of Consciousness," *History & Theory* 4 (1965) 196–211.

[40] Veblen, *LC*, p. 48.

[41] Robert K. Merton cited Veblen when he developed his theory of latent and manifest functions, noting that Veblen's gifts for observing the ironic and satiric dimensions of social life enabled him to perceive the ulterior intentions in ostensible conduct (*Social Theory and Social Structure* (New York, 1968).

[42] Veblen, *LC*, pp. 115–17.

[43] Veblen, *LC*, p. 145.

[44] Veblen, *POS*, pp. 387–408.

[45] Stephen Thernstrom, *Poverty and Progress: Social Mobility in a Nineteenth-Century City* (New York, 1970).

[46] Jonathan Cobb and Richard Sennet, *The Hidden Wounds of Class* (New York, 1972); see also Joseph Goldthorpe, et al., *The Affluent Worker in the Class Structure* (Cambridge, 1969).

[47] Studs Terkel, *Working* (New York, 1974), pp. xxiv–xxxv.

[48] Herbert Gutman, *Work, Culture and Society in Industrial America* (New York, 1975).

[49] Veblen, *LC*, p. 190.

7 . . . Veblen, Weber, and the "Spirit of Capitalism"

[1] Weber does cite Veblen twice in the reference notes to *The Protestant Ethic* and he describes *The Theory of Business Enterprise* as a "suggestive book." Max Weber, *The Protestant Ethic and the Spirit of Capitalism*, transl. Talcott Parsons (New York, 1958), pp. 258, 275. Veblen does not mention Weber specifically but he does, as we shall see, address himself to the thesis of *The Protestant Ethic*.

[2] Talcott Parsons, "Introduction," Max Weber, *The Theory of Social and Economic Organization* (New York, 1947), p. 40; Parsons, *The Structure of Social Action*, 2 vols. (New York: Free Press edn., 1968), II, p. 529.

[3] Weber, *Protestant Ethic*, p. 53; for useful summaries of Weber's thesis, see Anthony Giddens, *Capitalism and Modern Social Theory: an Analysis of the Writings of Marx, Weber, and Durkheim* (London, 1971), pp. 119–32; Reinhard Bendix, *Max Weber: An Intellectual Portrait* (Garden City, N.Y., 1960), pp. 49–79.

[4] Weber also suggested that the development of science and capitalism was related, although it was more a case of capitalists appropriating the technical possibilities of science than scientific discoveries giving rise to the "spirit" of capitalism. Veblen offered a different view of how scientific progress develops. See Weber, *Protestant Ethic*, pp. 13–15, 24, 168, 249; Veblen, *POS*, pp. 1–55; see also R. Hookyaas, "Science and Reformation," in *The Protestant Ethic and Modernization*, ed. S. N. Eisenstadt (New York, 1968), pp. 211–39; and Robert K. Merton, *Science, Technology and Society in Seventeenth Century England* (New York, 1970).

[5] Weber, *Protestant Ethic*, p. 162.

[6] Weber was by no means an uncritical admirer of the capitalist work ethic; see, for example, *Protestant Ethic*, pp. 69–72.

[7] Marianne Weber, *Max Weber* (Heidelberg, 1950), p. 731.

[8] See the various essays in *Protestantism and Capitalism: The Weber Thesis and Its Critics*, Robert W. Green, ed. (Boston, 1959), and in *The Protestant Ethic and Modernization*.

[9] Sheldon Wolin, *Politics and Vision: Continuity and Innovation in Western Political Thought* (New York, 1960), pp. 165–94; Michael Walzer, *The Revolution of the Saints* (Cambridge, 1965).

[10] Werner Sombart, *Luxury and Capitalism* (Ann Arbor, 1967); Philip Siegelman's informative introduction to this work contains an account of the Sombart-Weber controversy.

[11] Weber, *Protestant Ethic*, p. 55.

[12] *Ibid.*, pp. 181–82.

[13] Of Weber's visit C. Wright Mills and Hans Gerth have written (in curiously Veblenian terms): "Again and again, Weber was impressed by the extent of waste, especially the waste of human life, under capitalism." Gerth and Mills, "Introduction," *From Max Weber: Essays in Sociology* (New York, 1958), p. 15.

[14] Edmund S. Morgan, "The Puritan Ethic and the American Revolution," *William and Mary Quarterly* 24 (1967) 3–43.

[15] Perry Miller, *The New England Mind: From Colony to Province* (Boston: Beacon edn., 1961), pp. 40–52; Perry Miller and Thomas Johnson, "Introduction," *The Puritans,* 2 vols. (New York, 1965), I, pp. 1–79.

[16] Gabriel Kolko, "Max Weber on America: Theory and Evidence," *History & Theory* (1960) 243–60.

[17] Rex A. Lucas, "The Weber Thesis: Plymouth Colony," *History & Theory* 10 (1971) 318–46. For an excellent analysis of colonial attitudes toward work and wealth, which came to my attention too late to use in this study, see J. E. Crowley, *This Sheba, Self: The Conceptualization of Economic Life in Eighteenth-Century America* (Baltimore, 1974).

[18] Bernard Bailyn, "Introduction," *The Apologia of Robert Keayne: The Self-Portrait of a Puritan Merchant* (New York, 1964), p. xi.

[19] Richard Bushman, *From Puritan to Yankee: Character and the Social Order in Connecticut, 1690–1765* (Cambridge, 1967), pp. ix, 135–43, 188, *passim*.

[20] Marianne Weber, p. 231.

[21] Benjamin Franklin, *A Dissertation on Liberty & Necessity, Pleasure & Pain* (New York, 1930).

[22] Quoted in Paul K. Conkin, *Puritans and Pragmatists: Eight Eminent American Thinkers* (New York, 1968), p. 106.

[23] Thorstein Veblen, "The Independent Farmer" and "The Country Town" in *AO*, pp. 129–65.

[24] Weber, *Protestant Ethic,* pp. 53–54.

[25] *Ibid.*, p. 53.

[26] Benjamin Franklin, *Autobiography* (Berkeley, 1930), p. 112.

[27] Paul W. Connor, *Poor Richard's Politiks: Benjamin Franklin and His New American Order* (New York, 1965), pp. 43–46; on Franklin's views of luxury and consumption, see Franklin to Benjamin Vaughn, July 26, 1784, in *The American Enlightenment*, ed. Adrienne Koch (New York, 1965), pp. 100–04.

[28] Franklin, *Autobiography,* pp. 4, 82, 113; *The Writings of Benjamin Franklin,* ed. A. H. Smyth, 10 vols. (New York, 1905–07), II, p. 108.

[29] Gordon Wood, *The Creation of the American Republic, 1776–1787* (Chapel Hill, 1969).

[30] *Diary and Autobiography of John Adams,* ed. L. H. Butterfield, 4 vols. (Cambridge, 1961), IV, pp. 118–19.

[31] *The Political Writings of John Adams,* ed. George A. Peek (Indianapolis, 1954), pp. 175–94.

[32] *Ibid.*, pp. 148–49.

[33] C. B. Macpherson, *The Political Theory of Possessive Individualism* (New York, 1962), pp. 31–46; Albert O. Hirschman, *The Passions and the Interests: Political Arguments for Capitalism Before Its Triumph* (Princeton, 1977).

[34] Adams to Jefferson, Nov. 15, 1813, in *American Enlightenment*, pp. 218–19.

[35] Karl Marx, *Economic and Philosophical Manuscripts of 1844,* Transl. Martin Milligan (Moscow, n.d.), pp. 136–38.

[36] Daniel Bell, "Introduction," *The Engineers and the Price System* (New York, 1963), pp. 31–32.

[37] Quoted in Marvin Meyers, *The Jacksonian Persuasion: Politics and Belief* (New York: Vintage edn., 1960), pp. 18–23.

[38] Louis Harz, *The Liberal Tradition in America* (New York, 1955), pp. 89–142.

[39] Weber, *Protestant Ethic*, p. 37.

[40] *The Sociology of Georg Simmel,* pp. 293–94.

[41] Alexis de Tocqueville, *Democracy in America,* 2 vols. (New York: Vintage edn., 1945), II, p. 147.

[42] *Ibid.*, I, p. 11.

[43] Tocqueville, it must be admitted, discerned much in American society that Veblen missed. A case in point is the American Indian. While Veblen had considerable anthropological knowledge of the Southwest and North Pacific Coast Indians, and hence could cite the Pueblos and Eskimos as an example of peaceful, communal tribal life, Tocqueville concentrated on the Indians of the Northeast and found a martial culture that resembled the "barbarian habits" of European feudalism. Veblen was not unaware of the warlike culture of the Plains Indians and the Iroquois of the Northeast. But the irony is that Veblen believed the aggressive barbarism of the leisure class usually triumphs historically over peaceful, sed-

entary populations, whereas Tocqueville believed that the Indians devoted primarily to war and hunting and contemptuous of work, would follow the fate of the European aristocracy. Unlike the black slave, whose very condition compels him to accept the work ethic, the Indian is doomed to extinction because of cultural "pride."

> The natives of North America consider labor not only an evil, but also a disgrace, and their pride fights against civilization almost as obstinately as does their laziness.
>
> No Indian in his bark hut is so wretched that he does not entertain a proud conception of his personal worth; he considers the cares of industry degrading occupations; he compares the cultivator to the ox plowing a furrow and regards all our crafts merely as the labor of slaves. Granted he has formed a very high opinion of the power and intelligence of the white man; but while admiring the results of our endeavors, he scorns the means to obtain them, and though he admits our ascendancy, he yet considers himself our superior. He thinks hunting and war the only cares of a man. Therefore the Indian in the miserable depths of his forests cherishes the same ideas and opinions as the medieval noble in his castle, and he only needs to become a conqueror to complete the resemblance. How odd it is that the ancient prejudices of Europe should reappear, not among the European population along the coast, but in the forests of the New World. (*Democracy in America*, I, pp. 327–28.)

The differences between Tocqueville and Veblen extend beyond the American Indian and other inhabitants. On the subject of religion, for example, Tocqueville anticipates Weber when he observes that religious nations have often accomplished considerable industrial progress because people of faith "work as much in favor of happiness in this world as of felicity in the next." (*Ibid.*, I, p. 547.) A comparison of Tocqueville and Veblen may yield as many insights as that between Weber and Veblen. (One illustration of the contrasting perspectives is discussed in the footnote that follows.) The difference, of course, is that Weber, Veblen, and Marx gave priority to capitalist reality, while Tocqueville gave priority to the reality of democracy and the ideology of equality and liberty.

[44] Tocqueville considers this possibility in his chapter on "How An Aristocracy May Be Created By Industry." The division of labor, Tocqueville observes, leads to the division of social classes. Yet while this economic principle lowers the consciousness of the working class as labor becomes more repetitive and dull in proportion to its specialization, the position and intelligence of the capitalist class is enhanced. The successful entrepreneur must expand his knowledge of science and society in order to conduct his business with "vision." As the process of industrialization continues, the master becomes more and more like the "administrator of a great empire," and the workman is increasingly reduced to the condition of a "brute." Thus it first appears that an aristocracy may arise out of the "bosom of democracy." But Tocqueville denies this probability. In the first place, an aristocracy in American could never perpetuate itself, not only because the nature of competitive capitalism renders the status of the businessman forever insecure, but also because the wealthy elements share neither a "corporate spirit" nor any organic ties to established institutions. In addition, the dynamic and diffuse nature of capitalism is such that rich Americans enjoy no paternal control over the underlying populations. "Between workman and master there are frequent relations but no true association." Finally—and Tocqueville spells out this argument in his long chapter on "Concerning Honor In The United States And Democratic Societies"—the aristocratic code will never find nourishment in American society. In feudal Europe the nobility praised generosity and liberality as a social responsibility, military valor as the highest virtue, and personal loyalty to one's superiors as the essence of political obligation. In America, however, the categories of virtues and vices are reversed. In this mobile society with everyman on the make there is no stigma attached to avarice and cupidity. "To clear, cultivate, and transform the huge uninhabited continent which is their domain, the Americans need the everyday support of an energetic passion; that passion can only be the love of wealth." (*Ibid.*, I, pp. 555–58, 616–27)

Perhaps it was Tocqueville's own aristocratic background that prevented him from seeing that in a democratic society money can command power and influence as much as military valor, that its possession and display can be the means of social ranking as much as the titles of nobility, and that indeed the invocation of the strenuous work ethic can only indicate what John Adams feared and Veblen confirmed—with affluence and luxury would come a reemergence of the old leisure-class values of the past.

[45] Alan Tully, "Patterns of Slaveholding in Colonial Pennsylvania," *Journal of Social History* 6 (1973) 284–305.

[46] Edward Pessen, "The Egalitarian Myth and the American Social Reality: Wealth, Mobility, and Equality in the 'Era of the Common Man,' " *American Historical Review* 76 (1971) 989–1034.

[47] Edwin C. Rozwenc, ed., *Ideology and Power in the Age of Jackson* (Garden City, N.Y., 1964), esp. Part Two, "The Uncertainties of Status."

[48] William M. Gouge, "The Artificial Inequality of Wealth" in Rozwenc, pp. 109–21.

[49] Herbert Marcuse, *Eros and Civilization: A Philosophical Inquiry Into Freud* (Boston, 1955).

[50] On one occasion Veblen did let slip an utopian utterance. "With the abolition of private property, the characteristic of human nature which now finds its exercise in this form of emulation, should logically find exercise in other, perhaps nobler and socially more serviceable, activities; it is at any rate not easy to imagine it running into any line of action more futile or less worthy of human effort." Veblen, "Some Neglected Points in the Theory of Socialism," *POS*, pp. 387–408.

[51] Veblen, *LC*, p. 39.

[52] *The Prose of Ralph Waldo Emerson* (Boston, 1870), p. 154.

[53] Again without mentioning his name or his work, Veblen addressed himself briefly to Weber's thesis in *The Instinct of Workmanship*, as we saw in a previous chapter. There he questioned the historical validity of the thesis; in the essay discussed above he is concerned with its ethical implications. But it should be mentioned that Veblen was also concerned with the significance of the thesis for intellectual history. Indeed it might be said that while Weber was interested in what religion did for capitalism, Veblen was bemused by what capitalism did *to* religion. This is particularly true in regards to theology. Veblen understood perfectly that a theological residue continues into the sixteenth and seventeenth centuries to pervade the doctrine of political economy and its corollary natural law. But between the scholastic thought of the Middle Ages and the deified naturalism of modern rationalistic thought that results from the mechanistic temperament of capitalism lay a deep epistemological chasm:

> In the medieval speculations whether theological, philosophic or scientific, the search for truth runs back to the authentic ground of the religious verities,—largely to revealed truth; and these religious verities run back to the question, 'What hath God ordained?' In the course of the era of handicraft this ultimate question of knowledge came to take the form, 'What hath God wrought?' Not that the creative office of God in the divine economy was overlooked or in any degree intentionally made light of by the earlier speculators; nor that the sovereignty of God was denied or in any degree questioned by those devout inquirers who carried forward the work in later time. But in that earlier phase of faith and inquiry it is distinctly the suzerainty of God, and His ordinances, that afford the ground of finality on which all inquiry touching the economy of this world ultimately come to rest; and in the later phase, as seen at the close of the era of handicraft, it is as distinctly His creative office and the logic of His creative design that fill the place of an ultimate term in human inquiry—as that inquiry conventionally runs within the spiritual frontiers of Christendom. God had not ceased to be the Heavenly King, and had not ceased to be glorified with the traditional phrases of homage of the Most High, the Lord of Hosts, etc., but somewhat incongruously He had also come to be exalted as the Great Artificer—the preternatural craftsman. The vulgar habits of thought bred in the workday populice by the routine of the workshop and the marketplace had stolen their way into the sanctuary and the counsels of divinity. (Veblen, *IOW*, pp. 256–57.)

[54] Veblen, *EOC*, pp. 200–18.

[55] Walter Lippmann, *A Preface to Politics* (Ann Arbor: paperback edn., 1962), p. 48.

[56] "The guiding thread for the interpretation of this reality," wrote Karl Löwith of Weber's theory, "is the process of rationalization through which reality has

been disenchanted and rendered drab, flat, and matter-of-fact." Löwith, "Weber's Interpretation of the Bourgeois-Capitalist World in Terms of the Guiding Principle of 'Rationalization,'" in *Max Weber*, ed. Dennis Wrong (Englewood Cliffs, N.J., 1970), pp. 101–22.

[57] Lawrence is quoted in César Graña, *Modernity and Its Discontents* (New York, 1967), p. 208.

[58] Ortega y Gasset, "Man as Technician," p. 151.

[59] Veblen, *AO*, p. 255.

8 . . . The Barbarian Status of Women

[1] Adorno, p. 296.

[2] John Stuart Mill, "The Subjection of Women" in *John Stuart Mill and Harriet Taylor: Essays on Sex Equality*, ed. Alice S. Rossi (Chicago, 1970), pp. 128, 141 *passim*.

[3] These three articles are all reprinted in ECO.

[4] Veblen, *ECO*, pp. 51–52.

[5] *Ibid.*, p. 56.

[6] *Ibid.*, p. 58.

[7] *Ibid.*, p. 64.

[8] Veblen, "Professor Clark's Economics," *POS*, pp. 184–85.

[9] Frederick Engels, *The Origin of the Family, Private Property, and the State* (New York, 1972), pp. 44–68.

[10] Karen Sacks, "Engels Revisited," in *Women, Culture & Society*, eds. Michelle Zimbalist Rosaldo and Louise Lamphere (Stanford, 1974), p. 219; see also Ann J. Lane, "Women in Society: A Critique of Frederick Engels" in *Liberating Women's History: Theoretical and Critical Essays*, ed. Berenice A. Carroll (Urbana, 1976), pp. 4–25.

[11] Engels, *Origin*, pp. 151–52.

[12] Veblen, *IOW*, p. 78.

[13] *Ibid.*, pp. 94–96.

[14] Engels, *Origin*, pp. 44–65, *passim*.

[15] Veblen, *LC*, p. 32.

[16] On the problems in Marx's theory of alienation arising as a historical phenomenon, as opposed to a spiritual or metaphysical, see John P. Diggins, "Thoreau, Marx, and the 'Riddle of Alienation," *Social Research* 39 (1972), 571–98.

[17] See John Millar's chapter on "Of the Rank and Condition of Women in Different Ages," in his *The Origins of the Distinction of Ranks* (Glasgow, 1779).

[18] Claude Lévi-Strauss, *Structural Anthropology*, trans. Claire Jacobson and Brooke Grundfest Schoepf (London, 1972), p. 47.

[19] Margaret Mead, *Sex and Temperament in Three Primitive Societies* (New York, 1935), pp. 310–22; Carol P. Hoffer, "Madam Yoko: Ruler of the Kpa Mende Confederacy," in *Women, Culture & Society*, pp. 173–87; for a skeptical evaluation of Lévi-Strauss's theories, see Edmund Leach, *Lévi-Strauss* (London, 1974).

[20] Rosaldo and Lamphere, "Introduction," *Women, Culture & Society*, p. 7.

[21] Veblen, *LC*, pp. 229–30.

[22] Veblen, *EOC*, pp. 69–70.

[23] See, for example, René König, *A La Mode: On the Social Psychology of Fashion* (New York, 1973).

[24] Veblen, *LC*, p. 108.

[25] Veblen, *EOC*, p. 76.

[26] J. C. Flugel, *The Psychology of Clothes* (London, 1930), p. 137.

[27] George Simmel, "Fashion," *International Quarterly* 10 (1904) 130–55.

[28] Sombart observes that in eighteenth-century Parisian society the "respectable lady" had to compete with the mistress and adjust much of her own dress habits accordingly. After discussing the role of the *cocotte* and the *salon*, Sombart adds: "But the most important result of this development is that the style of life of the demimonde determined that of the women of the world, i.e., society. Hardly anything has changed in this respect since then. Even in the respectable middle-class world of today, the woman of secure position (I am not referring to the eccentric people in 'rational' dresses, vegetating in three-room apartments) studies the costumes worn by the *grandes cocottes* at the Spring races in Paris. All the follies of fashion, luxury, splendor, and extravagance are first tried out by the mistresses before they are finally accepted, somewhat toned down, by the reputable matrons. In those bygone days which we discuss here, when the burgher lived in a sphere of his own, far removed from what was then 'society,' the courtesan in her re-

stricted circle naturally exercised an influence which was more thoroughly and directly felt than is possible today." Weber Sombart, "The Secularization of Love," in *Luxury and Capitalism*, p. 57.

[29] Quentin Bell, *On Human Finery* (London, 1947), pp. 116, 126.

[30] Charles E. Rosenberg, "Sexuality, Class and Role in 19th Century America," *American Quarterly*, 25 (1973) 131–53; Sondra R. Herman, "Loving Courtship or the Marriage Market? The Ideal and Its Critics, 1871–1911," *ibid.*, pp. 235–52; Caroll Smith-Rosenberg, "The Hysterical Woman: Sex Roles and Role Conflict in 19th Century America," *Social Research* 34 (1972) 652–78; Carl Degler, "What Ought to Be and What Was: Women's Sexuality in the Nineteenth Century," *American Historical Review* 129 (1974) 1467–90; G. J. Barker-Benfield, *The Horrors of the Half-Known Life: Male Attitudes Toward Women and Sexuality in Nineteenth Century America* (New York, 1975); Sarah J. Stage, "Out of the Attic: Studies of Victorian Sexuality," *American Quarterly* 27 (1975) 480–85; Barbara Sicherman, "American History," *Signs* 1 (1975), pp. 461–85.

[31] Peter T. Cominos, "Late Victorian Sexual Respectability and the Social System," *International Review of Social History* 8 (1963), p. 216.

[32] Degler, pp. 1467–90; Rosenberg, pp. 131–53.

[33] All personal luxury springs from purely sensuous pleasure. Anything that charms the eye, the ear, the nose, the palate, or the touch, tends to find an ever more perfect expression in objects of daily use. And it is precisely the outlay for such objects that constitutes luxury. In the last analysis, it is our sexual life that lies at the root of the desire to refine and multiply the means of stimulating our senses, for sensuous pleasure and erotic pleasure are essentially the same. Indubitably, the primary cause of the development of any kind of luxury is most often to be sought in consciously or unconsciously operative sex impulses.

For this reason we find luxury in the ascendant wherever wealth begins to accumulate and the sexuality of a nation is freely expressed. On the other hand, wherever sex is denied expression, wealth begins to be hoarded instead of being spent; thus goods are accumulated, especially in such abstract forms as precious metals and, in more recent periods, money. (Sombart, *Luxury and Capitalism*, pp. xx–xxi.)

[34] Charlotte Perkins Gilman, *Women and Economics* (New York, 1966), p. 118.

[35] *Ibid.*, pp. 116–17.

[36] William Graham Sumner, "Sociology," in *American Thought: Civil War to World War I*, ed. Perry Miller (New York, 1954), pp. 72–92. On Darwinism and feminism see the following studies: Aileen S. Kraidtor, *The Ideas of the Woman Suffrage Movement, 1890–1920* (New York, 1965), pp. 18–42; Lester D. Stephens, "Evolution and Woman's Rights in the 1890s: The Views of Joseph LeConte," *The Historian* 33 (1976) 239–52; Rosalind Rosenberg, "In Search of Woman's Nature, 1850–1920," *Feminist Studies* 3 (1975), 141–54; Clifford H. Scott, "A Naturalistic Rationale for Women's Reform: Lester Frank Ward on the Evolution of Social Relations," *The Historian* 33 (1970), 54–67.

[37] Gilman was fascinated by the extent to which male insects are deliberately "sacrificed" by their own kind for the sake of the survival of the species, and in comparison this made the subordinate position of the human female sex seem only a minor and transient interlude in the creative processes of nature. "Never once in the history of humanity has any outrage upon women compared with these sweeping sacrifices of helpless males in earlier species. The female has been dominant for the main duration of life on earth. She has been easily equal always up to our own race; and in our race she has been subjugated to the male during the earlier period of development for such enormous racial gain, such beautiful and noble uses, that the sacrifices should never be mentioned nor thought of by a womanhood that knows its power. For the upbuilding of human life on earth she could afford to have her own held back; and—closer, tenderer, lovelier service—for the raising of her fierce sex-mate to a free and gentle brother-hood, for the uplifting of the human soul in her dear son, she could have borne not only this, but more,—borne it smilingly, ungrudgingly, gladly, for his sake and the world's." (*Women and Economics*, p. 135.)

[38] *Ibid.*, pp. 138, 257.

[39] Dorfman, II, p. 97; conversation with Dorfman, June 15, 1974.

[40] Riesman, p. 2.

[41] R. L. Duffus, *Innocents at Credo: A Memoir of Thorstein Veblen and Some Others* (New York, 1944), pp. 92–93.

[42] Quoted in John Dos Passos, *The Big Money* (New York, 1936), p. 100.

[43] The condition seems to have been much harder for her to bear than for him. Veblen refused to have children with his second wife, saying that he could not imagine himself a father. Ellen's plight has been poignantly described by a neighbor who wrote Dorfman after his biography appeared. "She [Ellen] would have given her life, I should almost say her soul, to bear a child." Dorfman, II, p. 131.

[44] Dorfman, I, p. 305.

[45] Isador Lubin, "Recollections of Veblen" in *Thorstein Veblen*, ed. Carlton Qualey (New York, 1968), p. 132.

[46] Scott's observations are cited in Riesman, p. 27.

[47] Veblen, *LC*, pp. 229–34.

[48] H. L. Mencken, *Prejudices: First Series* (New York, 1919), pp. 59–82.

[49] H. L. Mencken, *In Defense of Women* (New York, 1918), p. 51.

[50] Only once in his entire career did Veblen reply to his many critics, and that particular book reviewer later confessed, "I have often wondered how I could have been so blind." (Dorfman, I, pp. 507–08.) When Mencken's essay first appeared in *Smart Set* in 1919, Veblen's thoughts were on the war, peace, and the Russian Revolution, events that would leave him disillusioned in the twenties as he withdrew further into isolation and solitude. An exchange between Veblen and Mencken on the women question would have been a stimulating affair and may have helped keep the issue alive during the twenties, when, with the passage of the nineteenth amendment on suffrage, the apparent political battle was over and the real cultural struggle had begun.

[51] Veblen, "Barbarian Status," *ECO*, p. 63.

9 . . . The Tribes of Academe

[1] Heilbroner, pp. 180–213; Franco Ferrarotti, *Il pensiero sociologico da Auguste Comte a Max Horkheimer* (Milan, 1974), pp. 144–49.

[2] Dorfman, I, pp. 248–53; Heilbroner, 194–95.

[3] Dorfman, I, pp. 248–49; Heilbroner, p. 194.

[4] Dorfman, I, p. 118; Heilbroner, pp. 193–94; Lewis Mumford, "Thorstein Veblen," *New Republic* 68 (1931) 314–16; Mitchell is quoted in Joseph Dorfman, "Background of Veblen's Thought" in *Thorstein Veblen*, ed. Qualey, p. 129.

[5] Laski is quoted in Dorfman, I, pp. 450–51.

[6] Veblen, *HL*, pp. 51–52, 57.

[7] *Ibid.*, pp. 122–23.

[8] *Ibid.*, p. 163.

[9] *Ibid.*, pp. 152–62, *passim*.

[10] *Ibid.*, p. 209.

[11] J. M. Clark, "Thorstein Bunde Veblen: 1857–1929," *The American Economic Review* 19 (1929) 742.

[12] Edward Chase Kirkland, *Dream and Thought in the Business Community, 1860–1900* (Chicago: Quadrangle edn., 1964), pp. 83–113.

[13] Laurence R. Veysey, *The Emergence of the American University* (Chicago, 1965), pp. 368, 385.

[14] Riesman, p. 107.

[15] Veblen, HL, pp. 178–79.

[16] *Ibid.*, p. 163.

[17] Riesman, p. 106.

[18] Veysey, p. 6, passim.

[19] Riesman, p. 109.

[20] Veblen, *HL*, pp. 80–81.

[21] *Ibid.*, pp. 1–11, 85.

[22] *Ibid.*, pp. 162–63.

[23] *Ibid.*, p. 126.

[24] *Ibid.*, p. 111.

[25] *Ibid.*, p. 4.

[26] Riesman, p. 112.

[27] In a footnote in *The Higher Learning* Veblen asserts that although the "pioneers" of pragmatism denied the value of knowledge apart from utility, they later made their "peace" with the notion of idle curiosity (p. 4). Veblen frequently quoted or at least cited James in his essays; and when he later heard that James and Dewey were being attacked by a behaviorist, Veblen retorted: "He will never know as much as Dewey or James forgot." Dorfman, I, p. 450.

[28] Veblen, *POS*, pp. 1–31.
[29] *Ibid.*, p. 11; Veblen, *HL*, pp. 24–25.
[30] Veblen, *HL*, pp. 146–48.
[31] Ferrarotti, p. 140.

10 . . . America and the World

[1] John P. Diggins, *The American Left in the Twentieth Century* (New York, 1973), pp. 81–88.

[2] Veblen, *IG*, pp. v–vii, 3–12. Veblen spent much of his later years investigating theories about race and eugenics, and he referred in his own writings to such racial types as the "dolicho-blond temperament." But the idea of racial supremacy seemed to him arrant nonsense. After accompanying Isador Lubin to a movie house to see "The Birth of a Nation," Veblen commented: "Lubin, that is the finest example of concentrated misinformation that I've ever seen." Lubin, "Recollections of Veblen," in *Thorstein Veblen*, ed. Qualey, p. 133.

[3] Veblen, *IG*, p. 86.

[4] *Ibid.*, pp. 88–149.

[5] *Ibid.*, p. 103.

[6] *Ibid.*, p. 132.

[7] *Ibid.*, pp. 236–37.

[8] *Ibid.*, pp. 258–59.

[9] Dorfman, II, pp. 116–40, 199–232.

[10] Dorfman, I, p. 374.

[11] Veblen, *NOP*, pp. vii–viii.

[12] *Ibid.*, pp. 31, 33.

[13] *Ibid.*, p. 57, *passim*.

[14] *Ibid.*, p. 36.

[15] *Ibid.*, 178–298; "Outline of a Policy for the Control of the 'Economic Penetration' of Backward Countries and of Foreign Investments," in *ECO*, pp. 361–82; for a useful study of Veblen's attitudes toward war and peace, see Sondra Herman, *Eleven Against War: Studies in American Internationalist Thought, 1898–1921* (Stanford, 1969), pp. 150–78.

[16] Veblen, *NOP*, pp. 254–55.

[17] Veblen, *ECO*, pp. 399–414.

[18] Eastman quoted in Dorfman, I, p. 460.

[19] Veblen, *ECO*, pp. 423–36.

[20] Kallen quoted in Heilbroner, p. 210.

[21] Einstein to Ely Culbertson, August 8, 1942, in *Einstein on Peace*, eds. Otto Nathan and Heinz Norden (New York, 1960), pp. 321–22.

[22] See the essays by Allen Gruchy, Myron Watkins, Carter Goodrich, and Douglas Dowd in *Thorstein Veblen: A Critical Reappraisal*, ed. Douglas F. Dowd (Ithaca N.Y., 1958); on Germany, see Ralf Dahrendorf, *Society and Democracy in Germany* (Garden City, N.Y., 1967). For information on the influence of Veblen on contemporary German scholarship I am indebted to Professor Kenneth Barkin, who has discussed this in "Germany's Path to Industrial Maturity," *Revue de l'Université Laurentienne* 5 (1973) 11–33.

[23] See, for example, Reinhard Bendix, *Nation-Building and Citizenship: Studies of Our Changing Social Order* (New York, 1964), pp. 6–8, 168, 200, 210.

[24] The anthropologist, E. R. Service, is quoted in Dorfman, II, p. 123.

[25] Arnold J. Toynbee, *A Study of History* (London, 1934), IV, p. 430.

[26] Max Lerner, "Introduction," *The Portable Veblen* (New York, 1948), p. 13.

[27] Riesman, pp. 137–38; Dowd, pp. 100–03.

[28] Henry Wallace, "Veblen's 'Imperial Germany and the Industrial Revolution,'" *Political Science Quarterly* 55 (1940) 435–45.

[29] Walton H. Hamilton, "Veblen on the Munich Pact," *New Republic* 100 (1939) 107–08.

[30] Veblen, *ECO*, pp. 248–66.

[31] David Schoenbaum, *Hitler's Social Revolution: Class and Status in Nazi Germany, 1933–1939* (New York, 1966).

[32] See, for example, "Big Business in German Politics: Four Studies" (Fritz Stern, Gerald D. Feldman, Henry A. Turner, Ernst Nolte), *American Historical Review* 57 (1969) 37–78.

[33] John P. Diggins, *Mussolini and Fascism: The View from America* (Princeton, 1972).

[34] See, for example, Herbert W. Schneider, *Making the Fascist State* (New York, 1928).

[35] Quoted in Dorfman, I, p. 500.

[36] Lerner, p. 27.

[37] Kendall E. Bailes, "The Politics of Technology: Stalin and Technocratic

Thinking Among Soviet Engineers," *American Historical Review* 79 (1974) 445–69.

[38] Herbert Marcuse, *Soviet Marxism: A Critical Analysis* (New York: Vintage edn., 1961), p. 69.

[39] Veblen, *NOP*, p. 33.

[40] Veblen, "Economic Penetration," *ECO*, p. 368.

[41] John H. Schaar, "The Case for Patriotism," *New American Review* 17 (1973) 59–99.

11 . . . Disciples and Dissenters: Veblen's Legacy in American Thought

[1] Oscar Lewis, *The Big Four* (New York, 1938); Matthew Josephson, *The Robber Barons* (New York, 1934); Heilbroner, pp. 302–05.

[2] Discussion of this subject is based upon the following studies: Samuel Haber, *Efficiency and Uplift: Scientific Management in the Progressive Era* (Chicago, 1964); Edward Layton, *The Revolt of the Engineers: Social Responsibility and the American Engineering Profession* (Cleveland, 1971); Bell, "Introduction," *EPS*.

[3] Quoted in Dorfman, I, p. 511.

[4] David Seckler, *Thorstein Veblen and the Institutionalists* (Boulder, Colorado, 1975).

[5] Mencken, *Prejudices*, pp. 59–82.

[6] Dos Passos, *The Big Money*, p. 98.

[7] *The Fourteenth Chronicle: Letters and Diaries of John Dos Passos*, ed. Townsend Ludington (Boston, 1973), p. 443; See also John P. Diggins, "Dos Passos and Veblen's Villains," *Antioch Review* 23 (1963), 485–500.

[8] Lewis Corey, "Thorstein Veblen," *The Marxist Quarterly* (1937) 162–68; see also John G. Wright, "Thorstein Veblen: Sociologist," *The New International* 2 (1935) 20–23.

[9] Lerner, "Introduction," pp. 1–49.

[10] Commager, p. 236.

[11] White, pp. 89–90.

[12] Daniel Aaron, *Men of Good Hope* (New York, 1951), p. 213.

[13] Miller, "Introduction," *American Thought*, p. xlvii.

[14] David Noble, *The Paradox of Progressivism* (Minneapolis, 1958).

[15] Dowd, p. 158.

[16] Heilbroner, pp. 181–213.

[17] Mills, p. xvii.

[18] John Kenneth Galbraith, "A New Theory of Thorstein Veblen," *American Heritage* 24 (1973) 32–40. John Kenneth Galbraith, *The Affluent Society* (New York: Mentor edn., 1963) and *The New Industrial State* (Boston: Sentry edn., 1971); see also Charles G. Leathers and John S. Evans, "Thorstein Veblen and the New Industrial State," *Journal of Political Economy* 5 (1975) 420–37.

[19] Diggins, *Mussolini and Fascism*, pp. 454–55.

[20] Talcott Parsons, "Social Strains in America" in *The Radical Right*, ed. Daniel Bell (Garden City, N.Y., 1963), pp. 209–38.

[21] Arthur K. Davis wrote his doctoral dissertation on Veblen under Parsons' supervision at Harvard University. He chose to stress the "many serious failings" in Veblen's works. See, for example, Davis's "Sociological Elements in Veblen's Economic Theory," *Journal of Political Economy* 53 (1945) 132–49.

[22] Daniel Bell, *The End of Ideology: On the Exhaustion of Political Ideas in the Fifties* (New York, 1961), p. 403.

[23] Bell, "Introduction," *EPS*, pp. 4, 13.

[24] Not all Marxists who came of political age in the thirties went on to become critical of Veblen in the fifties. See, for example, Lewis A. Coser's respectful chapter on Veblen in *Masters of Sociological Thought: Ideas in Historical and Social Context* (New York, 1971), pp. 263–302; see also Bernard Rosenberg, *The Values of Veblen: A Critical Appraisal* (Washington, D.C., 1956).

[25] Lewis Feuer, "Thorstein Veblen: The Metaphysics of the Interned Immigrant," *American Quarterly* 5 (1953) 99–112; see also George Fredrickson, "Thorstein Veblen: The Last Viking," *ibid.* 11 (1958), 403–415.

[26] Riesman, pp. 7–8, 18, 41, 78–79, *passim*.

[27] For a critique of Riesman's psychological interpretation of Veblen, see

Ferrarotti, pp. 139–44; my own criticisms have been influenced by the methodological problems astutely discussed in Gerald Izenberg's "Psychohistory and Intellectual History," *History & Theory* 14 (1975) 139–55.

[28] Max Horkheimer, "Preface," *Studies in Philosophy and Social Science* 9 (1941) 365.

[29] Herbert Marcuse, "Some Social Implications of Modern Technology," *Ibid.*, 414–39.

[30] T. W. Adorno, "Veblen's Attack on Culture," *Ibid.*, 389–413.

12 . . . Conclusion: Whither Capitalism?

[1] Daniel Bell, "The Cultural Contradictions of Capitalism," *The Public Interest* 21 (1970) 35; for an elaboration of the argument in the context of intellectual history, see Bell, *The Cultural Contradictions of Capitalism* (New York, 1975).

[2] E. J. Hundert, "The Making of Homo Faber: John Locke Between Ideology and History," *The Journal of the History of Ideas* 33 (1972) 3–22.

[3] Veblen, *LC*, p. 145.

[4] See, for example, David Noble, "The Theology of Thorstein Veblen" in *Thorstein Veblen*, ed. Qualey, pp. 72–105.

[5] Mumford, pp. 322–23.

Index

79 – prob. of aberration
perhaps rooted
in human nature...